Recommended Bed & Breakfasts™ Series

Recommended Bed & Breakfasts™ Pacific Northwest

Myrna Oakley

The Globe Pequot Press

Old Saybrook, Connecticut

Recommended Bed & Breakfasts is a trademark of The Globe Pequot Press

Cover design by Lana Mullen
Cover illustration by Michael Crampton
All illustrations in this book are by Mauro Magellan except some that were reproduced from establishments' brochures or literature. These illustrations are courtesy of: page 5, Antique Rose Inn; page 32, Sandlake Country Inn; page 34, The Johnson House Bed & Breakfast Inn; page 40, Willowbrook Inn; page 44, Historic Orth House Bed & Breakfast; page 108, Falcon's Crest Inn; page 132, Sauvie Island Bed & Breakfast; page 220, Colonel Crockett Farm Bed & Breakfast Inn; page 242, Guest House Log Cottages; page 262, Roberta's Bed & Breakfast; page 298, Johnson Heritage House Bed & Breakfast.

Library of Congress Cataloging-in-Publication Data
Oakley, Myrna.
    Recommended bed & breakfasts. Pacific Northwest / Myrna Oakley. —1st ed.
        p.   cm. — (Recommended bed & breakfast series)
    Includes index.
    ISBN 0-7627-0331-8
   1. Bed and breakfast accommodations—Northwest, Pacifc—Guidebooks. I. Title. II. Title:
Recommended bed and breakfasts. Pacific Northwest. III. Title: Pacific Northwest. IV. Series.
   TX907.3.N96025   1999   99-18083
   647.94795'03—dc21   CIP

Recommended Bed & Breakfasts™
Pacific Northwest

Help Us Keep This Guide Up to Date

Every effort has been made by the author and editors to make this guide as accurate and useful as possible. However, many things can change after a guide is published—establishments close, phone numbers change, facilities come under new management, etc.

We would love to hear from you concerning your experiences with this guide and how you feel it could be made better and be kept up to date. While we may not be able to respond to all comments and suggestions, we'll take them to heart and we'll also make certain to share them with the author. Please send your comments and suggestions to the following address:

The Globe Pequot Press
Reader Response/Editorial Department
P.O. Box 833
Old Saybrook, CT 06475

Or you may e-mail us at:

Editorial@globe-pequot.com

Thanks for your input, and happy travels!

To all those folks—couples, singles, and families—who love traveling Pacific Northwest highways and byways, and who delight in discovering its scenic and historic treasures as well as its welcoming bed-and-breakfast inns.

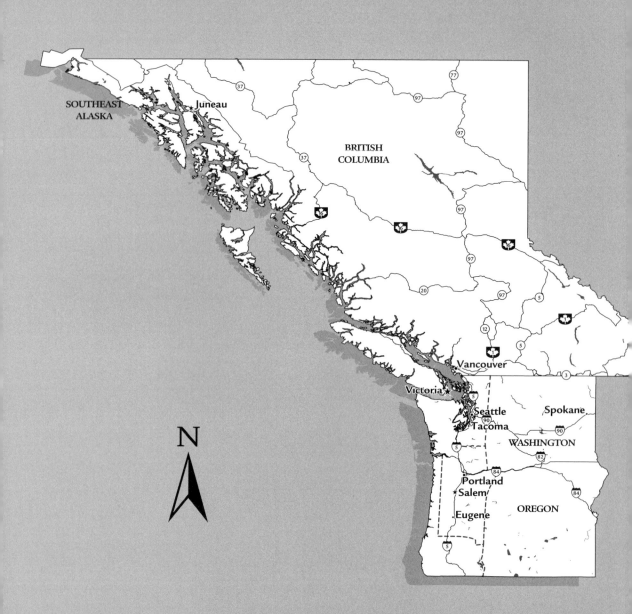

Contents

Acknowledgments

With much appreciation and grateful thanks to

. . . bed-and-breakfast innkeepers in Oregon, Washington, British Columbia, and Southeast Alaska for welcoming me to your communities, and offering personal tours of your inns, cups of hot tea, and muffins without raisins.

. . . my home group of bed-and-breakfast innkeepers—Melody and B. J., Mary, Judi, Charlene and Gary, Jan, Pat, Barbara and Jim, Barbara and Jack, Nancy, and Beverly—for making me an honorary member of the Associated Bed & Breakfasts of Mount Hood and Northern Willamette Valley, for always keeping the light on, and for much help with updating my research of this area.

. . . my colleagues at Marylhurst University for encouragement and support, particularly the PLA crew in the Learning Assessment Center—Marylee, Lonna, Simeon, and Cheri.

. . . my editors Laura Strom and Christina Lester at Globe Pequot, who kept me moving toward those deadlines and asking the tough questions like, "Precisely just what do you mean by sometime next week?" The e-mails and e-mail attachments flew through cyberspace with much regularity between Oregon and Connecticut.

Introduction

Bed-and-breakfast—whether offered in small country inns, rural farms, or restored Victorians; in mountain lodges, high desert ranches, or beachside guest houses; in elegant city dwellings, private homes, or hidden cottages—continues as a popular way to travel and plan one's vacation itineraries.

This first edition of *Recommended Bed & Breakfasts: Pacific Northwest* offers the latest information about the bed-and-breakfast experience Northwest style, and offers inns that are recommended to those who want to travel in the upper left-hand corner of the U.S. Also included is a sampling of inns in western British Columbia and in southeastern Alaska.

An adventurous spirit, a bit of flexibility, and a sense of humor will help to make your bed-and-breakfast stays memorable. These days you will most often have a private bath, but sharing a bath down the hall may happen too. Because most bed-and-breakfast inns in the Northwest are small and intimate (generally fewer than twelve rooms), guests are usually asked to leave children and pets at home. However, there are exceptions.

No bellman will carry your suitcases and you probably won't have maid service or soft drink and ice machines down the hall. What you will find is personal attention, an opportunity to meet congenial fellow guests over libations in the library or common room, and waist-bulging, gourmet breakfasts that are included in the price of the room.

Speaking of breakfast plan on leaving plain toast and cereal behind. Most innkeepers and hosts realize that not merely good, but great food is a must for a successful getaway. How about a hearty, delicious entree, such as French toast baked in a Grand Marnier-egg-orange peel batter and topped with warm syrup made of pure maple, honey, and dark rum? Or, cinnamon rolls hot from the oven drizzled with an almond glaze. The choices are many—Dutch babies, egg-shrimp stratas, artichoke fritattas, fresh seasonal fruits, freshly ground and brewed gourmet coffees, and a selection of teas.

You may eat on a sun-drenched deck or patio overlooking a river, a lake, a mountain, an ocean beach, even a sunrise. You may sit with other guests at a gleaming antique Jacobean-style table that looks as though it belongs in a baronial castle. Or you may even arrange to eat in bed, with breakfast presented on a wicker tray with French linens and fresh flowers.

Because it's both personal and sociable, the bed-and-breakfast experience often offers a soothing way to erase stress. Imagine cobbled lanes and woodland walks, peaceful vistas and driftwood-strewn beaches. The bed-and-breakfast phenomenon began in Europe, as a way to travel through the countryside on a budget. The idea then spread to the U.S. via the East Coast and then on to the West Coast by way of San Francisco in the early 1970s.

When I began writing about inns in the Pacific Northwest in the early 1980s, there were just three B&Bs in Ashland, home of Oregon's Shakespeare Festival. Today there are more than fifty here. This trend is occurring in a number of areas in the Northwest including British Columbia and southeastern Alaska. The American brand of bed-and-breakfast is somewhat more polished and sophisticated than the family-style European home-stays, and the prices are higher—from $85 to $150 and up for a couple is fairly standard in the late 1990s.

In my years of travel throughout my native Pacific Northwest, I have met some of the most extraordinary innkeepers, delightful people who create havens of rest and rejuvenation for travelers. These eclectic couples and individuals come from all walks of life, many are world travelers, most of them have great libraries, most of them love to cook—some of them are even gourmet cooks—and they love sharing their inns and their regions with travelers. Each bed and breakfast is unique and reflects the lifestyle and values of its owners. I try to capture this impression in words and narrative of the overall feeling so that readers can find their special niche,—their own special nest away from home. In the index are suggestions for

finding particular types of inns, for example ones in classy city areas, B&Bs with great water views, those on islands and reached by ferry, romantic B&Bs, and others that are far from city lights.

As we go to press all of the information included is current. However do not despair should you find a new proprietor at one of the inns you visit—most will gladly assist travelers with information, reservations, and provide the kind of experience that makes new friends. If an inn is full when you phone or e-mail, the innkeepers will usually be able to suggest other bed and breakfasts located in the area. If you have a negative bed-and-breakfast experience, we would appreciate a letter. Likewise accounts of especially happy experiences and information or recommendations about exceptional and/or new bed-and-breakfast inns in the Pacific Northwest, British Columbia, and southeastern Alaska will be most welcome.

Happy travels!

A few particulars:

Unless otherwise noted, the bed-and-breakfast inns in this edition are open year round; innkeepers' schedules do change, however, so it is best always to clarify when making telephone or e-mail inquiries.

Some inns request minimum stays on weekends and during busy holiday times; be sure to ask. Also inquire about seasonal rates.

Because nightly and weekend rates tend to

change, the following rate categories are used in this edition and specify per night double occupancy; many inns are required to collect a city or county tax that is added to this overall rate:

$	up to $79
$$	80–$119
$$$	120–$159
$$$$	160 and up

Many bed-and-breakfasts now have e-mail addresses and Internet sites, even their own domain names, and these electronic addresses have been included in the individual entries. These addresses can change without notice, but all information has been verified and is correct as we go to press.

How to be a Great Bed & Breakfast Guest

1. Call well ahead for reservations prior to traveling; collect maps, directions before leaving home. Pack cameras and lots of film and binoculars if you have them.
2. Inquire about services and amenities that are important to you, such as king or queen beds, private bath with shower or soaking tub; discuss with the innkeepers any special dietary restrictions and allergies.
3. If you will arrive at the B&B after 4:00 to 6:00 P.M., always call with your estimated time of arrival. Leave a voice mail if the innkeeper is away. Call again on the road if you will arrive even later.
4. During the day, don't camp out in the innkeeper's kitchen longer than one cup of coffee.
5. Plan your day of activities and sightseeing and get started early so that you can thoroughly immerse yourself in the city or town and region. Ask about off-the-beaten-path destinations, local theater and activities, good restaurants and eateries, shops, delis that can provide picnic makings, and about interesting and fun things to see and do in the immediate area. Answering such questions is what B&B innkeepers enjoy and do best.
6. Stop at local and border visitors information centers and at USDA Forest Service Ranger stations for current maps, local weather and road conditions, and to make emergency telephone calls. Take time to visit local historical society museums, historic centers, and historic sites—learn interesting history about the town, the area, and the region. Staff and volunteers at these various centers, ranger stations and sites can offer helpful information and good ideas about what to see and do in

---

The prices and rates listed in this guidebook were confirmed at press time. We recommend, however, that you call establishments before traveling to obtain current information.

I. Oregon

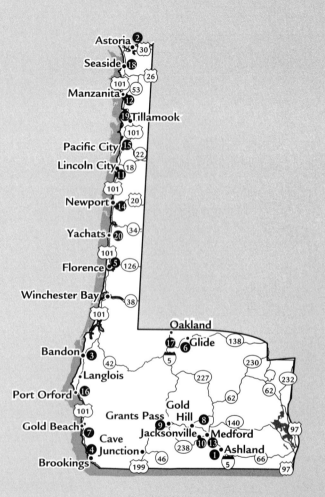

Astoria ● ❷
● 30
Seaside ● ⑱

101 26

Manzanita ● 53
⑫
⑲ Tillamook
101

Pacific City ● ⑮
22
Lincoln City ● 18
⑪
101

Newport ● 20
⑭

34
Yachats ● ⑳

101
Florence ● ⑤ 126

Winchester Bay ●
38
101

Oakland ●
⑰ ⑥ Glide
138
Bandon ● ❸ 5
42
230
Langlois ● 227
62 232
Port Orford ● ⑯
62
Gold
101 Grants Pass Hill
Gold Beach ● Jacksonville ● ❽ 140
❼ ❾ ● Medford 97
Cave ⑩ ⑬
❹ Junction ● ● Ashland
Brookings ● 238 ❶ 66
46
199 5 97

BC

AK

WA

OR

N

Southern Oregon and Oregon Coast

Numbers on map refer to towns numbered below.

1. Ashland,
   - Antique Rose Inn,   4
   - Ashland's English Country Cottage,   21
   - Country Willows Bed & Breakfast,   6
   - Cowslip's Belle Bed & Breakfast,   8
   - Hersey House Bed & Breakfast Inn,   10
   - The Iris Inn,   21
   - McCall House Bed & Breakfast,   21
   - Morical House Garden Inn,   12
   - Mount Ashland Inn,   14
   - The Pedigrift House Bed & Breakfast,   16
   - The Peerless Hotel,   18
   - Romeo Inn,   20
   - Wolfe Manor Inn,   22
2. Astoria,
   - Astoria Inn Bed & Breakfast,   27
   - Benjamin Young Inn,   27
   - Clementine's Bed & Breakfast,   24
   - Grandview Bed & Breakfast,   26
3. Bandon,
   - Bandon Beach House Bed & Breakfast,   115
4. Brookings,
   - Brookings South Coast Inn Bed & Breakfast,   31
   - Chetco River Inn Bed & Breakfast,   30
5. Florence,
   - The Blue Heron Inn,   35
   - The Johnson House Bed & Breakfast,   34
   - Oak St. Victorian B&B,   35
6. Glide,
   - Steelhead Run Bed & Breakfast,   36
7. Gold Beach,
   - Inn at Nesika Beach,   38
8. Gold Hill,
   - Willowbrook Inn,   40
9. Grants Pass,
   - Flery Manor,   42
   - Kerbyville Inn Bed & Breakfast,   55
   - Pine Meadow Inn Bed & Breakfast,   54
10. Jacksonville,
    - Historic Orth House Bed & Breakfast,   44
    - Jacksonville Inn,   47
    - McCully House Inn,   46
    - Touvelle House,   47
11. Lincoln City,
    - The Enchanted Cottage Bed & Breakfast,   48
12. Manzanita,
    - The Arbors Bed & Breakfast,   50
13. Medford,
    - Under the Greenwood Tree Bed & Breakfast,   52
14. Newport,
    - Cliff House Bed & Breakfast,   75
    - Newport Belle Bed & Breakfast,   72
    - Oar House Bed & Breakfast,   56
    - Ocean House Bed and Breakfast,   58
    - Solace by the Sea Bed & Breakfast,   74
    - Tyee Lodge Oceanfront,   59
15. Pacific City,
    - Sandlake Country Inn,   32
16. Port Orford,
    - Floras Lake House by the Sea,   71
    - Home by the Sea Bed and Breakfast,   64
    - Sixes Hotel Bed and Breakfast,   70
17. Roseburg,
    - Beckley House Bed & Breakfast,   60
18. Seaside,
    - Anderson's Boarding House Bed & Breakfast,   66
    - Cannon Beach Hotel,   69
    - Gilbert Inn Bed & Breakfast,   68
    - 10th Avenue Inn Bed & Breakfast,   69
19. Tillamook,
    - Eagle's View B&B,   63
    - SeaRose, A Bed & Breakfast,   62
20. Yachats,
    - The Kittiwake Bed & Breakfast,   76
    - New England House Bed & Breakfast,   78
    - Sea Quest Bed and Breakfast,   80
    - Serenity Bed & Breakfast,   79
    - Ziggurat Bed & Breakfast,   79

Antique Rose Inn

91 Gresham Street
Ashland, OR 97520
Phone: (541) 482-6285; (888) 282-6285
E-mail: antiquebnb@aol.com
Internet site: www.wvi.com/~dhull/antiquebnb

Innkeeper: Kathy Buffington
Rooms: 3 rooms with private baths; guest cottage with 2 rooms sleeps 2–6
Extras: Fresh flowers, terry robes, homebaked cookies; whirlpool tub for 2 in cottage
On the grounds: Flower gardens, views of nearby mountains
Smoking? Outdoors only
Visiting pets? No; 2 resident cats
Credit cards: Visa, MasterCard, American Express
Rates: $$–$$$
How to get there: From I-5 take either Ashland exit and head west to downtown; from the north turn right onto Gresham Street just before the library. From the south turn left just past Eufloria, cross Main Street and on up Gresham Street; for off-street parking turn right on Vista Street.

This restored three-story Queen Anne stick-style Victorian was constructed in 1888 by Henry B. Carter for his wife and five children for the princely sum of $4,000. "I learned that it was a 'catalogue house,'" explains Kathy. "It was shipped by railcar from Philadelphia." It was also reportedly one of the first homes in the area to have electric lights; Mr. Carter, a businessman and banker, established the first electric company here. "Most of the original light fixtures and switches are still intact," says the innkeeper.

The elegant home has thirty-seven windows, nine of which are stained glass. Cozy porches and deep verandas overlook the grounds, Grizzly Peak, and other surrounding hills and mountains. In the diary of Mr. Carter's sister on July of 1889 was written: "Brother H's house is on an elevation which overlooks the town and the view is very fine . . . no paint on the inside but a variety of Oregon woods, polished and varnished."

Now Victorian floral wallpapers adorn the walls and lovely floral chintzes dress the four-poster beds. Dark wood gleams as trim on upholstered chairs and on the elegant settee in the guest parlor. Antique laces drape the windows and bedside tables, and Tiffany lamps and stained-glass windows catch the sunlight filtering through tall windows. Although offering a decidedly Victorian ambience of yesteryear in every room, the innkeeper thoughtfully provides guests with one of modern life's daily necessities, that of fresh coffee, ". . . set out by 7:30 A.M.," smiles Kathy.

The large guest parlor on the main floor offers comfortable sitting areas, games and books as well as sherry, wines, soft drinks, and homemade cookies. A warm area rug in soft creams and blues graces the polished wood floor. A stained-glass window colors soft light.

Breakfast may consist of raspberry sorbet with fruit, freshly baked cinnamon rolls, and such delectible entrees as peach crepes, asparagus quiche, lemon soufflé, or cheese-and-crab bake. This meal is served at the large dining table in the formal dining room just off the guest parlor. The table is set with a lace tablecloth, fine china, silver, and fresh flowers.

What's Nearby

See What's Nearby Ashland on page 13.

Country Willows Bed and Breakfast Inn

1313 Clay Street
Ashland, OR 97520
Phone: (541) 488-1590; (800) WILLOWS
E-mail: willows@willowsinn.com
Internet site: www.willowsinn.com

Innkeepers: Dan Durant and David Newton
Rooms: 4 rooms with private baths in main farmhouse; large cottage adjacent to swimming pool and pond with private patio; 3 suites and 1 room in large barn, all with private baths; 1 handicap accessible room
Extras: Telephones; redwood-paneled library with fireplace, TV-VCR
On the grounds: Hiking trails through forested area behind inn; heated outdoor swimming pool; outdoor hot tub; families of goats, geese, and ducks; mountain views
Smoking? Outdoors only
Visiting pets? No
Credit cards: Visa, MasterCard, American Express, Discover
Rates: $$-$$$$
How to get there: From I-5 take exit 14, proceed west on Highway 66 and turn left on Tolman Creek Road; turn right at blinking red light onto Siskiyou Boulevard (Highway 99) and take the second left onto Clay Street following this to the inn at the end of the road.

Situated on five acres of rural farmland just south of downtown Ashland, the inn, a large two-story farmhouse with a wide second-floor balcony and main-level veranda, commands views of both the Siskiyou and Cascade Mountain ranges to the east and south. Willow outdoor furniture invites guests to sit and contemplate the grand panorama, or loaf in the swing under large graceful willows. This quiet time may be interrupted only by a gaggle of ducks or geese wad-

dling past on the rolling lawns. "We offer guests the use of our bikes for exploring nearby country roads," says Dan. "Or if you're into horses, we can arrange horseback rides at a nearby ranch."

The guest rooms are elegant havens with decor that one would often find pictured in the finest home decorating magazines. In each private bath guests find Turkish cotton robes, French milled and glycerin soaps, shampoo, bubble bath, shower caps, and an ample supply of thick towels. The most spacious accommodations are located in the enormous renovated barn. The Pine Ridge Suite has open-beam ceilings and several skylights in its combination living room/bedroom. A deep sofa and English lounge chair face the large fireplace and a custom lodgepole-pine king bed is placed so that it, too, has a view of the fireplace.

Early morning coffee is ready by 7:00 A.M., then breakfast is served from 8:30 to 9:30 A.M. at individual tables in the sun room, on the outside porches, or in the dining room. The morning meal may consist of freshly squeezed juices, poached pears with cranberry-orange relish, eggs Benedict, homemade sausage, and vegetables and fruits from the inn's gardens.

What's Nearby

Rafting, hiking, golfing, horseback riding, and skiing are close by. Ask the innkeepers about Oak Knoll and Eagle Point golf courses, both located close to the inn. Downtown Ashland is a seven-minute drive from the inn; see also What's Nearby Ashland on page 13.

Cowslip's Belle
Bed & Breakfast

159 North Main Street
Ashland, OR 97520
Phone: (541) 488-2901
E-mail: stay@cowslip.com
Internet site: www.cowslip.com/cowslip

Innkeepers: Jon and Carmen Reinhardt
Rooms: 4 rooms with private baths; evening turn-down service with truffles on the pillows; teddy bears and fresh rose bouquets from the garden placed in rooms
Extras: Hot and cold beverages, sherry, and home-made biscotti; imported English toiletries and extra thick towels in bathrooms; library in living room; free use of local racquet club with indoor tennis, indoor pool, workout center, and sauna
On the grounds: Flower garden; 3 rooms have outside decks with tables and chairs
Smoking? Outdoors only
Visiting pets? No; resident Yorkshire terrier, Tuffy "14 years young," arrangements can be made to board pet at a local kennel
Credit cards: No; personal checks accepted
Rates: $$-$$$
How to get there: If arriving from the north, take I-5 to exit 19 into Ashland to North Main Street; if arriving from the south take exit 11 from I-5 and proceed along Siskiyou Boulevard to North Main. The inn is located between Laurel and Bush Streets; parking off street to rear in paved alley off Bush Street.

I f you love chocolate and teddy bears as well as extra thick towels and the softest of bed linens, you'll probably fall in love with this bed and breakfast. "We also have a gourmet cookie business," explains Carmen, "so we invite our guests to taste-test for quality control—you know how important that is!"

The inn's down-to-earth homey atmosphere encourages long, inviting breakfasts, even forays into the kitchen for another tasty biscotti and a chat with Jon. He will most likely be whipping up another batch of his gourmet chocolate macaroon cookies.

The guest rooms are invitingly furnished with eclectic antiques, sumptuous window treatments, and cozy sitting areas. The Rosebud Suite has a color scheme of peach, moss green, terra cotta, light blue, and forest green. In its sitting room are a Victorian-style day bed, antique mahogany dresser, cushioned-wicker side chair, and French windows and garden windows dressed with balloon valances and floral patterned draperies with white lace floral sheers. In the bedroom is an antique iron-and-brass queen bed, an original built-in Douglas fir dresser and closet with Japanese cherry wood stain. The private bath has the original chrome and porcelain bathtub fixtures and its original 6' 6" tub along with a large tiled shower and Italian tile floor.

In the separate Carriage House two junior suites are decorated in an equally sumptuous manner. One offers a bent-willow handmade canopied queen bed with white silk roses intertwined throughout the canopy. Both of these suites have private entrances and private decks that overlook the garden area.

Breakfast is a gourmet affair with such marvelous entrees as crème fraîche scrambled eggs in dill crepes with smoked salmon; sour cream Belgian waffles with pecan maple cream; Secret French Toast with sour cream-cinnamon-strawberry sauce; and shrimp turnovers with sherry sauce. All this along with homemade muffins or bread and the usual selection of juice, coffee, teas, and a fresh fruit dish.

What's Nearby

See What's Nearby Ashland on page 13.

Hersey House
Bed & Breakfast Inn and
Hersey Bungalow

451 North Main Street
Ashland, OR 97520
Phone: (541) 482–4563; (888) 3HERSEY
E-mail: herseybb@mind.net
Internet site: www.mind.net/hersey

Innkeepers: Paul and Terri Mensch
Rooms: 4 rooms with antiques, private baths, telephones with voice mail; separate 1940s-style bungalow has 2 bedrooms, baths, kitchen, and dining-sitting room with cable TV
Extras: Fresh flowers in rooms; copy of Shakespeare's works in each room; guest refrigerator stocked with bottled water, soda, juice; collection of paperback novels for guests use; afternoon snacks and iced tea; piano in common area
On the grounds: English country garden that blooms from March through September; sitting area on rear deck shaded by sycamore tree; old-fashioned two-person swing attached to apple tree next to bungalow
Smoking? Not allowed
Visiting pets? No; 2 friendly resident golden retrievers, Ophir and Kira
Credit cards: Visa, MasterCard, Discover
Rates: $–$$; $$–$$$ for bungalow
How to get there: If arriving from the north, take I-5 to exit 19 into Ashland to the corner of Main and Nursery Streets. If arriving from the south, take I-5 to exit 11 and proceed along Siskiyou Boulevard and Lithia Way to North Main.

"**B**ecause we have a play season that runs from late February through summer and to early November," explains Terri, "guests enjoy having the works of Shakespeare in the rooms—good for brushing up before going to see *Merchant of Venice* or *Merry Wives of Windsor,* or whatever is currently playing!"

A desire to exit the corporate scene and a love of theater brought the couple to Ashland. Both Terri and Paul express a love of the innkeeping life. "What could be more fun than serving grape juice from your own Concord grape arbor, ripe raspberries and blueberries from your own bushes, or applesauce and apple-oat pancakes made from apples from your own tree," smiles Terri. In addition the waist-expanding breakfast may include such tasty items as cheese blintzes with strawberry-rhubarb compote, spiced-nut French toast, roasted vegetable hash with poached eggs, or potato-onion frittata with Gorgonzola.

If this isn't enough guests are served a beverage and snack—such yummy treats as cherry cake, cheese torte and crackers, brownies, or homemade cookies—when checking in or when returning from the day's activities. The inn is within walking distance to downtown shopping, Lithia Park and the intimate Japanese Garden, and the theaters.

The wonderful old house was built in 1904; in 1916 James and Carrie Hersey purchased the house and five generations of their family lived here until it was sold in 1974. In 1983 the house was renovated by two sisters and brought to life as a bed-and-breakfast inn. One senses a good feeling in this space, a feeling that surely emanates from many happy family times spent here.

What's Nearby

See What's Nearby Ashland on page 13 and What's Nearby Jacksonville on page 47.

Morical House Garden Inn

668 North Main Street
Ashland, OR 97520
Phone: (541) 482-2254; (800) 208-0960
E-mail: moricalhse@aol.com
Internet site: www.garden-inn.com

Innkeepers: Gary and Sandye Moore
Rooms: 7 rooms with private baths; some rooms offer fireplaces and double whirpool tubs; 2 rooms have wheelchair access
Extras: Afternoon refreshments, 24-hour beverage bar; rooms contain shampoos, bath gels, conditioners, moisturizing lotions, sewing kits; parlor has baby grand piano and fireplace
On the grounds: Two acres of landscaped gardens; 3 ponds, large deck, tall shade trees; sun porch with mountain and garden views
Smoking? Outdoors only
Visiting pets? No; innkeepers can assist with arranging to board pets at a nearby kennel
Credit cards: Visa, MasterCard, American Express, Discover
Rates: $$–$$$$
How to get there: From I-5 take exit 19 and follow signs into Ashland. At traffic light, turn left onto Highway 99 (North Main Street); after passing under the railroad overpass the inn is located ½ mile on the left.

"**B**ecause we both have backgrounds in theater and arts management," says Gary, "we enjoy assisting guests with activities in the area and with scheduling play tickets." Playgoers might see *A Midsummer-Night's Dream, The Comedy of Errors,* or *Hamlet;* and *Blithe Spirit, The School for Scandal,* or *Les Blancs.* Each year a new selection of plays by Shakespeare and contemporary playwrights is unveiled and runs from mid-February until the first of November. "The town really sings with theater-lovers young and old, actors, actresses, and local vendors," says Sandye. "We love it!"

The innkeepers produce a quarterly newsletter that details all of the upcoming play offerings and their dates as well as other interesting activities like special garden-design weekends at the inn, winter ski packages, even recipes from the inn's kitchen (like Ginger Pears and Holiday Pears). Guests choose from lovely rooms with names like The Berries, Garden Party, French Lace, Sage, Foxglove, Quail Run, and Aspen Grove. The latter two are new garden rooms with vaulted ceilings, king beds, fireplaces, double whirlpool tubs and showers, and wet bars with refrigerators and microwaves. Both of these rooms have private entrances.

Breakfast is served between 8:00 and 9:30 A.M. at individual tables in the dining room or on the sun porch. Tasty dishes may include fresh fruit smoothies, oatmeal soufflé, Oregon salmon, breakfast breads, and local fresh fruits and berries. Plus lots of steaming hot coffee and teas, as well as grand views out a wide expanse of windows of the inn's outstanding gardens. The entire property is registered with the National Wildlife Federation's backyard habitat program.

What's Nearby Ashland

The Oregon Shakespearean Festival offers historic and contemporary plays nearly year-round in two indoor theaters as well as on the splendid outdoor Elizabethan Stage. Oregon Cabaret Theatre hosts musicals, revues, and comedies. Downtown areas offer a plethora of charming shops, boutiques, and eateries. Travelers enjoy Lithia Park, the intimate Japanese Garden, and outdoor music concerts at the park's band shell. Nearby Jackson Hot Springs spa offers warm mineral swimming pools. Hiking paths and trails are accessible in nearby nature areas. The Ashland Visitors Information Center is located at 110 East Main Street, P.O. Box 1360, Ashland, OR 97520; Telephone: (541) 482-3486.

Mount Ashland Inn

550 Mount Ashland Ski Road
Ashland, OR 97520
Phone: (541) 482-8707; (800) 830-8707
Internet site: www.mtashlandinn.com

If the notion of sleeping in a 5,500-square-foot, handcrafted mountain log inn sounds appealing, travelers can easily drive the paved road that leads up to 7,528-foot Mount Ashland. "We're just above the 5,000-foot level and about 16 miles south of Ashland," explains Chuck. "And about 6 miles from I-5." The original owners, Elaine and Jerry Shanafelt, built the inn in the late 1980s selecting trees on site from their 160 acres. After cutting and stripping some 275 incense cedar logs, Jerry, an architect, per-

Innkeepers: Chuck and Laurel Biegert
Rooms: 5 rooms with private baths, 2 with gas fireplaces; 1 room is handicap accessible
Extras: Beverages and snacks available; extensive music library in common areas; in-room CD players; handmade quilts; hair dryers, slippers, spa slippers, and robes; snowshoes, cross-country skis, sleds; guided cross-country ski tours and dog sled tours from the inn; mountain bikes in summer; outdoor spa and sauna; newsletter for guests
On the grounds: Pacific Crest Trail located at inn's door; forest of ponderosa pine, incense cedar, and white and Douglas fir; views of Mount Shasta and Siskiyou Mountains
Smoking? Not allowed
Visiting pets? No; two resident golden retrievers, Aspen and Whistler, not allowed in indoor guest areas but they are often invited to accompany guests on summer hikes and winter snowshoeing forays
Credit cards: Visa, MasterCard, Discover
Rates: $$-$$$$
How to get there: From Ashland, take I-5 10 miles south to exit 6 and turn right onto Mount Ashland Ski Road; the inn is located 5½ miles up the mountain. Note: The road is regularly plowed during winter months but traction devices may be required; guests should be prepared for snow November through May.

formed most of the construction, plumbing, wiring, and finishing work.

"We feel privileged to continue offering fine lodging to guests," say the Biegerts, "and we've continued to add more amenities as well." One of the latest additions is the relocation of the luxurious Sky Lakes Suite to the top floor of the inn. It offers a stunning view of 14,162-foot snowy Mount Shasta some 50 miles to the south in very northern California. Perhaps the ultimate in privacy, the suite offers a cozy reading nook, king bed with a handmade quilt, river-rock gas fireplace, comfortable antiques, wet bar, refrigerator, and microwave. A skylight bath/spa for two is entered through a handcrafted log archway; a miniature rock waterfall fills the tub.

Other guest rooms, including Mount Ashland, Cottonwood Peak, Mount Shasta Suite, and Mount McLoughlin Suite, are equally as inviting and offer queen or king beds, handmade quilts, and antique dressers. A large stone fireplace warms the inn's common room on the main floor, welcoming guests to snuggle up on the couch in front of the crackling fire or browse a bookcase filled with games, books, magazines, and memorabilia from the innkeepers' travels. Outdoor activities beckon both summer and winter and guests are welcome to use any of the inn's cache of equipment available for mountain biking as well as for cross-country skiing, sledding, and snowshoeing. During winter months guests can also arrange for a ride on the Sled Dog Express that, snow permitting, departs from the inn's door; veteran musher Pat Campbell and his dogs whisk folks through the surrounding snowy wonderland.

Breakfast is served between 8:00 and 9:00 A.M. at tables in the sunny dining area along with more stunning views of Mount Shasta. "I like to describe breakfast as gourmet, on the healthy side of decadent," chuckles Laurel. And that it is—try orange creamsicle smoothies, honey-lime pears with toasted almonds, and lemon-cheese French toast. Or perhaps enjoy cold cantaloupe soup with kiwi, fresh baked focaccia bread, and fresh spinach-mushroom frittata or baked Marsala eggs on a bed of ham and dilled sour cream with onion crouton topping. For evening dining ask the innkeepers about eateries such as Firefly, Cucina Biazzi, and Chateaulin in nearby Ashland.

What's Nearby

Alpine skiing is available at Mount Ashland generally from November through April. Also see What's Nearby Ashland on page 13.

The Pedigrift House Bed & Breakfast

407 Scenic Drive
Ashland, OR 97520
Phone: (541) 482–1888; (800) 262–4073
Internet site: www.opendoor.com/pedigrift

Innkeepers: Dorothy and Richard Davis
Rooms: 4 rooms with private baths
Extras: Afternoon beverages, cheeses, fruits served buffet-style in dining room; soft drinks and wines available in guest refrigerator; fresh flowers in common rooms and guest rooms; warm dessert with ice cream available after evening theater; telephone jacks in each guest room; gas fireplace in common room
On the grounds: Patio sitting areas near terraced gardens in the rear; wide views of southern Rogue Valley and Grizzly Peak
Smoking? Outdoors only
Visiting pets? No; 1 resident cat
Credit cards: Visa, MasterCard
Rates: $$–$$$
How to get there: From downtown Ashland, travel north on North Main Street to Wimer Street; turn left and proceed to Scenic Drive.

Constructed in 1888 by S. and Sarah J. Pedigrift, the two-story home is a fine example of the double-bay front variation of the late Victorian Queen Anne style. The truncated hip roof resembles the mansard roof of Second Empire houses, while the gable dormers and wide cornice band and bracketry add an Italianate quality to the design. "Among the several owners of the house were the Kingsbury family and later the Ashcraft family, both families from New York," explains Richard. "We also share New York roots so this has been a very special project,

opening the wonderful old house for bed-and-breakfast travelers from all across the country."

The Davises purchased the house in 1993 undertaking extensive remodeling in 1994 and opening their wide front door to guests in May 1995. East Room on the main floor offers from its cushioned window seat and bay window splendid views of the east valley and Grizzly Peak. Garden Room, a spacious corner room with skylights, overlooks the terraced garden and patio. Cypress Room and Spruce Room both offer valley and mountain views as well; the room is named for the large Monterey cypress that grows at the corner of the property planted by the Pedigrifts when the house was constructed. Guests find a comfortable mix of traditional and antique furnishings, soft comforters, and fresh flowers in addition to desks, comfortable chairs, and good lighting in their abodes.

Breakfast is served at three round tables in the large dining room where a small grandfather clock overlooks the proceedings. Tantalizing smells from the inn's kitchen may indicate such morning fare as French toast, quiche, or blueberry pancakes along with bacon, sausage, roasted potatoes, and fresh baked muffins, scones, or coffeecake. Freshly squeezed orange juice and steaming hot coffee and tea are also plentiful every morning.

What's Nearby

See What's Nearby Ashland on page 13, What's Nearby Medford on page 53, and What's Nearby Jacksonville on page 47.

The Peerless Hotel & Restaurant

243 Fourth Street
Ashland, OR 97520
Phone: (541) 488–1082; (800) 460–8758
E-mail: peerless@mind.net
Internet site: www.mind.net/peerless

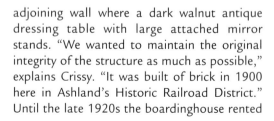

Innkeepers: Crissy and Steve Barnett
Rooms: 6 rooms with telephones and private baths, some with whirlpool tubs, his and hers claw-foot tubs, or 2-person shower; gas-burning wood stove in 1 room; 1 handicap accessible room; nightly turndown service
Extras: Italian bed linens; 30 channels of cabled in-room music; Private Butler honor bars in each room; health club access; bicycles; room service available from inn's restaurant; Sunday champagne brunch; afternoon tea served Monday–Saturday; after-theater dessert and wine also are available
On the grounds: Historic Railroad District is nearby
Smoking? Outdoors only
Visiting pets? No
Credit cards: Visa, MasterCard, American Express
Rates: $$–$$$$
How to get there: If arriving from the north or south, take I-5 to exit 11 and proceed along Siskiyou Boulevard to Main Street; turn right onto Second Street, then turn right onto B Street; at Fourth Street turn left.

Offering an eclectic mixture of exotic antique furnishings from New Orleans to the West Indies to the Hawaiian Islands, each room is crowned with hand-painted ceilings and walls. One of the guest rooms offers a captivating trompe l'oeil garden painted on the wall in the bed's alcove; original bricks face an adjoining wall where a dark walnut antique dressing table with large attached mirror stands. "We wanted to maintain the original integrity of the structure as much as possible," explains Crissy. "It was built of brick in 1900 here in Ashland's Historic Railroad District." Until the late 1920s the boardinghouse rented small rooms to Southern Pacific railroad workers; "the fourteen rooms all shared one bath," says Crissy. She also arranged to have the large beverage sign restored on the inn's exterior brick wall—"it was originally painted around 1915."

The inn's guests often take in a game of golf during the day at Quail Point, Eagle Point, Cedar Links, or other municipal courses. Nightly plays beckon guests as well. The inn's Garden Grill is open for lunch, dinner, cocktails and private parties. The hotel's Connoisseur Menu is also quite popular, and all the delectable entrees and offerings are designed and prepared by executive chef Daniel Durfort. After-theater dessert and wine are also available with prior arrangement.

Breakfast, served from 8:45 to 10:30 A.M. in the sunny Back Porch Room on the main floor, may consist of freshly squeezed orange juice, mango bread, traditional eggs Benedict, hash browns, and Kona coffee. A weekend special at the inn could be grilled lamb sausage with sweet pepper ratatouille on soft garlic polenta, a choice of champagne mimosa or Peerless Fizz along with a basket of freshly baked breads and muffins and an exotic fresh fruit salad.

What's Nearby

See What's Nearby Ashland on page 13.

Romeo Inn

295 Idaho Street
Ashland, OR 97520
Phone: (541) 488-0884; (800) 915-8899

Innkeepers: Deana and Donald Politis
Rooms: 6 rooms with private baths
Extras: Teas, soft drinks, cookies; afternoon snacks; daily newspapers; library with large selection of books and magazines; thick terry robes and luxury soaps in baths; fresh flowers in guest rooms; homemade chocolates placed in rooms each evening
On the grounds: Heated outdoor swimming pool and hot tub; landscaped flower gardens
Smoking? Not allowed
Visiting pets? Some pets with restrictions; inquire with innkeepers
Credit cards: Visa, MasterCard, Discover
Rates: $$-$$$$
How to get there: From downtown Ashland proceed south on Main Street; turn right onto Gresham Street, then left onto Iowa Street, and right onto Idaho Street. The inn is on the corner of Idaho and Holly Streets.

This is the kind of comfortable inn that invites one to ease into a soft overstuffed chair or curl up on a cozy love seat near the fireplace with a great novel, a glass of wine, and thou. There is plenty of space here, plus light from wide windows and views of the expansive rear garden. You might decide to open the French doors and amble outside for a dip in the large heated swimming pool or float on an air mattress and contemplate the fluffy white clouds and blue sky overhead. You could relax on a lounge chair and watch others swim their laps. Later you might sink into the outdoor hot tub for a warm soak before retiring for the night. The guest rooms are spacious and equally as comfortable as the rest of the inn. For a couple who desires a special hideaway, the separate Stratford Suite offers a romantic haven with its own two-person whirlpool tub, sitting room with marble fireplace and views of the Cascade Mountains, raised king bed, and complete kitchen.

"We like our quiet residential area," says Donald. "We both were insurance executives before becoming innkeepers; we enjoy our wonderful guests and the challenge of owning our own business." The innkeepers serve a three-course breakfast between 8:30 and 9:30 A.M. in the dining room. Coffee and tea are available at 7:30 A.M., however, for early risers. Your breakfast might include fresh juices, pineapple with maple cream and granola, apricot scones, and a ham soufflé with chile potatoes.

Besides the plays offered by the Oregon Shakespearean Festival, other plays are offered at the Ginger Rogers Craterian Theater, the Oregon Cabaret Theatre, the Actors' Theatre of Ashland, and the Southern Oregon University Theatre Arts. "There's also Monday night ballet in Lithia Park," offers Deana. "And during the winter, ice skating in Lithia Park at our new Darex Family Ice Rink." Ask the couple about favorite spots for dining out such as Chateaulin, Monet, Beasy's on the Creek, Primavera, Quinz, Winchester House, and Plaza Café.

What's Nearby

See What's Nearby Ashland on page 13.

Other Recommended B&Bs Nearby

Ashland's English Country Cottage, a Tudor-style inn with rooms named after English flowers; innkeepers Shirley and Brian Wallace, 271 Beach Street, Ashland, OR 97520; Telephone: (541) 488-4428. **The Iris Inn,** a cozy 1905 Victorian near downtown shops and parks; innkeeper Vicki Lamb, 59 Manzanita Street, Ashland OR 97520; Telephone: (541) 488-2286. **McCall House,** historic 1883 Victorian, one of the oldest and largest in town; innkeepers Bobbie and Ed Bludau, 153 Oak Street, Ashland, OR 97520; Telephone: (541) 482-9296.

Wolfe Manor Inn

586 "B" Street
Ashland, OR 97520
Phone: (541) 488-3676; (800) 801-3676
Internet site: www.wolfemanor.com

Innkeepers: Sybil and Ron Maddox
Rooms: 5 rooms with private baths
Extras: Bathrobes and toiletries in baths; down comforters; four-poster queen bed in 1 room; some rooms have mountain views; fresh flowers from garden; after dinner port and truffles; mini 24-hour beverage and snack center
On the grounds: Wicker furniture on front veranda; sitting places in private rear garden; landscaped flower beds and shade trees
Smoking? Not allowed
Visiting pets? No; 4 outside neighborhood cats visit occasionally
Credit cards: Visa, MasterCard, American Express, Discover, Diners
Rates: $-$$$
How to get there: Turn north off Siskiyou Boulevard at the Safeway store onto Sherman Street; go one block to East Main and jog to the left on this street; turn right on Fifth Street and proceed two blocks to B Street; the inn is on the corner of Fifth and B Streets.

"The original owners, Mamie and Julius Wolfe, had the house built in 1910 and they loved to party and entertain in high style," smiles Sybil. "Their grand ballroom is now our combined parlor and dining room." It is a wonderful space filled with comfortable French provincial furniture, has large bay windows, and it contains some of the original lighting fixtures. The dining room table is set with fine linens, specially folded napkins, elegant arrangements of fresh flowers, and individual place settings of white china. Tall cane-back chairs await guests who will arrive for a hearty breakfast, " . . . at 0900," says Sybil. "But fresh brewed coffee is available at 0700 in the foyer."

The cozy library-reading room has wicker furniture, an Oriental rug, seascape oil painting, small antique desk, and guest telephone. Relax on the veranda, picnic on the patio in the garden, or curl up with a book in your cozy room.

The Swazi Safari room, with its private entry and two full-sized beds with down comforters, reminds Sybil of her youth; she was born and raised in Kenya and in South Africa. Alyce's Alcove is a romantic space decorated in shades of blue and white. Norman's Nook is furnished with Norman Rockwell memorabilia, and Lynette's Lair has an antique four-poster queen bed. Before retiring guests are offered chocolate truffles and port as a way of saying "pleasant dreams."

Sybil and Ron can offer ideas for day trips such as rafting on the Rogue and Klamath rivers. For dinner out options ask about local restaurants like Firefly, Chateaulin, and Cucina Biazzi.

What's Nearby

See What's Nearby Ashland on page 13. For information about fishing, boating, rafting, hiking, and other wilderness experiences, contact the Ashland Ranger District and Siskiyou Welcome Center, 645 Washington Street, Ashland, OR 97520; Telephone: (541) 482-3333.

Clementine's Bed & Breakfast

847 Exchange Street
Astoria, OR 97103
Phone: (503) 325-2005; (800) 521-6801
E-mail: jtaylor@clementines-bb.com
Internet site: www.clementines-bb.com

Innkeepers: Judith and Cliff Taylor
Rooms: 5 rooms with private baths, 1 with gas fireplace; 2 suites in separate cottage
Extras: Sweet treats and beverages served evenings in common room; baby grand piano; gourmet cooking classes taught in gourmet kitchen; fresh flowers in the rooms
On the grounds: Lavish English-style garden of annuals and fragrant perennials, rose garden, cutting garden
Smoking? Outdoors only
Visiting pets? No; 2 resident Australian shepherds, P. K. and Yinnie
Credit cards: Visa, MasterCard
Rates: $-$$
How to get there: From downtown Astoria turn onto Eighth Street and proceed 4 blocks away from the Columbia River to Exchange Street. The inn is located across from the Flavel House Museum.

"We're located downtown in the historic district," explains Judith, "right across from the wonderful Flavel House Museum." The inn is also within easy walking distance to shopping, dining, and other historic houses and museums in Astoria, the oldest U.S. city west of the Mississippi River. The town dates back to 1811 when John Jacob Astor developed a fur trading post here at the mouth of the Columbia River.

Judith, originally from the Northwest, was the executive director of the Nevada Symphony for seven years. Cliff formerly worked as a guide on the Colorado River, rowing for Grand Canyon Dories. "I enjoy talking 'boat talk' with guests," says Cliff. Moving to Astoria in 1993, the husband-and-wife team tackled the renovation of this large 1888 classic Italianate Victorian. "We decided to name the inn after its first mistress, Clementine, and we opened our doors to bed-

and-breakfast guests that summer," recalls Judith. The couple also got involved in the local Master Gardner program, completely redesigned the landscaping, and planted both a wonderful English garden and an exceptional rose garden on the grounds.

The spacious guest rooms have names like Clementine's Suite, Sunriser Room, French Violet, Garden Room, and The School Room. The suite features a wide view of the Columbia River from a large bay window and private balcony. An antique mirrored armoire stands next to the white-iron queen bed; a gas fireplace warms the room. Bedside reading lamps are included in all the rooms. The main floor School Room catches the morning sun and is embellished with late 1800s and early 1900s school artifacts including a vintage U.S. school flag that hangs next to the antique dresser. In a separate renovated cottage two suites are suitable for families and for longer visits. This structure dating back to 1850 once housed the city's Moose Lodge.

Judith prepares generous continental breakfasts in the gourmet kitchen located on the main level next to the dining area. Sparkling white open shelves that extend from counter to ceiling display glassware, cookware, and cooking utensils. Copper skillets, pots, and kettles gleam on the stovetop. Gourmet cooking classes are offered at the inn throughout the year, coordinated and taught by Judith.

What's Nearby

See What's Nearby Astoria on page 27 and What's Nearby Seaside on page 67.

Grandview Bed & Breakfast

1574 Grand Avenue
Astoria, OR 97103
Phone: (503) 325-0000; (800) 488-3250
E-mail: grandvu@postbox.com
Internet site:
www.bbonline.com/or/grandview/

Innkeeper: Charleen Maxwell
Rooms: 9 rooms, 7 with private baths; several have canopy beds
Extras: Snacks such as cookies, apples, almonds, dried cranberries
On the grounds: Flower gardens, view down the bluff to Columbia River
Smoking? Outdoors or on Treetops balcony
Visiting pets? No; one resident female German shepherd, Kearsarge
Other restrictions: No alcoholic beverages allowed on the premises
Credit cards: Visa, MasterCard, Discover
Rates: $-$$; two room suites $$-$$$
How to get there: Access Astoria via Highway 30 from Portland or via Highway 26 from Portland to Seaside, then Highway 101 north to Astoria; from the downtown area turn south, uphill, on Sixteenth Street for 4 blocks; turn right onto Grand Avenue to second house on right.

"We especially welcome families with children," says innkeeper Charleen Maxwell. "The youngsters as well as their moms and dads enjoy seeing the views of historic Astoria and the Columbia River from the bullet turret, the bay windows, the five-sided tower, and the balconies." Charleen shares some history about the house explaining that Eben Tallant and his brother Nathan came to Astoria to build a salmon-packing cannery, and that they commissioned Andrew Ferguson to design the Richardson shingle-style residence. "My research indicates that the house was built in the late 1890s," says Charleen.

Additional research on the house and its original owners reveals that Eben had spent some time as first officer on a clipper ship and also had held a similar post for a time on a passenger ship that sailed between Shanghai and Hong Kong. This love of the sea may account in part for the tower capped with an open balcony on the northwest corner of the house that gives the feeling of standing on the prow of a ship. It points toward the mouth of the Columbia River far below, which churns against and with the changing tides as it converges with the Pacific Ocean.

The well-appointed guest rooms have charming names like The Rose Bower, The Leopard's Lair, The Iris Garden, The Gazebo, The Treetops, Cloud 9, The Secret Garden, Anastasia's Room, Peaceable Kingdom, and The Bird Tweet. Families can ask about the availability of two-bedroom suites. The Gazebo may be the most popular

room with its queen canopy bed and views of the Columbia River from tower windows and balcony.

Breakfast is served in the dining room with its bullet-style turret allowing views down the bluff of the river, several one-hundred-year-old churches, and nearby Victorian homes. Guests enjoy fresh-squeezed orange juice, homemade muffins, smoked salmon, cream cheese, bagels, fresh fruit in season, and hot beverages. For pleasant dinner-out options, ask Charleen about Pier II, Café Uniontown, Ira's, and Ship Inn.

What's Nearby Astoria

In addition to historic walking tours of both downtown and residential areas, visitors can enjoy waterfront boutiques, galleries, antiques shops, and cafes. Close by are the historic Astor Column (atop Coxcomb Hill), the Columbia River Maritime Museum, the elegant Flavel House Museum, Uppertown Firefighters Museum, and the restored Fort Astoria. Within a short drive are living history programs at historic Fort Clatsop. For an extra treat, drive across the 4-mile-long Astoria-Megler bridge that spans the river and ocean between Oregon and southern tip of Washington state to visit the World Kite Museum on the Long Beach Peninsula. Ships from many nations dock at Astoria and some allow Sunday tours. The Astoria/Warrenton Visitors Information Center is located at 111 West Marine Drive, P.O. Box 176, Astoria, OR 97103; Telephone: (503) 325-6311.

Other Recommended B&Bs Nearby

Astoria Inn Bed & Breakfast, an 1890s Victorian, offers rooms with private baths and Columbia River views from the veranda; contact innkeeper Mickey Cox at 3391 Irving Avenue, Astoria, OR 97103; Telephone: (503) 325-8153. **Benjamin Young Inn** features river-view rooms in an elegant 1888 Queen Anne Victorian with traditional tower; contact innkeeper Carolyn Hammer at 3652 Duane Street, Astoria, OR 97103; Telephone: (503) 325-6172.

Bandon Beach House Bed & Breakfast

2866 Beach Loop Drive
Bandon, OR 97411
Phone: (541) 347-1196
E-mail: beachhouse@harborside.com
Internet site: www.bandonbeach.com

Innkeepers: Adrienne and Steve Casey
Rooms: 2 rooms with private baths
Extras: Suite-sized ocean view rooms; river-rock fireplaces; morning tray with hot beverages
On the grounds: The Pacific Ocean, sandy beach, offshore sea stacks, water birds
Smoking? Outdoors only
Visiting pets? No; no resident pets
Credits cards: None at this time; personal checks accepted
Rates: $$$
How to get there: From Highway 101 in Bandon, continue 1 mile south of the traffic light at Eleventh Street, then turn west off Highway 101 onto SeaBird Lane. Proceed to Beach Loop Drive which edges the ocean bluff; the inn is located five houses to the right (north) on the ocean side of the drive.

"**W**e're located on a gently sloping 50-foot bluff right at the edge of the ocean," explains Steve. And the views are stunning. Try taking in about 250 degrees of sandy beach, ocean surf and far horizon, and the oddly shaped sea stacks that are so characteristic of this section of the coast. The sea stacks, jutting upward at various heights near the shore, are actually basaltic remnants of eons-ago volcanic activity deep under the ocean. They provide transient nesting places for hundreds of gulls, puffins, cormorants, and petrels—among some of the many seabird species that range up and down the Oregon coast.

After checking in, guests often relax in the Great Room with its large river-rock fireplace and comfortable sofas and overstuffed chairs. These afford front-row seats for views through the large windows facing west and the setting sun. "Our sunsets are marvelous," says Adrienne. Or you can soon disappear into your large suite with its own smaller version of the river-rock fireplace. From the cozy sitting places and from the king bed with a handsome quilt, you'll also have the wonderful ocean views. The decor is casual but at the same time luxurious. Guests feel well taken care of here. It feels much like an elegant lodge, especially with the use of river rock for the fireplaces and with the collection of early California art displayed in the common areas.

Before breakfast a welcome tray of coffee or tea appears at your door, a thoughtful amenity for those who appreciate an early morning "cuppa." Breakfast is served at the dining table in the Great Room usually around 8:30 or 9:00 A.M., giving guests time to walk on the beach or have a morning run. The first course is fresh fruit in season, such as cantaloupe and bananas or papaya and slices of lemon, followed by homemade breads and, perhaps, an egg soufflé or baked cranberry French toast.

What's Nearby Bandon

Charming Old Town offers numerous weaving, gifts, and sweets shops, bookstores, and good restaurants. Ask about the Coquille River Museum housed in the refurbished Coast Guard building along the river, as well as the old Coquille River Lighthouse Museum on the jetty, about jetty fishing, and where to see the cranberry bogs and the process of cheesemaking. In nearby Coos Bay-North Bend travelers can find Shore Acres Gardens, Sunset Bay, and Charleston Harbor. The Visitor's Information Center is located at the entrance to Old Town, P.O. Box 1515, Bandon, OR 97411; Telephone: (541) 347-9616.

Chetco River Inn

21202 High Prairie Road
Brookings, OR 97415
Phone: (541) 670-1645; (800) 327-2688
(Pelican Bay Travel in Brookings, open week-
days 9:00 A.M. to 5:00 P.M.)
Internet site: www.chetcoriverinn.com

Innkeeper: Sandra Brugger
Rooms: 5 rooms with private baths
Extras: The solitude of being in an area with no electricity and near a wilderness area
On the grounds: The Wild and Scenic Chetco River, herbal garden, wooded flower garden, acres of mixed fir, pine, and myrtlewood forest; near Kalmiopsis Wilderness
Smoking? Outdoors only
Visiting pets? No; 2 resident Scotties, Maggie and Max, and 2 outside cats, Louie and Clark
Credit cards: Visa, MasterCard (the innkeeper prefers payment by check)
Rates: $$–$$$
How to get there: From Highway 101 in Brookings turn east onto North Bank Road following the Chetco River 16 miles; you will pass Loeb State Park and Little Redwood Campground and cross three bridges along the way. Continue across the fourth bridge, South Fork Bridge, then turn left for ³⁄₁₀ mile and left again at the inn's sign.

By the time you reach the inn, any doubts about being far away from freeways and city lights will have evaporated. At this point travelers have crossed several bridges over the meandering Wild and Scenic Chetco River and are close to the Kalmiopsis Wilderness in the heart of the Siskiyou Mountains in the Beaver State's southernmost region. Next stop: California. "Actually I'm so far off the beaten path that the power company decided it was too far to bring in electricity," explains Sandra.

So are we sleeping in tents and sitting around a campfire? Far from it. Instead guests find an elegant and contemporary back-country retreat with expanses of windows that afford serene views of the river, herb and wooded flower gardens, and forests. Whatever power is needed indoors is generated by alternative means such as solar propane batteries and wood stoves.

Guests also find in the comfortable Great Room on the main floor soft Oriental rugs on an elegant marble floor, a fireplace fashioned of local rock, cozy wingback chairs, and comfortable sofa. On the open balcony landing is a well-stocked library. Brass and wrought-iron beds with down comforters and handmade quilts are found in the comfortable guest rooms, located on the second floor. One room offers twin beds. A fifth room is located on the main level; this new room offers a whirlpool tub and a view of the gardens.

Outdoors the loudest sounds you hear may be soft winds chattering through the trees, mountain birds offering a morning chorus, or water lapping gently against the river shore. In the morning guests gather around the polished wood table adjacent to the Great Room while Sandra serves baked apples with raisin brandy sauce, Dutch baby pancakes with fresh lemon and sugar and maple syrup, locally made banger sausage, or chef's potatoes with cheese and chives along with biscotti and hot steaming coffee and teas. "'Not bad for back-country living' one couple said recently," the innkeeper told me with a grin.

Note: Make prior arrangements with the innkeeper well ahead of your visit for dinner; don't even think of popping into town for supper.

What's Nearby Brookings

Both saltwater and fresh water options are many—try, for example, deep-sea fishing, drift boat fishing, kayaking, canoeing, or rafting. For back-country and wilderness hiking information contact the Chetco Ranger Station, 555 Fifth Street, Brookings, OR 97415; Telephone: (541) 469-3025. The Brookings-Harbor Visitors Information Center is located at the Port, 16330 Lower Harbor Road, P.O. Box 940, Brookings, OR 97415; Telephone: (541) 469-3181.

Other Recommended B&B Nearby

Brookings South Coast Inn Bed & Breakfast, 1917 Craftsman-style home overlooks Brookings and the ocean; innkeepers Ken Raith and Keith Pepper, 516 Redwood Street, Brookings, OR 97415; Telephone: (541) 469-5557.

Sandlake Country Inn

8505 Galloway Road
Cloverdale, OR 97112
Phone: (503) 965-6745

Innkeepers: Femke and David Durham
Rooms: 4 rooms, 2 with TV/VCR, private baths, all with whirlpool tubs; 1 handicap accessible room
Extras: Breakfast en suite includes Femke's Baked Apple Oatmeal, cookies, and hot cider
On the grounds: Two streams, tall Douglas fir, rhododendron, country rose garden
Smoking? Outdoors on patio
Visiting pets? No; one resident dog, Chaucer, and one outdoor cat, BJ
Credit cards: Visa, MasterCard, American Express, Discover
Rates: $$-$$$
How to get there: Take Highway 26 west from Portland to Highway 6; southwest to Tillamook then south on Highway 101 11 miles to Sandlake turnoff; 5½ miles to Three Capes Scenic Loop turning south to Galloway Road (near Fire Station). The inn is about 115 miles from Portland.

For a comfortable overnight stop far away from city lights, consider the romantic Sandlake Country Inn located a few miles north of Pacific City. Nestled about 1 mile from the ocean in a green bower of rhododendron, old roses, and Douglas fir, the large farmhouse was built in 1894 out of virgin red-fir bridge timbers from a ship that had wrecked four years earlier off the coast near here. The home had been in the same family for eighty years when the original innkeepers purchased and refurbished it for a bed-and-breakfast in the late 1980s.

"We purchased the inn in 1995," explains Femke, "and we have enjoyed continuing and enhancing the romantic tradition here." Guests may choose from four lovely rooms—The Rose Garden offers a canopied king bed to snuggle into as well as wicker furniture and French doors; the rose garden is just outside. On the entire second floor, The Starlight Suite is a spacious hideaway with a plum paisley half-canopy queen bed and private deck overlooking the rear gardens. A double-sided fireplace warms both the bedroom and sitting room. The luxury bath is equipped with a whirlpool tub for two plus a claw-foot tub and shower.

In The Timbers room you can see those huge 3' x 12' bridge timbers exposed; colors and prints in woodsy green, rose, and gold warm the walls and also the comforter on the king bed. The fireplace offers a warm glow as well. This room has a private entrance from the country garden. The Cottage and its private deck are separate from the main house, nestled alongside the stream and shaded by lush rhododendron and tall trees. Guests can warm themselves by the gas fireplace in the living room or in the warm waters of the whirlpool tub.

Breakfast is served on a handsome tray delivered to your door allowing for a private tête-à-tête, and may include such goodies as country orange juice, Dave's special smoothies, zucchini frittata, Sunny Day Muffins, Oregon hazelnut toast and jam, and the inn's specialty, Baked Apple Oatmeal. Also available during the day are Sandlake Country Inn cookies, hot apple cider or raspberry lemonade, and hot water for teas, hot chocolate and such. For evening dinner options ask about restaurants and eateries in Pacific City and Oceanside.

What's Nearby

In addition to sand dunes and beach walks, horseback riding on the beach, hiking at Cape Lookout State Park, and winter storm watching, see What's Nearby Oceanside on page 63.

The Johnson House Bed & Breakfast Inn

216 Maple Street
P.O. Box 1892
Florence, OR 97439
Phone: (541) 997–8000; (800) 768–9488
E-mail: fraese@presys.com
Internet site:
www.touroregon.com/TheJohnsonHouse

Innkeepers: Jayne and Ron Fraese
Rooms: 6 rooms, 3 with private baths, 1 handicap accessible room with private bath
Extras: Gourmet breakfasts with special European recipes particularly from France
On the grounds: Lovely garden that emphasizes herbs, edible plants, roses, and Northwest perennials
Smoking? Outdoors only
Visiting pets? No; no resident pets
Credit cards: Visa, MasterCard, Discover
Rates: $$-$$$
How to get there: From Highway 101 turn away from the ocean onto Maple Street (just across from the Chevron service station); the inn is located at the corner of Maple and First Streets and just one block north of the Old Town waterfront area.

Dating back to 1892 and reportedly the oldest house in Florence, the structure was built by Dr. O. F. Kennedy as a residence and clinic. The planed lumber and trim molding were probably brought in by ship from San Francisco. Over the years the house served as a private residence for several owners, the last of whom were Milo and Cora Johnson, who lived here for sixty years. "We bought the Johnson house in 1982 and began major restoration," explains Jayne. They opened the bed & breakfast in 1984.

The Fraeses became intrigued with the bed-and-breakfast experience through travels in Europe, particularly in France. He had been stationed at an Air Force base near Paris during the 1950s; in September 1998 the couple traveled again to France for an Air Force reunion of his original group. "We go to France almost every year; we love the people and we love the food!"

Jayne brings back wonderful recipes from France to use at the inn. Guests are invited down to the dining room for breakfast at 8:30 A.M. and may be treated to such gourmet fare as frittata with chanterelles and goat cheese, omelette *aux fines herbes,* special crepes, or a light soufflé. All specialties of the house are made with fresh herbs and ingredients from the kitchen garden, and special breads and scones are baked daily at the inn. "I like to use fresh seafood in season for other breakfast surprises," smiles Jayne.

The nineteenth-century parlor features plain but comfortable farm-style furnishings of the late 1890s, including a pump organ of the period. Cozy guest rooms are located on the second floor of the inn. For dining out try Lovejoy's, an English restaurant, pub, and tea room; Bay Street Grill for pasta, fresh seafood, and microbrews; Mo's for informal fish and chips on the river; or the Windward Inn for steaks.

What's Nearby Florence

Freshwater fishing is available in both the Siuslaw River and in many freshwater lakes located close by. There are also opportunities for deep-sea fishing, clamming and crabbing, and hiking and dune buggy riding in the nearby sand dunes. Visitors can beachcomb, beach walk, and bird watch out at the South Jetty area; the flat terrain there is also fine for bicycling. Cozy cafes, restaurants, and delightful shops line the street in Old Town along the waterfront. The Performing Arts Center offers fare on the weekends and a wonderful old movie theater from the 1930s has been restored in Old Town. Ask for information about horseback riding on the beach from one of the stables located north of town. Devil's Elbow Beach and the picturesque Heceta Head Lighthouse are just north of town a few miles. The Florence Visitors Information Center is located at 270 Highway 101; Telephone: (541) 997-3128.

Other Recommended B&Bs Nearby

The Blue Heron Inn, 1940s ranch home with views of Siuslaw River, innkeepers Doris Van Osdell and Maurice Souza, 6563 Highway 126, P.O. Box 1122, Florence, OR 97439; Telephone: (541) 997-4901. **Oak St. Victorian B&B,** a 1904 cottage with antiques, flowers, and lace; innkeepers Paul and Hazel Arellanes, 394 Oak Street, P.O. Box 2799, Florence, OR 97439; Telephone: (541) 997-4000.

Steelhead Run
Bed & Breakfast

23049 North Umpqua Highway
P.O. Box 807
Glide, OR 97443
Phone: (541) 496-0563; (800) 348-0563
Internet site: www.moriah.com/inns

Innkeepers: George and Nancy Acosta; Dick Moeller, Sr.

Rooms: 5 rooms with private baths; 1 handicap accessible room; 1 family unit with a small kitchen; 4 rooms open onto decks with views of the river

Extras: Guest parlor with library; large screen TV in Little Theatre Room; TV/VCRs in each room; selection of more than 400 videos; game room with billiards, darts, and board games; gallery and gift shop on the premises

On the grounds: North Umpqua River; barbeque and picnic tables available in picnic areas along the river

Smoking? Outdoors only

Visiting pets? Yes, if well-trained, only in family kitchen unit

Credit cards: Visa, MasterCard, Discover, American Express, Novus

Rates: $–$$; the inn is closed during December and January

How to get there: From I-5 at Roseburg turn east onto scenic Highway 138 and wind along the North Umpqua River to the small community of Glide; continue beyond Glide to the 20-mile marker and look for the inn's mailbox and driveway.

This is a family friendly inn and favorite haunt of those who love fly fishing and riverbank fishing—fishermen of all types call the scenic North Umpqua River home. It is reported that Zane Grey, early writer of western novels, often visited this area and loved to fish in secret holes in the Umpqua River. "The house was actually built in the 1930s," says Dick. His daughter, Nancy, and son-in-law, George, are now managing the inn, which is situated on five acres along the river. "Folks seem to like the views from the upper decks as well as from the picnic areas down by the riverbank," smiles Nancy.

A family would rarely run out of things to

do here. The game room offers a pool table, darts, parlor games, and sitting areas. A little theater room next to this offers a large TV and VCR; a satellite dish brings in 300 channels of television programming and the library of more than 400 videos offers new and classic films to choose from. Outdoors more than four acres of woods, trails, and picnic areas along the river offer plenty of space for the kids to run about and play.

The Shiloh Room, a studio-kitchenette unit, sleeps six and opens onto the lower river-view deck; it has a private entrance. The Umpqua Room sleeps three and also has a private entrance and views of the garden and small patio area. April's Garden Room sleeps four and has an entrance to the upper deck from the bedroom. Sally's Gibson Room sleeps four, has a private entrance, and access to the upper deck. All the guest rooms have TV and VCRs.

A large country breakfast is served in the dining room along with wide views of the river. Moms, dads, and the kids can dive into such hot entrees as scrambled eggs with ham, crisp bacon, hash browns, apple turnovers, French toast, or Belgian waffles with fruit topping along with orange juice, milk, coffee, hot chocolate, and teas.

What's Nearby

Premier fly fishing as well as river rafting and swimming are available on the North Umpqua River. The area offers hiking trails, many that lead to scenic waterfalls. Boating and fishing are offered at Diamond Lake. Fisherman's dinners can be enjoyed at nearby Steamboat Inn; ask about special dinners and music at Idleyld Inn. The Roseburg Area Visitors Information Center is located at 410 SE Spruce Street, P.O. Box 1262, Roseburg, OR 97470; Telephone: (541) 672-9731.

Inn at Nesika Beach

33026 Nesika Road
Gold Beach, OR 97444
Phone: (541) 247-6434

Innkeeper: Ann Arsenault
Rooms: 4 rooms with private baths, 2 rooms have private decks, all have views of the ocean
Extras: Whirlpool tubs in all baths; 3 rooms have black marble fireplaces and feather beds
On the grounds: Panoramic views of the Pacific Ocean; porch swing faces the ocean
Smoking? Outdoors only
Visiting pets? No; no resident pets
Credit cards: No; personal checks preferred
Rates: $$–$$$
How to get there: Heading south on Highway 101 about 20 miles from Port Orford just beyond the Ophir Rest Stop, look for a small sign that says Nesika Beach; turn right and proceed about .two mile to the inns sign and driveway on the right. Heading north from Gold Beach a little more than 5 miles turn off Highway 101 at the flashing yellow light onto Nesika Road; proceed to the inns sign and driveway on the left.

"I want my guests to relax here on our bluff at the edge of the ocean," says Ann, "and to have a memorable night's sleep." The Arsenaults built the inn, a decidedly Victorian style with wraparound porches and characteristic "gingerbread" accents, in the early 1990s. They wanted to provide their guests the ultimate in privacy so each guest room has a private bath with a two-person whirlpool tub. Three rooms feature black marble fireplaces, cozy sitting areas, and king or queen feather beds; two rooms also have their own decks that look out onto the expanse of ocean to the west. The other two rooms offer cozy chaise lounges and bay windows for ocean watching. One room has twin beds.

Morning brings gourmet breakfast aromas from Ann's kitchen on the main floor. She taught gourmet cooking classes and French when she lived in the Bay Area near San Francisco. "I've also lived in France and in the Philippines," she explains. Breakfast may consist of juices and a fresh fruit course followed by warm scones, a puffed soufflé or mushroom omelet, or crepes filled with peaches, roulades, and a special meat course. After this sumptuous meal guests often go for walks along the bluff, eyes squinting toward the ocean for the possibility of a whale sighting. Or they relax on the enclosed porch that also faces the ocean if the weather is stormy or breezy.

But whatever else you do on this section of the south coast, don't miss one of the mailboat rides up the Rogue River from nearby Gold Beach. Snugly ensconced in safe, open hydrojet boats, you and about a dozen others enjoy a round trip of 32 miles up and back down the river. Genial river pilots point out wildlife, bird species, and river life along the way. A longer round trip of 64 miles is also available. For evening dining, especially for good seafood, ask about local eateries like Rod & Reel, Norwester, and The Rogue Landing, all near Gold Beach.

What's Nearby

The Gold Beach area offers all kinds of fishing opportunities including trout, salmon, and steelhead fishing on the Rogue River. The nearby eighteen-hole Cedar Bend golf course welcomes visitors. Storm watching is a popular winter activity along the coast. The Gold Beach–Wedderburn Visitors' Information Center is located at 29279 South Ellensburg, Gold Beach, OR 97444; Telephone: (541) 247-7526.

Willowbrook Inn

628 Foots Creek Road
Gold Hill, OR 97525
Phone: (541) 582-0075
E-mail: willowbr@chatlink.com
Internet site: www.chatlink.com/~willowbr

Innkeepers: Tom and JoAnn Hoeber
Rooms: 3 rooms with private baths
Extras: Sherry served in dining room; lemonade or iced tea available during summer months
On the grounds: Wraparound porch with hammock and willow porch furniture; outdoor swimming pool (unheated); hot tub outdoors under aromatic cedars; extensive herb garden
Smoking? Outdoors on the front porch or in the garden
Visiting pets? No; 2 friendly resident dogs, Tucker and Wally, and 1 friendly cat, LeKitty
Credit cards: Visa, MasterCard
Rates: $–$$
How to get there: From I-5 east of Grants Pass take exit 45-A (Savage Rapids Dam) and turn left onto Rogue River Highway (Route 99); proceed for 1½ miles then turn left onto Foots Creek Road; continue ½ mile to the inn on the right.

"**W**e previously owned a kitchenware store," says JoAnn, "so a lot of our focus is on cooking and food." The couple makes extensive use of fresh vegetables and berries from their garden as well as using freshly picked herbs from their large herb garden. It feels quite a bit like staying at grandmother's place in the country. "The farmhouse was built in 1905," explains Tom. "We fell in love with the house and with southern Oregon, being transplants from the East Coast."

In the common area guests find a cozy fireplace, comfortable sofa and chairs, and ample supplies of books and magazines. You might take a good read outside to the hammock or porch swing, or you might wander through the herb garden and around back to the swimming pool. There's croquet on the lawn. A warm soak in the hot tub, situated under the aromatic cedars, may sound appealing at day's end. Then a glass of sherry with Tom and JoAnn before disappearing upstairs to your guest room.

Morning often brings the sun streaming through the east windows and always is accompanied by the smell of freshly brewed coffee wafting up to the second floor. Breakfast on the sun porch may start with mixed berries with mango yogurt, nutmeg muffins or sweet bread, followed by a main entree such as baked apple pancakes and crisp bacon.

What's Nearby

See What's Nearby Grants Pass on page 43 and What's Nearby Jacksonville on page 47.

Flery Manor

2000 Jumpoff Joe Creek Road
Grants Pass, OR 97526
Phone: (541) 476-3591
E-mail: flery@chatlink.com
Internet site: www.flerymanor.com

Innkeepers: Marla and John Vldrinskas
Rooms: 3 rooms, 1 suite, all with private baths; the suite has a fireplace, whirlpool tub, and private balcony
Extras: Telephones and TV outlets in each room; music with volume control in each room; triple sheeting on beds; turndown service with truffles and flowers on the pillows; fax and other business services in library and parlor
On the grounds: Barbeque grill for guests use; pond and gazebo
Smoking? Not allowed
Visiting pets? No
Credit cards: Visa, MasterCard
Rates: $-$$$
How to get there: From I-5 north of Grants Pass take exit 66 and proceed east on Jumpoff Joe Creek Road for 1⁷⁄₁₀ miles to the inn.

Don't most folks have a nine-foot tall mahogany armoire in their living room? Well probably not, but in this inn's living room, which reaches two stories upward and also contains a massive stone fireplace, the large piece of furniture looks right at home. Through the wall of windows, guests look out across the rolling countryside to forested foothills in the Siskiyou Mountain Range. "We just fell in love with this place," says Marla. The couple moved here from southern California. "But it was so quiet at night," says John, "that we actually had trouble sleeping at first!"

On the second floor guests find four royally appointed rooms with the Moonlight Suite being the crown jewel. This 850-square-foot suite has a king bed, a fireplace, and large bath outfitted with a double vanity, double whirlpool tub, and glassed-in shower. French doors open onto a private balcony with a view of the grounds and a specially constructed waterfall that is turned on for guests.

John, a master craftsman specializing in seventeenth-century period finishing and furniture restoration, has fashioned elegant moldings and special faux finishes throughout the inn. One example of his work, faux clouds painted on the ceiling over the whirlpool tub in the Moonlight Suite, is especially romantic. The couple has also used interesting antiques as massive headboards for the queen and king beds. For one such headboard, an antique English pine buffet with inset mirrors, Marla designed and hand-crafted a canopy of lush velvets and sheers. Surrounded by this sumptuous romantic ambience, and on such a grand scale, a couple will feel as though they're staying in the castle of a Norse king and queen.

This impressive scale is further experienced in the morning with breakfast served in the baronial dining room amid yards of antique linen and lace as well as fine china, silver, and crystal. You may be served baked apples stuffed with wild blackberries, Egg on a Cloud with fresh poached salmon, breakfast pudding, or a fresh herb and vegetable frittata.

What's Nearby Grants Pass

Water activities often predominate here—fishing, rafting the Rogue River, and taking a jet boat excursion down wild and scenic stretches of the Rogue River from Grants Pass. The Stardust Theater, Barnstormer Theater, and Rogue Music Theater, all have live local theater offerings. An extraordinary farmer's and crafts market is offered on weekends in Grants Pass. The Grants Pass Visitors Information Center is located at 1501 NE Sixth Street, Grants Pass, OR 97526; Telephone: (541) 476-7717. This is also a gateway to the Oregon Caves and to the scenic redwood groves of the northern California coast, via Highway 199 and heading southwest from Grants Pass.

Historic Orth House Bed & Breakfast

105 West Main Street
P.O. Box 1437
Jacksonville, OR 97530
Phone: (541) 899-8665; (800) 700-7301
E-mail: orthbnb@medford.net
Internet site: www.historicorthhousebnb.com

Innkeepers: Lee and Marilyn Lewis
Rooms: 4 rooms, 3 with private baths
Extras: Tandem bicycle for guest use; collections of teddy bears and pedal cars on display; player piano in one parlor; guest refrigerator on patio with sodas and ice; afternoon snacks and tea
On the grounds: Vintage two-person buggy; wooden swing on front lawn; porch with wicker furniture
Smoking? Outdoors only
Visiting pets? No
Credit cards: Visa, MasterCard,
Rates: $$-$$$$
How to get there: From I-5 east of Grants Pass take the Gold Hill-Jacksonville exit and proceed southeast on Old Stage Road for 10 miles to Jacksonville. From the Ashland-Medford area take either the South Stage Road from exit 24 off I-5 or Highway 238 from Medford west to Jacksonville. The inn is located 1 block south of California Street, the main street of town, and between Oregon and Third Streets.

"We're located close to the Britt Festival grounds," explains Marilyn. "Guests can walk from the inn to Oregon Street and up past the small rose garden to the open-air seating area." Throughout the summer months, travelers flock to Jacksonville to hear a plethora of musical groups and vocalists—from classical and bluegrass to jazz and big band favorites. The festival has hosted such notables as Mel Torme, Diane Schuur, and Lorin Hollander. Before the evening's concert, music lovers will often collect picnics, blankets, lap robes, pillows, or lawn chairs and find just the right spot on the wide sloping lawn or on wooden benches, all under tall Douglas fir trees.

Back at the inn, guests enjoy two comfortable parlors that are filled with books, magazines, games, a player piano, and a TV. The Lewises serve afternoon snacks and tea in the dining room. Guests who are into athletic pursuits may enjoy pedaling about historic Jacksonville on the inn's tandem bicycle. "Lots of couples have fun exploring the side streets and seeing all our historic houses on the bicycle built for two," chuckles Lee.

The inn was built by early resident John Orth in 1880. The house has been faithfully restored and is now listed on the U.S. National Register of Historic Homes. There are more than eighty restored homes and commercial structures in Jacksonville. While in the area be sure to visit the Pioneer Cemetery located on a small bluff just west of downtown. Old headstones, many tilted off center and covered with trailing vines, offer intriguing looks into the region's past. Living history programs are offered during summer at Beekman House, located on California Street near the restored 1854 Methodist Church.

For a good night's sleep, guests choose from Josie's Room with its Victorian decor, brass king bed, and teddy bears; Flora's Room with antique furnishings, queen bed with a carved headboard, and toys and teddy bears; and Celia's Suite, two cozy rooms with two balconies, period furnishings, king and queen brass beds, and, of course, teddy bears.

Breakfast served at 8:30 A.M. in the dining room may consist of such delightful entrees as stuffed French toast, egg casserole, or apple-pecan French toast along with muffins or breakfast breads, fresh fruit, and hot beverages. "Coffee is always ready by 7:30 A.M.," says Marilyn.

What's Nearby

See What's Nearby Jacksonville on page 47, What's Nearby Medford on page 53, and What's Nearby Ashland on page 13.

Innkeepers: Dennis and Mary Ann Ramsden

Rooms: 3 rooms with private baths

Extras: Restaurant on the premises serving gourmet dinners, open to the public; McCully Merchantile next door offers local wines, picnic baskets, and deli sandwiches

On the grounds: Test garden for Jackson & Perkins Company roses—some 250 rose varieties; English country rear garden with waterfall and gazebo

Smoking? Outdoors only

Visiting pets? No

Credit cards: Visa, MasterCard, American Express, Discover

Rates: $$

How to get there: From I-5 east of Grants Pass take the Gold Hill-Jacksonville exit and proceed southeast on Old Stage Road for 10 miles to Jacksonville; the inn is on the main street at the eastern edge of downtown shops. From I-5 north of Ashland and near Medford take exit 24, Phoenix exit, and follow signs 6 miles via South Stage Road to Jacksonville.

McCully House Inn

240 East California Street

P.O. Box 13

Jacksonville, OR 97530

Phone: (541) 899-1942

Internet site: www.wave.net/upq/mccully

"**O**ur inn is perfect for travelers who love good food, good wine, and beautiful roses," smiles Mary Ann Ramsden. "This is a labor of love for us and we love doing it."

The historic inn was completed in 1861 and is reportedly one of Jacksonville's first six dwellings. Although the house was built by John W. McCully, a physician and real estate speculator, he ran into financial difficulties and made a hasty exit one day on the local stagecoach leaving behind his wife Jane with three children to support.

"Jane must have been a spunky lady," says a local historian. "Not only did she become the town's first schoolteacher, but she may have opened the first bed-and-breakfast in southern Oregon—she turned her home into a boardinghouse and later a school." Old records show that the *Oregon Sentinal* newspaper reported in 1862: "Amos E. Rogers has taken Mrs. J.W.

McCully's new dwelling on California Street for the above purpose [boardinghouse] . . . his table will be furnished with the best market affords and gotten up in Apple-pie order. Cost $7.00/week or 50 cents for a single call." It is also reported that Jane sold her tasty apple pies to the town's gold miners for one dollar per pie.

Lining the walkway leading to the door are elegant 24-inch high tree rose varieties, such as Sun Flare, Crimson Lace, and Intrigue, and a charming English country garden thrives in the rear. On the second floor, McCully Room, the original master bedroom, is furnished in massive Renaissance Revival pieces of solid black walnut that traveled around the Horn to the West Coast. A cozy fireplace offers cheery warmth on chilly evenings and a claw-foot bathtub offers a comfortable place to soak away one's worldly cares. Doll Suite offers a charming two-room boudoir that is suitable for families.

Breakfast is served at 9:00 A.M. in the light and airy Garden Patio Lounge or in the backyard English country garden. The chef prepares a sumptuous surprise entree every morning that generally begins with a fresh fruit plate. Guests can reserve a table for dinner in the inn's main floor dining room and enjoy such luscious fare as grilled portobello mushrooms with French Brie sauce; sautéed prawns with mushrooms, garlic, and lime; and smoked salmon fusilli. Other eateries in town include the Jacksonville Inn and Bella Union.

What's Nearby Jacksonville

Visit the historic Pioneer Cemetery, Jackson County Historical Society Museum, and Children's Museum. Take in living history at Beekman House. The annual Britt Music Festival offers top name performers between mid-June and Labor Day. Browse antiques shops, boutiques, and eateries. The Jacksonville Visitors Information Center is located at 185 North Oregon Street, P.O. Box 33, Jacksonville, OR 97530; Telephone: (541) 899–8118. Also see What's Nearby Medford on page 53 and What's Nearby Ashland on page 13.

Other Recommended B&Bs Nearby

Jacksonville Inn, 1861 bed-and-breakfast hotel and restaurant including three honeymoon cottages; innkeepers Linda and Jerry Evans, 175 East California Street, P.O. Box 359, Jacksonville, OR 97530; Telephone: (541) 899–1900. **Touvelle House,** a 1916 Craftsman-style mansion at the edge of downtown Jacksonville and near the Pioneer Cemetery; innkeepers Dennis and Carolee Casey, 455 North Oregon Street, P.O. Box 1891, Jacksonville, OR 97530; Telephone: (541) 899–8938.

The Enchanted Cottage Bed & Breakfast

4507 SW Coast Street
Lincoln City, OR 97367
Phone: (541) 996-4101; (800) 788-1669
E-mail: daythia@wcn.net
Internet site: www.lincolncity.com

Innkeepers: David and Cynthia Gale Fitton
Rooms: 3 rooms, 1 handicap accessible; all rooms have private baths, plush bathrobes, and cable TV
Extras: Appetizers of regional and local seafood and local cheeses served on arrival
On the grounds: Large ocean-view deck; beach access
Smoking? Outdoors only
Visiting pets? Small pets allowed with own pet bed/carrier; inquire
Credit cards: Visa, MasterCard
Rates: $$–$$$$
How to get there: Take Highway 101 south through Lincoln City and look for the Inn at Spanish Head on the bluff facing the ocean; take second right onto SW Coast Street, which fronts the ocean and beach.

World travelers, David and Cynthia Fitton decided to pack up and move to the West Coast, exchanging their southern roots in Arkansas and Alabama for salt air and sandy beaches. They have welcomed travelers to Lincoln City since 1991. And they've done so with a decided southern brand of hospitality. For starters on arrival guests are served a delectable appetizer such as smoked king salmon from Alaska, Tillamook cheeses, and hot or cold beverages. If you can glance away from the stunning views of the Pacific Ocean and beach, located

just 300 feet from the wide deck, you might also enjoy meeting other guests and hearing about the myriad activities available in the busy Lincoln City area.

You could plan an evening out at the new Chinook Winds Casino taking in top-star performers and trying out the gaming tables. Or you could plan a shopping foray at the city's sixty-nine-store Factory Outlet located nearby. Stroll the sandy beach, go crabbing or fishing, even boating on freshwater Devil's Lake, or buy a kite and catch the wind with other beachcombers and kite lovers on the wide beach at the D River Wayside.

Or you could hole up at the inn and surf the sixty-channel cable color TV with its five premium movie channels that is located in the large fireplace common area. "The coffee pot is always on," smiles Cynthia. When you see your well-appointed quarters, you may decide never to leave Coast Street. Guests choose from Natalie's Garden Room, California Suite, Victoria's Secret, and the enormous ocean-view fireplace suite, S Arthur's View. "Our decor is a blend of contemporary and Victorian," explains Cynthia. "The inn is full of antiques and our guests find pleasure in seeing something that reminds them of their childhoods."

Breakfast is served between 8:00 and 10:00 A.M. in the Wuthering Heights Dining Room complete with wide ocean views and such delicious fare as Breakfast Strata or Breakfast Pizza, pancakes or waffles with apple compote, or French toast along with the usual fresh juices, individual fruit cups, teas, and steaming coffee. For evening dining ask Cynthia and Dave about such spots as Tidal Raves, Kylos, Kernville Steak House, and the romantic Chez Jeanette, which is located a few miles south at Gleneden Beach.

What's Nearby Lincoln City

The bustling Lincoln City area offers much to see and do as well as great shopping in small boutiques, antiques shops, and factory outlet stores. To observe seals and shore birds such as the great blue heron, find the Nature Trail that skirts tiny Siletz Bay just north of the MarketPlace that is located directly across from Salishan Lodge a few miles south of Lincoln City toward Gleneden Beach; there's also beach access here. The Connie Hansen Garden offers a stroll through a true botanical paradise on two city lots; it is now cared for by dedicated volunteers. The Lincoln City Visitors Information Center is located at the far north end of town (near the garden) at 801 SW Highway 101; Telephone: (541) 994-2164.

The Arbors Bed & Breakfast

78 Idaho Avenue
P.O. Box 68
Manzanita, OR 97130
Phone: (503) 368-7566
E-mail: arbors@doormat.com

Innkeepers: Judd and Lee Burrow
Rooms: 3 rooms with private baths including 1 handicap accessible room
Extras: Homemade cookies ; enclosed sun porch with sitting places, books, magazines, games, puzzles
On the grounds: Extensive landscaped beds of annuals and perennials; patio and lawn; front deck; vegetable and herb gardens; view of the ocean
Smoking? Not allowed
Visiting pets? No; 2 resident cats, Cosmos and RoseBud
Credit cards: Visa, MasterCard, American Express
Rates: $$
How to get there: From the Highway 101 exit at Manzanita, drive west on Laneda Avenue through the Manzanita business district to the ocean, about ½ mile; the street turns right and becomes Ocean Road. Idaho Avenue is the first right turn and the inn is on the right hand side of the street.

Located just 200 feet from the sandy beach and within hearing range of the ocean surf, the 1920s English-style cottage bed and breakfast offers travelers a quiet haven away from the hustle bustle of the larger coastal towns. "We decided to settle in Manzanita because we liked the small village character and friendly feeling here," says Lee. She is a retired nurse, loves cooking and gardening, and runs a small antiques and giftware business in addition to writing a column on living for the local newspa-per that her husband Judd publishes. The inn reflects Judd's interest in restoring fine furniture and in graphic design. He's also a member of Manzanita's volunteer fire platoon.

The guest rooms are light and airy and feature period and antique furnishings along with comfortable queen beds and soft down comforters. Henrietta's Room looks beyond the garden to the ocean. Priscilla's Room offers a peek at the ocean and restful surf sounds. Each has a spacious private bath with full tub/

shower. The common area is outfitted with a cozy fireplace, TV with VCR, music system, and lots of reading materials. The enclosed sun porch offers another place to relax, to enjoy a cup of coffee or tea, and munch some of Lee's delicious oatmeal-date cookies.

You could decide to walk on the beach in the early morning or afternoon, or take a romantic stroll at sunset; guests also like to plan some time to explore nearby tide pools. Kites and sand toys are available for beach use as well. "Our garden and yard have many places for sunning and relaxing too," says Lee. The two resident cats may stop and say hello. "Cosmos is a black shorthair and is mister genteel," chuckles Lee. "Then RoseBud, a balanese/calico mix, thinks she is the neighborhood princess and will certainly let you know!" For evening dining there are two excellent local eateries—the Blue Sky Café and Jarboe's.

Breakfast is served family style at 8:30 A.M. with hot coffee on by 6:30 A.M. Lee and Judd usually join their guests at the breakfast table. The morning's fare along with lively conversation may include a fresh fruit plate, orange juice, and home baked scones along with Lee's special Eggs Manzanita Soufflé and oven roasted potatoes.

What's Nearby Manzanita

There are places close by for bicycling, hiking, kayaking, fishing, and golf. One lovely hike is found at nearby Short Sand Beach near Oswald West State Park. For more strenuous hikes, travelers can check out the trails at Neah-Kah-Nie Mountain. A few miles south at both Nehalem and Wheeler are excellent antiques shops and sports and fishing rental facilities. Nehalem Bay offers saltwater fishing.

Under the Greenwood Tree
Bed & Breakfast

3045 Bellinger Lane
Medford, OR 97501
Phone: (541) 776-0000
E-mail: grwdtree@cdsnet.net
Internet site: www.greenwoodtree.com

Innkeeper: Renate Ellam
Rooms: 5 rooms with private baths
Extras: Afternoon high tea; sherry, candies, and cookies available; selection of fine toiletries in baths along with thick towels; triple sheeting on beds and turndown service with truffles on pillows; fresh flower bouquets throughout the inn
On the grounds: Towering oaks; iris and rose gardens, large deck overlooking the lawn areas; historic weigh station structure including vintage scales; bicycles, table tennis, lawn croquet; 10 acres of grounds and trees; gazebo; hammocks in the trees; pond
Smoking? Outdoors only
Visiting pets? No; several songbirds, one resident outside cat, one Angora rabbit, Harvey, and several sheep
Credit cards: Visa
Rates: $$–$$$
How to get there: From I-5 take exit 27 Barnett Road at Medford, and turn immediately onto Stewart Street for 3 miles; this becomes Hull Street. Follow Hull Street one block and turn right on Bellinger Lane to the inn, the first house on the left side of the lane.

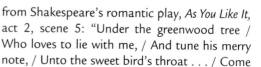

On a charming old fence post is nailed a weathered board with a knothole on which is lettered, 1 MPH. Beneath this a clutch of fresh flowers—old roses and hollyhocks peek from a vintage basket. Guests turn into the circular driveway and discover an inn that offers an unhurried bed-and-breakfast experience. Indeed, slowing to 1 mile per hour may seem very appealing about now. The inn's name comes from Shakespeare's romantic play, *As You Like It*, act 2, scene 5: "Under the greenwood tree / Who loves to lie with me, / And tune his merry note, / Unto the sweet bird's throat . . . / Come hither . . ."

Explains convivial innkeeper, Renate, "I think that living under the greenwood tree means, in old English, in the forest, the home of shepherds and milkmaids." The beautifully restored farmhouse exudes both comfort and romance, sitting comfortably amid enormous old oak trees and lush green lawns and gardens. Shade dapples the lawn and birds twitter in the trees and shrubs; an Angora rabbit hops about. The farm served as the area's weigh station in the 1870s and 1880s for weighing hay and grain from surrounding farms. The original scales are still here and can be inspected on a tour of the grounds and barns.

For sleeping guests choose from rooms on the second floor that are named for pears, many varieties of which grow in lush orchards here in the Rogue Valley near Medford. Bartlett Room with its Chippendale and chintz offers a cozy sitting room of white wicker that overlooks the gardens. Bosc Room offers a brass-and-iron bedstead and scalloped lace curtains; D'Anjou Room is lush with roses, lace, and velvet. Comice Room offers an elegant four-poster canopy bed and sitting nook of willow twig furnishings.

In the common room on the main floor a Persian rug lies on a polished wood floor, a deep sofa beckons one to sit for tea, and oil paintings and English and German etchings are seen on the walls. Breakfast served at a French Provincial table in the adjacent dining area is a three-course gourmet affair. Guests may be served such delicious treats as honeydew melon with raspberry sauce; local smoked ham with white potatoes, tomatoes, onions, and eggs and topped with sour cream and parsley; and strawberry blintzes filled with egg and yogurt and topped with preserves. This is just the first day; the second and third day's menus are just as intriguing.

What's Nearby Medford

Southern Oregon History Center, (541) 773–6536, in Medford includes two floors of exhibits, gifts and bookshop, and a fine research library. The Bear Creek Nature and Bicycling Trail meanders through the area. Harry and David's outlet store and Jackson & Perkins Rose Nursery and rose test gardens are both located close by. The Medford Visitors Information Center is located at 101 East Eighth Street, Medford, OR 97501; Telephone: (541) 779–4847. Also see What's Nearby Jacksonville on page 47 and What's Nearby Ashland on page 13.

Pine Meadow Inn
Bed & Breakfast

1000 Crow Road
Merlin, OR 97532
Phone: (541) 471-6277; (800) 554-0806
E-mail: pmi@pinemeadowinn.com
Internet site: www.pinemeadowinn.com

Innkeepers: Nancy and Maloy Murdock
Rooms: 4 rooms with private baths
Extras: Telephones; pillow-top queen mattresses; irons and ironing boards; fresh flowers; current magazines; turn-down service with mints on pillows and cookies at the bedside; hot and iced tea; personalized soaps, bath oils for tubs and showers in each bath
On the grounds: Meadow, woods, cutting-flower gardens, koi pond, paths for strolling; hot tub outdoors on redwood deck; herb and vegetable gardens
Smoking? Not allowed
Visiting pets? No; no resident pets; visiting deer
Credit cards: Visa, MasterCard
Rates: $–$$
How to get there: Take I-5 north of Grants Pass to exit 61 and proceed west 5 miles to Crow Road; turn right onto Crow Road for 1 mile then left at the inn's sign.

"We designed and built the inn as a haven and retreat," explains Nancy, "so we've included many places to sit, relax, read, and just rest—on the porch, on the deck, by the koi pond, and in the woods." Nestled in a pine forest and meadow with views of Mount Walker, guests immediately feel the peaceful and romantic atmosphere created by these caring innkeepers. You may even see deer amble through the grounds as you relax in your chosen nook.

Guests settle into light, airy, and comfortable rooms decorated with Early American antiques and find comfortable sitting places like maple rocking chairs, comfy wingback chairs, or cozy cushioned window seats with pillows. Garden Room offers a bay window that overlooks the rear gardens, the koi pond, and trees. Laurel Room offers an elegant antique oak bed, writing desk, long window seat, and view of the meadow. Willow Room, the most spacious, has a sitting area with loveseat and rocker as well as a window seat with a view of Mount Walker. Heather Room, cozy and sunlit, features a white iron bed and view of the gardens and woods.

Couples can enjoy a leisurely soak in the outdoor hot tub, walk or ride bicycles on shady trails and paths, and stroll through the grounds to inspect the flowering perennial beds, the koi pond, and its gentle waterfall. This miniature waterfall may be the loudest sound you hear other than the gentle breezes playing through the branches of the trees.

Breakfast, served in the formal dining room on the main level, is memorable because it is healthy and light yet gourmet. Nancy and Maloy might serve a fresh vegetable-egg bake, country potatoes, and Morning Glory muffins along with strawberries in sour cream and sprinkled with brown sugar. Another favorite is baked pears with marionberry sauce and Granny Smith waffles. "We like to use seasonal fruits and veggies from our gardens," explains Maloy.

Lowering the stress level and leaving city cares behind are pleasant norms here; the care and attention to details combine to make this an extraordinary bed and breakfast. For evening dining ask the innkeepers about Laughing Clam, Morrison's, Legrand's, and Yankee Pot Roast, eateries in nearby Merlin and Grants Pass.

What's Nearby

See what's Nearby Grants Pass on page 43.

Other Recommended B&B Nearby

Kerbyville Inn Bed & Breakfast, is located near the Oregon Caves and the California redwoods; innkeeper Carolyn Koistner, 24304 Redwood Highway, Kerby, OR 97531; Telephone: (541) 592–4689.

Oar House Bed & Breakfast

520 Southwest Second Street
Newport, OR 97365
Phone: (541) 265-9571; (800) 252-2358
E-mail: oarhouse@newportnet.com
Internet site:
www.newportnet.com/oarhouse

Innkeeper: Jan LeBrun
Rooms: 5 rooms with private baths
Extras: Guest refrigerator stocked with soft drinks; selection of teas and instant hot water
On the grounds: Top floor enclosed cupola with widow's walk and ocean views
Smoking? Not allowed
Visiting pets? No
Credit cards: Visa, MasterCard
Rates: $$–$$$
How to get there: From Highway 101 in Newport, turn west on Hurbert Street to Southwest Second Street. The inn is located between Hurbert and Brook Streets.

"**I**'ve learned that the house was first a boardinghouse in the early 1900s," explains Jan. "Then new owners turned the place into a bordello, with red lights and everything." In the early 1980s another couple purchased the large home and began major renovations including the addition of a lighthouse tower and widow's walk. When Jan bought the inn in the early 1990s, she continued the nautical decor and added her own touches with international art, Persian carpets, Oriental objets d'art. When she added red and green lights in the lighthouse tower, local townsfolk inquired about their meaning. "Well of course green is for starboard

and red is for port, but if you wish, you may call me Madam!"

Located in the historic Nye Beach area, Jan offers guests a warm welcome and a choice of five well-appointed rooms located in different areas of the house. The Chart Room offers a queen sleigh bed, comfortable overstuffed chairs, its own library, and west windows that look over the roofs to the ocean. The Starboard Cabin has its own library along with north views of the ocean and, in the distance, the Yaquina Head lighthouse. The Crow's Nest is the third-floor attic room with dormer, gables, and slanted ceilings along with a wonderful ocean view. The Captain's Quarters on the south second floor offers a small sitting room with chair and ottoman; the bedroom has an English cottage-style queen bed, a secretary and chair, and an ocean view from its west window. The cozy Deckside Berth is located on the first floor.

A fireplace sitting room offers guests a music system and the large living room offers cable TV, movie channels, and bar area with guest refrigerator stocked with soft drinks; a selection of teas and instant hot water are also available. A large outside deck is sheltered from ocean breezes.

Breakfast, a tradition at Oar House, consists of group seatings in the dining room and individual tables in the morning room, and is served from 8:30 to 9:30 A.M. One of Jan's special breakfast favorites is preparing and serving Lemon Ricotta Pancakes along with sautéed apples and sausage. For dining out ask Jan about local spots such as Tables of Content, Canyon Way, and Mo's (for great clam chowder and slumgullion).

What's Nearby Newport

For golf check out the lovely Agate Beach Golf Course. Visit the Oregon Coast Aquarium (where Keiko the whale learned how to live in the wild), the Hatfield Marine Science Center, Yaquina Bay Lighthouse Museum, and Yaquina Head Outstanding Natural History Area with its lighthouse, bird sanctuary, and interpretive center. There's always lots going on at Newport's Performing Arts Center and at the Visual Arts Center. Both the historic bayfront and historic Nye Beach areas offer cozy cafes, shops, galleries, and historic memorabilia. The Greater Newport Visitors Information Center is located at 555 Southwest Coast Highway, Newport, OR 97365; Telephone: (800) 262-7844.

Ocean House
Bed and Breakfast

4920 Northwest Woody Way
Newport, OR 97365
Phone: (541) 265–6158; (800) 562–2632
E-mail: garrard@oceanhouse.com
Internet site: www.oceanhouse.com

Innkeepers: Bob and Marie Garrard
Rooms: 5 rooms with private baths, 3 rooms offer whirlpool tubs
Extras: The inn offers a well-stocked library
On the grounds: Oceanfront setting, half-acre garden, decks, private trail to tide pools and Agate Beach
Smoking? Outdoors only
Visiting pets? No; one resident Amazon parrot
Credit cards: Visa, MasterCard, Discover
Rates: $$–$$$
How to get there: From Highway 101 turn onto Woody Way about ½ mile north of the Newport city limits.

The Garrards offer guests an oceanfront setting surrounded by a sweeping lawn, well-tended perennial gardens, and decks tucked here and there for sitting and viewing the vast nautical landscape as well as listening to the crashing surf. A private staircase and trail lead down to the tide pools and to the beach; morning walks and sunset strolls are a must.

All of the guest rooms in this charming 1940s-era home have great views of the ocean and the gardens. Overlook Room offers a fireplace, spa, private deck, and king bed. Rainbow Room is spacious with a cathedral ceiling and offers a spa, private deck, and four-poster queen bed. Melody's Room has inviting bay windows, a spa, and four-poster. Michele's Room offers an enclosed sun room, daybed, and canopied queen bed. And Windrift Room is cozy with a small sitting room, deck, bay window, and king bed.

Guests are invited to enjoy the spacious common area, especially at sunset, or to cozy up to the fireplace when a storm is brewing over the Pacific. Find a good novel in the inn's library, snuggle on the sofa and listen to music, or enjoy the wide-angle views and ocean sounds from your own room with its comfortable sitting areas.

An ample breakfast is served family-style between 8:00 and 9:00 A.M. in the kitchen area.

And of course the coffee is always on.

What's Nearby

See What's Nearby Newport on page 57.

Other Recommended B&B Nearby

Tyee Lodge Oceanfront, with wide ocean views, in Newport; innkeepers Mark and Cindy McConnell, 4925 Northwest Woody Way, Newport, OR 97365; Telephone: (541) 265-8953.

Beckley House
Bed & Breakfast

338 Southeast Second Street
P.O. Box 198
Oakland, OR 97462
Phone: (541) 459-9320
E-mail: neuharth@users.wizzards.net
Internet site: www.makewebs.com/beckley

Innkeepers: Karene and Rich Neuharth
Rooms: 3 rooms, 2 with private baths
Extras: Vintage 1930s magazines, Victrola, and TV in common room; snacks and beverages available; innkeeper is trained chef; walking tours of restored Victorian homes
On the grounds: Covered patio, swing, flower garden
Smoking? Outdoors only
Visiting pets? No; 2 resident cats
Credit cards: Visa, MasterCard, American Express
Rates: $–$$
How to get there: From I-5, south of Cottage Grove or north of Roseburg, take exit 138 and proceed into town onto Front Street; turn onto Locust Street 1 block to Second Street turning right for 3 blocks; the inn is located at the corner of Second and Chestnut streets.

Visitors to the small community of Oakland often feel as though they have stepped back in time to the late 1800s and early 1900s. Walking along Locust, the main street of town, as well as ambling around the surrounding neighborhoods, gives one a nostalgic connection with the past. In the small business district once thrived such businesses as the Page and Dimmick Drug Store, Beckley Brothers General Mercantile, and the Thomas Hotel along with several livery stables, a dentist's office, a restaurant, and a confectionery. A number of these original brick buildings built in the 1890s have been preserved, including the ornate cast-iron fronts that were popular exterior decoration during this period. One of these buildings houses a favorite local eatery, Tolley's Restaurant. There are several antiques stores to explore as well.

Records indicate that Oakland was the second town settled in Oregon and the first to have an organized school district. In those earlier days, with the construction of the Oregon & California Railroad through Oakland in 1872, the town became a busy agricultural and shipping center—stockyards were built for cattle, sheep, hogs, and turkeys and warehouses were constructed for produce such as prunes and hops. Located about halfway between Seattle and San Francisco, Oakland was the main stopping and distribution point to other cities and towns in the region. The mail arrived once a week and was picked up by riders who delivered to coastal towns and to other towns in the Willamette Valley as well as east across the Cascade Mountains into Central Oregon.

On the corner of Second and Chestnut Streets, guests find The Beckley House Bed & Breakfast, a two-story Classic Revival that was built in 1900 by Charles Beckley. "We encourage our guests to wind up the old Victrola in the parlor or enjoy browsing our collection of 1930s magazines," smiles Karene. Two rooms on the second floor, Spring Suite and Garden Suite, offer antiques and soft colors. The innkeeper is a trained chef so breakfast here is an event in fine dining; you might enjoy such treats as Grand Marnier French toast, Wisconsin cheddar cheese cake, or puffs filled with scrambled eggs and topped with hollandaise sauce, all served with Karene's special American potatoes. Fresh fruit, herbal breads, special muffins, and the usual hot and cold beverages are also available.

What's Nearby Oakland

Visitors enjoy the self-guided Historic Walking Tour of the Oakland Historic District and of neighborhoods nearby. In September folks take in the Umpqua Valley Wine, Arts and Jazz Festival. For further information contact Oakland City Hall; Telephone: (541) 469–4531. The area also offers winery tours and an eclectic mix of antiques and gift shops.

SeaRose, A Bed & Breakfast

1685 Maxwell Mountain Road
Oceanside, OR 97134
Phone: (503) 842-6126
E-mail: searosebb@oregoncoast.com

Innkeepers: Judith Gregoire and daughter, Antoinette Gentile
Rooms: 2 rooms, private baths; no TV
Extras: Homemade cookies on arrival; piano; special Writer's Block package during the week
On the grounds: Private garden, gazebo, arbor in rose garden, views of ocean
Smoking? Outdoors, covered area
Visiting pets? No; resident cat, Puddin
Credit cards: Visa, MasterCard
Rates: $$
How to get there: Follow Three Capes Scenic Loop 9 miles from Tillamook to Oceanside; turn right at stop sign onto Maxwell Mountain Road and drive up hill to first driveway; park off street in garage.

Decidedly off the beaten path (actually at the end of the road), tiny Oceanside nestles at the base of 500-foot Maxwell Mountain. "This is where all the intrepid hang-gliders come to fly," explains Judith. "They launch from atop the mountain and glide on the air currents out over the ocean, then land on the beach. It's quite a sight!"

Guests check into one of the inn's two rooms, either Nicole Room with its white wicker furniture, oak writing desk, and soft restful colors, or Antoinette Room with antique table and chairs, cozy rocker, and a private deck plus a covered ocean view seating area. In the private baths are large fluffy towels, homemade soaps, and bath bubbles for relaxing in large claw-foot tubs with brass fixtures. The view includes the ocean and Three Arch Rocks National Bird and Sea Lion Refuge, where hundreds of tufted puffins set up housekeeping, stellar sea lions and their sea pups bark and roar, and various pods of whales migrate past. You may want to bring your binoculars, telephoto lenses, and lots of film.

Sea Rose also offers writers, "or writer

wannabes," smiles Judith, a Writer's Block haven from Monday evening through Thursday morning. "Sort of a room of one's own," she says. You'll pretty much have the whole place to yourself.

Coffee, tea, and homemade cookies are offered guests upon arrival in the cozy common area located between the two guest rooms. Local cheeses and popcorn are on hand as well as a coffee maker, microwave, and small refrigerator (stocked with ice and ice cream) for guests use. For dining out Judith suggests Roseanna's Café or Anchor Tavern, which has good pizza.

Breakfast is served in the ocean view dining room or on the deck, weather permitting, and consists of delicious fare such as homemade cranberry-almond granola with yogurt, fresh fruit platter, shrimp quiche, lemon/blueberry muffins, *apfelkuchen,* and hot beverages. A piano is close by and, says Judith, "We've had lovely impromptu concerts."

There is a quiet, intimate, "at home" feeling here—the kind of atmosphere that encourages taking off one's shoes and padding about in stocking feet. And for a time, there is no television, no sitcoms, and no national news.

What's Nearby Oceanside

There is golfing at Alderbrook Golf Course and at Bay Breeze Golf & Range; there are tours and hiking trails at nearby Cape Meares Lighthouse. In Tillamook, the Tillamook County Pioneer Museum is one of the best to visit on the coast. Find an abundance of antiques shops in nearby Wheeler and Nehalem. The Tillamook Visitors Center is located at 3705 Highway 101 North, Tillamook, OR 97141; Telephone: (503) 842-7525. Additional information, particularly about Three Capes Scenic Drive, the dory fleet, and dory fishing trips, can be obtained from the Pacific City–Woods Visitors Information Center, P.O. Box 331, Pacific City, OR 97135; Telephone: (503) 965-6161.

Other Recommended B&B Nearby

Eagle's View B&B, a romantic inn with an ocean view; innkeepers Mike and Kathy Lewis, 37975 Brooten Road, P.O. Box 901, Pacific City, OR 97135; Telephone: (503) 965-7600.

Home by the Sea Bed and Breakfast

444 Jackson Street
P.O. Box 606-B
Port Orford, OR 97465
Phone: (541) 332–2855
E-mail: alan@homebythesea.com
Internet site: www.homebythesea.com

Innkeepers: Alan and Brenda Mitchell
Rooms: 2 rooms with private baths
Extras: McIntosh is spoken here; the innkeeper is a computer wizard
On the grounds: Views of the Pacific Ocean, Battle Rock, shoreline, forested hills, Siskiyou Mountains
Smoking? Outdoors only
Visiting pets? No; resident canary, lovebird, and cockateel
Credit cards: Visa, MasterCard
Rates: $$
How to get there: As Highway 101 curves to the east through Port Orford, turn onto Jackson Street 1 block to the inn.

Nestled on a bluff overlooking a half-moon shaped cove that tilts around to the east, the inn offers outrageous views of the ocean, shoreline, and headlands. The Mitchells have embraced this stunning panorama for more than thirty years and have been sharing it with bed-and-breakfast guests for some twelve years. It would be difficult to ever think of leaving this pristine spot. "We call our south coast the 'banana belt,'" says Alan. "Especially during the fall, winter, or spring months. The temperatures are often mildest here when summer crowds are long gone."

Guests choose between the Blue Suite and Coral Room located on the second floor of the home; both have wonderful beds with myrtle-wood headboards and wood accents. Both rooms offer the dramatic ocean shoreline views to the east and south including nearby Battle Rock and 1,756-foot Humbug Mountain. In the morning around 8:30 A.M., the Mitchells serve a full breakfast in the main floor common area; it offers the fabulous view as well. The friendly morning bird songs often heard come from three feathered residents, a canary, a lovebird, and a cockateel named Screech. The day's meal may include such delicious items as waffles with warm maple syrup, German sausage, fresh fruit, and steaming hot coffee. "We like to serve locally made products," says Brenda. "Two of our favorites are a roadside family business that makes jams and syrups, Misty Meadows, located between Bandon and Sixes, and the place where we get the freshly made sausage, Black Forest Kitchen south of here near Humbug Mountain."

The Mitchells are also pleased to share helpful information about the area with their guests; their Web site offers Alan's informal guide to the south coast that readers can print out and take along in the car. "Be sure to save time for the close walk out to our local harbor, just five minutes from the house," suggests Alan. "It's quite a sight!" Each day that the sport and fishing boats go out in search of prime salmon, crab and bottom-fishing locales, the crafts are first hoisted into the churning ocean waters with an enormous converted log boom. The process is reversed in the late afternoon when the boats are hoisted back up to the dock by the same crane. They rest high and dry on long trailers on the large dock during the night.

What's Nearby Port Orford

The area is well known for its glass-blowing artists, woodworking artisans, contemporary basket weavers, and prolific quilters; ask about Laughing Baskets Studio, Hawthorne Studio, The Wooden Nickel, and Quilter's Corner. Hike the Humbug Mountain trail, well maintained but steep; visit ancient forest sites; picnic under old growth myrtlewood trees at Humbug Mountain State Park. Ask, too, about the Mail Boat trips up the Rogue River from Gold Beach. The Port Orford Visitors Information Center is located at Battle Rock City Park; Telephone: (541) 332-8055.

Anderson's Boarding House
Bed & Breakfast

208 North Holladay Drive
P.O. Box 573
Seaside, OR 97138
Phone: (503) 738-9055; (800) 955-4013
E-mail: bedwards@transport.com

Innkeeper: Barbara Edwards
Rooms: 6 with private baths, 1 handicap accessible; miniature Victorian cottage with fully equipped kitchen sleeps 1–6 persons (does not include breakfast)
Extras: Pillow-top mattresses, down comforters; Barb's homemade Vanilla Bath Salts
On the grounds: gardens, close to the banks of the tidal Necanicum River
Smoking? Outdoors only
Visiting pets? No; one resident cat
Credit cards: Visa, MasterCard
Rates: $–$$
How to get there: From Highway 101 south or north to Roosevelt Street, then turn west on Second Avenue to Holladay Drive.

With its fir tongue-and-groove walls, beamed ceilings, and paneling, the Craftsman-style house dates back to 1898 and lived many of its early years as a boardinghouse for the Seaside area. "This is where many railroad workers and travelers stayed," explains Barb. "They would share their stories and experiences around the breakfast table."

The charming parlor on the main floor offers a gas fireplace, comfortable chairs for reading or for conversation with fellow travelers along with a vintage Victrola, an upright piano, and lots of books and magazines. You could also curl up on the comfortable upholstered window seat. Breakfast, served from 8:30 to 9:30 A.M. at the antique dining table or at tables for two, may include such fare as cinnamon coffeecake, hot gingered fruit compote, blueberry Finnish pancake, egg-sausage-cheese frittata, and yogurt parfait. "A bit more sumptuous than the boardinghouse days, I think," smiles the innkeeper.

Barb's background well-prepared her for the innkeeping role—she was a registered nurse from the *Bridges of Madison County* area of Iowa before moving to the West Coast some twenty-three years ago. Combining a love of cooking and gardening with a love of people, music, and reading works well for her here on the Oregon coast. "I love hearing guests' stories and adventures," she says. "It's a bit like those earlier days when railroad workers and travelers stayed here."

Redecorated and refurbished again in 1996, each guest room is furnished in antiques from the decades of 1900 through 1940 and also offers pillow-top mattresses, down comforters, and TVs. Four baths sport claw-foot tubs with showers, two offer tub/shower combos, and all contain ample supplies of Barb's homemade Vanilla Bath Salts.

For dining out ask about Pacific Café in nearby Gearhart, and Doogers, The Stand, and Vista Sea eateries in Seaside.

What's Nearby Seaside

The wide, flat beach here is perfect walking and for kite flying. Check out the famous Turn-Around at the ocean's end of Broadway Street, walk the historic 2-mile-long Seaside Promenade with its great views of the beach and surf, and poke into myriad shops along Broadway and adjacent streets. Try the Coaster Theater in nearby Cannon Beach for excellent local live theater; a five-theater movie complex in Seaside also offers entertainment options. Golfers enjoy four nearby public golf courses—Gearhart, Highlands, Seaside, and Astoria Country Club. The Seaside Visitors Information Center is located at 7 North Roosevelt Street, P.O. Box 7, Seaside, OR 97138; Telephone: (503) 738-6391. Also see What's Nearby Astoria on page 27.

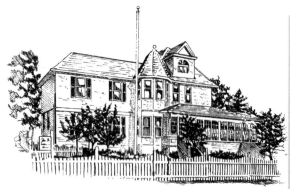

Gilbert Inn Bed & Breakfast

341 Beach Drive
Seaside, OR 97138
Phone: (503) 738–9770; (800) 410–9770
E-mail: gilberti@pacifier.com
Internet site: www.clatsop.com/gilbertinn

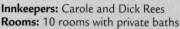

Innkeepers: Carole and Dick Rees
Rooms: 10 rooms with private baths
Extras: Fresh flowers, color TV in all rooms, gourmet breakfasts
On the grounds: One block from Seaside Promenade, Pacific Ocean, and wide beach
Smoking? Outdoors only
Visiting pets? No; resident orange tabby cat, Gilbert the Great
Credit cards: Visa, MasterCard, American Express, Diner's Club
Rates: $–$$
How to get there: Follow signs from Highway 101 to city center; the inn is located on the corner of Third Street and Beach Drive, 1 block from the ocean and 1 block south of Broadway, the main street.

If one subscribes to the notion of accomplishing a major feat during one's life, a magnum opus shall we say, then the Rees's gargantuan task of completing the restoration, preservation, and decoration of this stunning circa 1885 Queen Anne Victorian more than qualifies. "The house was built by Alexander and Emma Gilbert for their summer home," says Carole. The Gilberts had emigrated from France, making their way to the West Coast and living first in Astoria. But when their home was lost in a fire that consumed most of early Astoria, Mr.

Gilbert moved the family permanently to Seaside. Carole explains that the Gilberts were also asked by the governor of Oregon to represent the state at the dedication of the Eiffel Tower in Paris in 1889. "Emma's dress worn at the grand event is on display at the Heritage Museum in Astoria," she says.

The original fir tongue-and-groove paneling has been preserved on the ceilings and walls on the first two floors of the inn. The impressive fireplace with its dark polished molding is featured in the main parlor, now flanked by two comfortable sofas richly upholstered in a Victorian floral print of hunter green, mauve, and pink. Guests entering the parlor from the entry porch are also often greeted by Gilbert the Great, the twenty-pound orange-and-white resident feline; he's also featured in one of the photos on the inn's Web site. "He's quite a guy," chuckles Dick.

Guests have ten comfortable rooms to choose from throughout the house, including The Garret on the third and top floor, Turret Room on the second floor, and the 1880s Suite on the main floor. The elegant Turret Room, originally the Gilberts' sitting room, features a tall four-poster rice bed and the expanse of turret windows dressed with antique lace curtains. All the rooms have color TVs and private baths.

Carole's gourmet breakfast is served from 8:30 to 9:30 A.M. in the spacious garden sitting room that was, in the early days, a party room and side porch. Filled with baskets of lush greenery and white wrought-iron tables and chairs, this is where guests gather for a sumptuous repast that might include French toast filled with walnuts and cream cheese and served with warm apricot sauce along with a fruit medley of fresh pineapple, bananas, and blueberries garnished with fresh mint from the kitchen herb garden. Freshly brewed coffee is always out early in the sitting room, and soft music is often heard in the background. Some of Carole's favorite haunts for shopping include the Judith M. Gift Shop, Raintree Garden & Gifts, and Pacific Way Bakery & Café for interim coffee and pastries.

What's Nearby

See What's Nearby Seaside on page 67 and What's Nearby Astoria on page 27.

Other Recommended B&Bs Nearby

Cannon Beach Hotel, a petite European-style inn near village boutiques, galleries, cafes, and the beach near Haystack Rock; innkeeper Linda Toler, 1116 South Hemlock Street, Cannon Beach, OR 97110; Telephone: (503) 436-1392. **10th Avenue Inn Bed & Breakfast** on the beach near the Promenade in Seaside; innkeepers Francie and Vern Starkey, 125 Tenth Avenue, Seaside, OR 97138; Telephone: (503) 738-0643.

Sixes Hotel
Bed and Breakfast

93316 Sixes River Road
Sixes, OR 97476
Phone: (541) 332-3900; (800) 828-5161
E-mail: innkeeper@sixeshotel.com
Internet site: www.sixeshotel.com

Innkeepers: Bert and Elizabeth Teitzel
Rooms: 5 rooms with private baths
Extras: Recreation room with regulation size pool table, dart games, and TV/VCR; dinner may be arranged with advanced planning
On the grounds: Sixes River, benches for sitting, eight acres of grounds extending to and along the river are being further developed into gardens with private sitting areas and gazebo
Smoking? Outdoors only
Visiting pets? No; 1 resident dachshund, Ashley
Credit cards: Visa, MasterCard, American Express
Rates: $-$$
How to get there: Take Highway 101 and between Bandon and Port Orford, turn east onto Sixes River Road and ¼ mile to first driveway on right.

Former bed-and-breakfast innkeepers in the northern Willamette Valley college town of Newberg, the Teitzels decided to head south into the pristine Siskiyou Mountains of southern Oregon and they found just the right place on the south coast, the historic Sixes Hotel. "The site was originally used as a campsite by Sikhas Indian families who fished both the Sixes and Elk rivers," explains Bert. The hotel is the last remaining structure of the Sixes town site. The Teitzels explain that much of the hotel was built of white Port Orford cedar and Douglas fir; the southern portion of the building sits on hand-sawn cedar beams hand-notched to carry the floor joists and wall studs. The floors and ceilings are vertical grain tongue-and-groove Douglas fir. "And the light hanging in the dining room is of cast aluminum and hand-painted," says Elizabeth. "It was installed in the early 1940s when electricity first came to rural Curry County!"

The front section of the hotel, circa 1900–1905, was built on the eastern hillside; this was later moved down from the hill by horse and logs to its present site. The northern half of the hotel, circa 1915, sat on the riverbank and was a bunkhouse for mill workers and miners. The architecture of these two historic buildings blends nicely in its present transformation. "We love the history here," echo the couple. "There are many fascinating stories."

The inn has been carefully restored by former owners and now by the Teitzels, and also features a small, fully licensed restaurant for the convenience of their guests. Drawing from their personal travel experiences, the couple knows the frustration of traveling late, being hungry, and finding all the local eateries closed for the evening. "Especially down in our territory," smiles Elizabeth. "We're quite a ways off the beaten path here on the south coast."

Afternoon refreshments are offered on arrival—coffee, tea, soft drinks as well as homemade cookies and other baked treats are served to guests in the main parlor or on the wraparound porch weather permitting. The dining room and parlor are furnished with comfortable antiques, large wingback chairs, and art and collectibles of earlier eras. It feels like stepping back into the 1920s, 1930s, and 1940s. Breakfast, however, served between 7:30 and 9:30 A.M., feels very contemporary and gourmet and may include such items as Belgian waffles with sausage, Mexican strata egg dish, smoked sausage with apples and cream cheese scrambled eggs, buttermilk pancakes with local syrups, or blueberry-orange crepes.

What's Nearby Sixes

There is much to see and do on the south Siskiyou coast—view work of local artists in galleries and open studios; tour the historic 1898 Hughes House and visit the circa 1870s Cape Blanco Lighthouse; watch the windsurfers on Floras Lake; try bankside salmon and steelhead fishing; poke into antiques shops in Langlois; go hiking in nearby Grassy Knob Wilderness; find a quiet beach for walking at Paradise Point.

Other Recommended B&B Nearby

Floras Lake House by the Sea, near Floras Lake, offers windsurfing rentals and lessons; innkeepers Liz and Will Brady, 92870 Boice Cope Road, Langlois, OR 97450; Telephone: (541) 348-2573.

Newport Belle
Bed & Breakfast

H-Dock, Newport's South Beach Marina
P.O. Box 685
South Beach, OR 97366
Phone: (541) 867–6290
E-mail: sporter@newportbelle.com
Internet site: www.newportbelle.com

Innkeeper: Sharon (Sherry) Porter
Rooms: 6 rooms with private baths
Extras: Binoculars for watching birds and wildlife
On the grounds: Views of South Bend Marina, everyone is asked to wear deck shoes when aboard
Smoking? No smoking on or near the boat; main dock area available
Visiting pets? No; one resident cat, Peaches
Credit cards: Visa, MasterCard, American Express
Rates: $$$
How to get there: From Highway 101, at Newport, proceed to South Beach Marina and to H-Dock

Newport Belle Bed & Breakfast has been up and running, with Sherry at the helm, since 1996. "I always thought I'd like to own a boat, but I thought it would be a sailboat," says Sherry with a chuckle. She's standing amidship iin the gleaming main salon with its polished wood ceiling, hardwood floors, and large windows that overlook the marina, moored boats, and the low-forested hills that hug the distant shoreline. She explains that it took six hours to first tow the 97-foot sternwheel riverboat from Bandon to Salmon Harbor. Once docked, "the remodeling began!"; this included new countertop in the galley, new cupboards, new sinks, and bigger entrances.

The remodeling also included six updated staterooms, each with its own theme. The Montana Room, the Toy Room, the Australian Room, and the President's Suite, complete with a Truman election poster, are among them. An old Victrola, family photographs, a vintage milk can, dried flowers, a butter churn, seashells, and nautical coffee-table books decorate the main salon. "I call them my treasures," Sherry explains. "In my previous life I owned two kitchen stores; I brought all of my things from Billings, Montana, and have used them to decorate the inn." This includes 3,100 square feet of living space on the three decks of the 1900s-style riverboat. If several sea gulls settle into the water nearby, guests move to the windows and pick up the binoculars waiting for them on the windowsills. Other birds and waterfowl present may include grebes, buffleheads, and loons. At sunset everyone may troop out to the afterdeck to catch the deep gold and magenta hues on the western horizon, coloring the sky over the Pacific Ocean.

In the morning smells of freshly ground and brewed coffee waft through the galley into the main salon, where small, polished wood tables are set for breakfast. Soft classical music plays in the background and a wood pellet stove warms the room. During my visit Sherry served fresh pineapple, homemade French bread with artichoke butter, and crab quiche, hot, bubbly, and just from the oven. "I love to cook," she says. "I wanted my boat to reflect a welcoming warmth to travelers; classy and comfortable is what I wanted this boat to be." The riverboat now resides in Newport.

What's Nearby

See What's Nearby Newport on page 57.

Solace by the Sea Bed & Breakfast

9602 South Coast Highway
South Beach, OR 97366
Phone: (541) 867-3566; (888) 4SOLACE
E-mail: solace@newportnet.com
Internet site: www.moriah.com/solace

Innkeepers: Todd and Lisa Whear
Rooms: 3 rooms with private baths
Extras: Robes and towels for the hot tub; sodas in guest refrigerator; complimentary coffee and tea bar; wine, champagne, flowers, and chocolates are available on request for special occasions
On the grounds: Views of the Pacific Ocean; stairway leads down to the sandy beach
Smoking? Outdoors only
Visiting pets? Yes, dogs only, must be kept in dog run or in kennel on site; resident Labrador retriever, Bailey
Credit cards: Visa, MasterCard, Novus
Rates: $$-$$$$
How to get there: Via Highway 101 the inn is located 3½ miles south of Newport and south of the Yaquina Bay Bridge, or 4 miles north of Seal Rock and between mileposts 145 and 146 on the west, the ocean side.

The elegant contemporary structure with seeming acres of glass and cedar rises from a seaside bluff at the South Beach section of the greater Newport area. Its lines are straight and rectangular, its proportions oversized in order to better blend with and fit its stunning ocean view location. And looking at the ocean seems always to invite immediate relaxation.

"We think of the word 'solace' as meaning total comfort," explains Todd. If anyone knows it would certainly be this innkeeper who is also a certified massage therapist. Guests can arrange an appointment to have him tackle their aching muscles or aching backs. Gently, of course. They might decide to walk down the stairway to the beach and run for a couple of miles on the warm sand to get the kinks out. Bailey, the resident Labrador retriever, would probably love to join anyone who promised to throw a stick or two. This invigorating outing could be followed by a relaxing soak in one of the whirlpool tubs—there is one outdoors that is partially enclosed with a tiled deck and another in the elegant Neptune's Garden room.

Neptune's Garden offers a wide view of the ocean, a private deck, large bath with whirlpool tub, and walk-in closet with a vanity. One may decide never to emerge from the massive four-poster king feather bed that seems suitable for old King Neptune himself. The Agate Room is decorated with polished agates displayed against mirrors, and offers a romantic queen sleigh feather bed along with a stunning ocean view. Iola's Room encourages one to float away to the Far East in its four-poster mahogany queen feather bed. "We've decorated this room with Grandmother LaLa's Asian treasures," says Lisa. "She traveled a number of times to the Orient." This room like almost every room in the house also offers views of the ocean.

Breakfast is Lisa's domain since she has worked for a number of years in the food service and restaurant business. The four-course morning meal, accompanied first by freshly ground gourmet coffee blends and fine teas is served at 9:00 A.M. to guests seated around the large round table in the dining area. Fresh baked goods such as cranberry-orange bran muffins are served next and this is followed by a fruit dish like baked and broiled grapefruit. Lisa's main entree might be Egg Blossoms, which are lightly poached eggs in a filo dough flower.

What's Nearby

See What's Nearby Newport on page 57.

Other Recommended B&B Nearby

Cliff House Bed & Breakfast offers personal pampering, romantic bridal suite, panoramic ocean views, in Waldport; innkeeper Gabrielle Duvall, 1450 Adahi Street, P.O. Box 436, Waldport, OR 97394; Telephone: (541) 563-2506.

The Kittiwake Bed & Breakfast

95368 Highway 101 South
Yachats, OR 97498
Phone: (541) 547–4470
E-mail: jszewc@orednet.org
Internet site:
www.ohwy.com/or/k/kittiwbb.htm

Innkeepers: Brigitte and Joseph Szewc
Rooms: 2 rooms with private baths; each bath has two-person whirlpool tub with ocean view
Extras: Of interest to nature lovers, the inn is preserving habitat for silverspot butterfly; coffee and tea bar open all day
On the grounds: Access to ocean and beach; decks facing ocean to the west
Smoking? Outdoors only
Visiting pets? No; no resident pets
Credit cards: Visa, MasterCard, American Express, Discover
Rates: $$–$$$
How to get there: Take Highway 101, 7 miles south of Yachats, turn toward ocean at mile marker 171.2 just north of Ten Mile Creek.

"**O**ur two-and-a-half-acre parcel was overrun with blackberry vines and salal," explains Joseph. "The house was completed in 1993 but we're selectively cultivating the grounds in order to save the habitat of the Oregon silverspot butterfly; it's an endangered species." The 4,000-square-foot contemporary home snuggles on a bluff about 100 feet from the ocean and the crashing surf. Guests enjoy visiting the whale watching common area-lounge with its comfortable overstuffed chairs and sofa, a coffee and tea bar, and magazines and games; this offers an opportunity to meet other guests and to share ideas for sightseeing and for dinner forays into Yachats or the nearby area. Or they can relax and watch the seagulls sail by or spot the seals playing in the surf.

Guests will often decide to either don their own beach attire or borrow from a handy all-season collection provided by the innkeepers including boots, hats, scarves, rain ponchos, warm jackets, even flashlights for late night walks. Winds can be brisk on the Oregon coast and rain squalls are common, too, of course. This is where the weather begins!

Guest rooms offer queen beds, handmade afghans, down comforters, and cozy window seats for sitting and watching the ocean. It may sound as though the surf is just outside the French doors that open to the decks. "We like to think that our guests can relax and let go of stresses as the tide ebbs and flows," smile the Szewcs. "Ours is an unhurried, private, romantic atmosphere."

A light but delicious continental breakfast is served on a tray to each guest room on weekdays but an optional full breakfast is offered on weekends. This ample repast may include baked grapefruit, muffins and cheeses, *Kaiser Schmarren* (Austrian pancakes), breakfast sausage and pears, stuffed crepes, coffee, teas, and dessert. Note: Brigitte will be happy to translate for German tourists passing through the area.

What's Nearby Yachats

Ask the innkeepers about beach walking, beachcombing, agate collecting, hiking, summer swimming, and bicycling. Drive up to 800-foot Cape Perpetua, visit its interpretive center, and participate in guided tide pool walks. Stop at Strawberry Hill State Park to watch sea lions during low tide. Photograph a vintage covered bridge and see a resident elk herd on an auto tour up Yachats River Road. Visit Yachats Bay at low tide and walk on the beach. The New Morning Coffee House and Back Porch Gallery on Highway 101 at Fourth Street offers great espresso, pastries, and lunch Wednesday through Sundays.

For dining out try either LaSerre in Yachats, the restaurant at nearby Adobe Resort, or ask about other eateries in the nearby area. One such option is to drive north to Seal Rock for Japanese cuisine at Yuzen's. Or drive north to Waldport then turn west on Highway 34 about 10 miles to Kozy Kove Kafe, a floating restaurant on the Alsea River in the hamlet of Tidewater; call (541) 528–3251 for current hours and for reservations.

Annual events include The Smelt Fry and The Yachats Music Festival, both in July. The Arts and Crafts Fair is held in March. The city of Yachats internet site is: www.ohwy.com/or/y/yachats.htm

New England House Bed & Breakfast

227 Shell Street
P.O. Box 411
Yachats, OR 97498
Phone: (541) 547–4799; (800) 508–6455
E-mail: nehouse@pioneer.net
Internet site: www.moriah.com/nehouse/

Innkeepers: Lily and Lee Banks
Rooms: 1 suite with private bath
Extras: Fresh flowers; elegant linens; high tea served in late afternoon
On the grounds: wide views of ocean, Yachats Bay, village, and coastal hills
Smoking? Not allowed
Visiting pets? No
Credit cards: Visa, MasterCard, Discover
Rates: $$$; open Friday through Sunday and holidays
How to get there: From Highway 101, ¼ mile south of Yachats over the bridge, turn toward the ocean onto Shell Street to last residence on the ocean side.

This lovely bed and breakfast is often said to be one of the most romantic accommodations found on the central Oregon coast. Innkeepers Lily and Lee Banks offer guests exclusive use of a large suite; this is actually the entire second floor of the ocean view house, 900 square feet of living room with wide windows overlooking the ocean along with a bedroom and bath. The decor is English country with Old World paintings, Oriental rugs, antiques, and fresh flower arrangements from Lily's extensive gardens.

The couple married in 1968 and traveled the world for twenty years before moving to the Oregon coast. Lee had spent twenty years in the Marine Corps and had met Lily in Indonesia; she was the daughter of a Chinese businessman. "I think it was love at first sight," Lily smiles. "Lee proposed to me by mail after I was sent to school in the Netherlands." In their travels abroad the couple stayed at wonderful hotels and in comfortable bed-and-breakfast inns.

The guest suite's bright and airy bedroom reflects this refined European style of hospitality, and furnishings including a king feather bed with a goose down comforter, a large closet, fresh flowers from the garden, and the best of linens.

Special soaps, shampoo, hairdryer, more fresh flowers, and thick towels are found in the bath. Guests are offered high tea in the late afternoon. Lily prepares a sumptuous breakfast that is served at a cozy table set with fine china and linen by the large windows in the guest suite. Breakfast may consist of quiche made with sun-dried tomatoes and spinach from the garden, bacon or sausage, country red potatoes, a basket of blueberry bran muffins, and a plate of fresh fruit along with coffee, teas, hot cocoa, and juices.

What's Nearby

See What's Nearby Yachats on page 77.

Other Recommended B&Bs Nearby

Serenity Bed & Breakfast, sumptuous forested retreat a few miles away from the ocean; innkeepers Sam and Baerbel Morgan, 5985 Yachats River Road, Yachats, OR 97498; Telephone: (541) 547-3813; **Ziggurat Bed & Breakfast,** elegant contemporary home on the beach; innkeepers Mary Lou Cavendish and Irv Tebor, 95330 Highway 101, P.O. Box 757, Yachats, OR 97498; Telephone: (541) 547-3925.

Sea Quest Bed and Breakfast

95354 Highway 101
P.O. Box 448
Yachats, OR 97498
Phone: (541) 547–3782; (800) 341–4878
E-mail: seaquest@newportnet.com
Internet site: www.seaq.com

Innkeepers: Elaine and George Ireland
Rooms: 5 rooms with private baths
Extras: Whirlpool tubs in rooms; many sitting places with views
On the grounds: Views of the Pacific Ocean; beach access
Smoking? Outdoors only
Visiting pets? No; one resident cat, Clouseau, and a resident schnauzer, Sebastian
Credit cards: Visa, MasterCard
Rates: $$$
How to get there: From Highway 101 about 6 miles south of Yachats, between milemarkers 171 and 172, turn west toward ocean.

"If you time your visit right, you'll be able to watch whales as they move up or down the Oregon coast," says George. "We're located on a bluff just 100 feet from the ocean." Of the seven different kinds of whales plying the Pacific Ocean, the gray whales tend to maneuver closest to the shoreline. The whales migrate south to Baja California from November to January and return north to Alaskan waters from March to May. Guests will often congregate on the large decks that wrap around the inn, eyes shaded and squinting toward the ocean to spy the enormous mammals. "The whole central Oregon coast is great whale-watching territory," says Elaine.

With more than 1,500 square feet of comfortable places to settle in, along with a steaming cup of coffee or tea and freshly baked chocolate cookies or coffeecake, one might elect to stay several days. The second-floor great room, with its massive floor-to-ceiling brick fireplace, is a cozy place to curl up with the binoculars, a book, or a game.

The guest rooms are designed for privacy each having its own entry from the ground level. Queen beds with cozy comforters, lots of pillows, and sitting places with views of the ocean are offered along with large baths with bubbling whirlpool tubs for two. A warm soak may sound like an appealing option after a brisk walk on the beach.

After a good night's rest, lulled to sleep by surf sounds, guests amble up to the second-floor great room for a sumptuous breakfast. At small tables set for four, they enjoy such treats as baked blintzes, baked Brit-Chilean puffs, salmon and bagels, homemade granola, coffeecake, and a large assortment of fruit. The coffee and tea are on by 6:00 A.M. and breakfast is served at 9:00 A.M.

What's Nearby

See What's Nearby Yachats on page 77.

30

47

26

30

Hood River 6 The Dalles

84 12

Beaverton
Newberg
10 Portland

26 Welches
13 35

McMinnville 9
7 5

99W

99E
11

Monmouth 8 ★ Salem

5

Government
Camp
5

20 2

Corvallis

99W

99E

20

Veneta 99 Springfield

126 4 Eugene

Cottage 58 14 Westfir
Grove 3

5 Oakridge

138 5

58

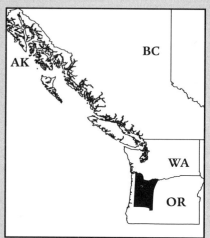

AK

BC

WA

OR

N

Portland Environs, Willamette Valley, Columbia Gorge, and High Cascades

Numbers on map refer to towns numbered below.

The Inn at Aurora

15109 Second Street Northeast

P.O. Box 249

Aurora, OR 97002

Phone: (503) 678–1932; (888) 799–1374

E-mail: weaver@hevanet.com

Internet site:

www.ohwy.com/or/i/innataur.htm

Innkeepers: Fay and Dave Weaver

Rooms: 4 rooms with private baths; 1 suite with gas fireplace and whirlpool tub

Extras: Homemade cookies; California king beds in guest rooms; 2 rooms have gas fireplaces; 3 rooms have outside balconies

On the grounds: Large trees, meadow, view of Pudding River

Smoking? Outdoors only

Visiting pets? No; no resident pets

Credit cards: Visa, MasterCard, American Express

Rates: $$–$$$

How to get there: Traveling north or south on I-5 take exit 278 Donald/Aurora, and proceed east on Ehler Road for 4 miles; you will cross railroad tracks coming into Aurora. Cross Highway 99E and turn immediately onto Second Street passing the post office and Ox Barn Museum and continuing 1 block to the inn; guest parking is clearly marked. Aurora can also be reached from the West Linn-Oregon City area via Highway 99E in approximately 10 miles.

"The inn was built in the early 1990s and was designed to reflect the style of the Old Aurora Colony," explains Fay. Shaded by large maple and old walnut trees, the modified Colonial-style house looks as though it's been here for decades. From the wide balcony on the second level, several of the original houses of the Old Aurora Colony can be seen; they date to the 1860s. A fine museum is housed in the restored ox barn and behind this structure is a charming garden, the Emma Wakefield Herb Garden. "Guests also enjoy inspecting the assortment of farm machinery on display here," says Dave. In the museum you can see many of the brass musical instruments used by colony members, including the *schellenbaum*, a rare bell tree. Wonderful handmade quilts are on display as well.

The guest rooms are located on the second floor of the inn and all contain California king beds with handmade quilts, bedside reading lamps, green plants, and wicker or antique furniture. The suite offers an oval whirlpool tub and a romantic gas fireplace as well as a section of the wide balcony, accessible through French doors. A second room gets the other section of the balcony and also has a gas fireplace. On the main floor are two comfortable common areas, one in the front of the inn that features a fireplace, couch, and book-filled bookcases. The other common area adjoins the open kitchen and offers light from a wide expanse of windows that look out on the meadow. This large room where breakfast is also served has a gas "wood stove" that warms guests on chilly mornings.

An amenable early morning tradition at the inn is the appearance of trays at the doors of each guest room laden with freshly brewed coffee and tea about a half-hour before breakfast. Breakfast may consist of Dutch baby pancakes, a seasonal fruit tray, juice or fruit smoothies, and coffee made in a French press. Steaming lattes or tea are also available. For dining out ask the innkeepers about local restaurants like Chez Moustache and Langdon Farms; for high tea ask about Angelina's French Country Tea Parlor.

What's Nearby

The area offers a number of fine antiques shops, cafes, delis, and coffee shops. Plan a visit to the Old Aurora Colony museum and to the one-hundred-year-old Aurora Presbyterian Church. A Spinner's Festival is held annually in the fall with demonstrations of hand spinning, spinning with vintage spinning wheels, and wool-dying. Contact the museum complex at (503) 678-5754. The nearby Aurora Airport can accommodate small aircraft. Also see What's Nearby Portland on page 125.

The Yankee Tinker
Bed & Breakfast

5480 Southwest 183rd Avenue
Beaverton, OR 97007
Phone: (503) 649-0932; (800) 846-5372
E-mail: yankeetb7b@aol.com
Internet site: www.yankeetinker.com

Innkeepers: Jan and Ralph Wadleigh
Rooms: 3 rooms, 1 with private bath
Extras: Fresh flowers in guest rooms; homemade fudge at evening turndown; afternoon tea and cookies; guest refrigerator stocked with juice, pop, beer, and wine; telephones and work areas in rooms
On the grounds: Well-established perennial beds, flowering trees and shrubs in serene backyard setting; deck with outdoor furniture
Smoking? Outdoors only
Visiting pets? No; no resident pets
Credit cards: Visa, MasterCard, Discover, American Express
Rates: $-$$
How to get there: From downtown Portland follow signs to Highway 26 West and Beaverton; proceed west to 185th Avenue taking exit 64 and immediately turning left. Cross over the highway and continue about 3½ miles to Tualatin Valley (TV) Highway, Route 8; continue on 185th to Deline Street, just beyond Aloha High School. Turn left onto Deline Street 2 blocks to 183rd Avenue and turn left.

On a quiet residential street in Portland's outer environs lives a couple who brings a bit of the East Coast to their bed-and-breakfast home. "My grandfather was a true New England craftsman," says Ralph. "He was a tinker." A number of special tinware pieces such as cups, pitchers, candlesticks, and match holders, are found in the comfortable common area. Guests often gather here in the evening with the hosts to enjoy cheese and crackers, a glass of wine, and good conversation. On chilly nights a fire burns brightly in the fireplace.

Later when guests say good night and repair to their rooms, they will find the handmade quilts on the queen beds neatly turned down, small votive candles lit at the bedside, and pieces of delicious homemade fudge or chocolates placed nearby. Jan also places her fresh flower arrangements in the rooms and she enjoys answering questions about the many antiques used in the rooms decor. You might wonder about the cricket rocker and the Empire-style dresser in The Maine Room or about the large leather trunk and the antique commode and washstand in The Massachusetts Room. "The old trunk belonged to Ralph's grandfather," explains Jan. "And the dresser was my grandmother's and came from Mount Desert Island."

Breakfast, served from 7:00 to 9:00 A.M., in the spacious dining room-country kitchen, starts with oranges freshly cut and squeezed into delicious juice and Longbottom's gourmet coffee beans freshly ground and brewed into steaming coffee. Guests visiting around Valentine's Day, may be served chilled strawberry soup, anise toast, and pear-hazelnut bread pudding with hazelnut custard sauce. Other mornings might bring baked apples topped with homemade cranberry-walnut granola and gingery yogurt, blueberry pancakes, and crisp bacon. On warm mornings they might have a second cup of coffee just outside on the deck, with relaxing views of the couple's extensive beds of flowers including lush roses, colorful iris, and deep green hostas. "We host a number of business travelers," says Ralph, "and they seem to enjoy the stress-free environment we provide here."

What's Nearby

The Washington County area offers a number of challenging public golf courses, a wide variety of shops, and many good restaurants. Touring wine country vineyards and tasting rooms is a popular pursuit as are hot-air ballooning, bicycling, jogging, and walking. The area is also home to many high-tech companies such as Intel, Sequent, and Tektronix. Also see What's Nearby Portland on page 125. The Washington County Visitors Association can be reached at (503) 644–5555 or (800) 537–3149.

Other Recommended B&B Nearby

Woven Glass Bed & Breakfast Inn, rambling country house features handwoven items, custom designed stained-glass windows, and healthy gourmet breakfasts; innkeepers Renee and Paul Giroux, 14645 Beef Bend Road, Tigard, OR 97224; Telephone: (503) 590–6040.

Bridal Veil Lodge
Bed & Breakfast

46650 East Historic Columbia River Highway
P.O. Box 10
Bridal Veil, OR 97010
Phone: (503) 695-2333
E-mail: lbslater@aol.com

Innkeepers: Laurel Slater
Rooms: 1 room in main lodge with private bath; 2 rooms in adjacent cottage with private baths
Extras: The inn is a TV-free zone; radio/tape player in rooms; coffee pot, coffee, teas, and cocoa in cottage rooms; current magazines, travel guides, paperback novels, and old books available
On the grounds: Near waterfalls along scenic highway and hiking trails/picnic areas in gorge
Smoking? Outdoors only
Visiting pets? No; no resident pets
Credit cards: No; checks preferred
Rates: $–$$
How to get there: From Portland take I-84 east 25 miles to the Bridal Veil exit 28; proceed right ½ mile to main intersection and turn right (west) onto Highway 30, the Historic Columbia River Highway. Continue 1 mile to the inn located on the left of the road and across from Bridal Veil State Park. From points east and heading west on I-84 take the Historic Highway/Ainsworth Park exit 35; travel about 8 miles on the Historic Columbia River Highway passing Multnomah and Wahkeena Falls and continuing to Bridal Veil Falls State Park. The inn is directly across from the park.

Imagine that it's 1926. You have thirty acres of forest, in the Columbia River Gorge near Portland. The land borders Highway 30, a road that winds through a scenic section of the narrow gorge, passing waterfalls, basalt outcroppings, and skirting the Columbia River. You have a lodge built, a place where travelers can stop for a meal and a room or to camp. "My great-grandfather, Virgil Amend, built this place after great-grandmother passed away," says Laurel.

Virgil operated the lodge and auto camp with his daughter, and, later, it became Laurel's family home. She grew up in what was a small logging community amid waterfalls, rocks, and tall trees. In the late 1980s, Laurel and her family opened Virgil's historic lodge to bed-and-breakfast travelers visiting the narrow gorge through which the Columbia River flows.

As a guest here, your room may be either in the main lodge or in the guest cottage just next door. The inviting guest rooms feature vintage quilts, country crafts, historic logging community memorabilia, and antique furniture. The double- or queen beds are outfitted with firm mattresses, fluffy down comforters, and extra quilts. The lodge room features a cozy window seat and sitting area, lustrous knotty pine accents, and hand-stenciled wallpaper. The private bath is a few steps down the hallway. The light and airy cottage offers two charming guest rooms with open-beam ceilings, skylight windows, wide- cushioned window seats, and private baths. Each cottage room also has its own private entrance and deck, amply sized.

Most mornings Laurel serves a country breakfast in the main lodge dining room. This large common area holds comfortable wicker furniture, reading lamps, and a vintage player piano with its music rolls neatly stacked close by. Occasionally breakfast may be delivered to guests who are staying in the cottage rooms. Morning fare may consist of waffles, crepes, or thick French toast topped with fresh fruit and dollops of whipped cream. Bacon or sausage and coffee and juices complement the hearty meal. For romantic dining in the evening, guests often make reservations at nearby Multnomah Falls Lodge Restaurant

What's Nearby

Hike on the great trails in the gorge, many of which follow alongside rocky creeks and culminate at small waterfalls or near wide-angle vistas. The Vista House at nearby Crown Point offers panoramic views of the river and gorge; helpful maps and information are available here. At Cascade Locks take the Bridge of the Gods (nominal toll charged) over to the Washington side of the river and drive east a couple miles to visit the impressive Columbia Gorge Interpretive Center and have lunch at the elegant Skamania Lodge. Charburger Restaurant on river bluff on the Oregon side offers great burgers and homemade desserts.

Other Recommended B&B Nearby

McMenamins Edgefield, built in 1911 as the Multnomah County Poor Farm, now hosts bed-and-breakfast rooms, restaurant, beer garden, brewery, winery, pub and movie theater, herb gardens; located at the entrance to the Columbia Gorge; 2126 SW Halsey Street, Troutdale, OR 97060; Telephone: (503) 669-8610.

Brightwood Guest House Bed & Breakfast

64725 East Barlow Trail Road
P.O. Box 189
Brightwood, OR 97011
Phone: (503) 622–5783; (888) 503–5783

It would be difficult to imagine a more serene, intimate, and private space in which to rest one's travel-weary body. Simply walking across the miniature Oriental-style bridge, looking into the koi pond and hearing the sounds of its small

Innkeepers: Jan Estep-Colgan
Rooms: 1 suite with loft in private guest house
Extras: Variety of bath oils and other toiletries in bath; kimonos and slippers; freshly ground gourmet coffee and coffee maker; conventional, herbal, and exotic teas as well as popcorn, condiments, spices, and herbs; board games, watercolors, oil pastels, calligraphy set, stationery, books, videos; telephone/intercom; guest packages
On the grounds: Private deck with Japanese water garden, waterfall and koi; fish food; birdseed; gazebo, barbecue, Hackett Creek, paths and two mountain bikes with helmets
Smoking? Outdoors only
Visiting pets? No; resident cat, Hedgerow
Credit cards: No; personal checks accepted
Rates: $$$
How to get there: From the Welches-Wemme area continue west on Highway 26 1 mile to the Brightwood turn-off; turn right and continue approximately 1 mile passing Mount Hood Coffee Roasters and residences to "Y." Immediately veer to the right, passing Brightwood Tavern and Brightwood Store and crossing the Sandy River; turn right onto Barlow Trail Road and continue 1 mile to the inn's sign on the left. Turn into driveway, veer right, and park next to the small guest house. From Portland-Gresham area take Highway 26 through Sandy and continue 15 miles to the Brightwood turn-off, turning left off the highway and proceeding to "Y." Immediately veer left, passing the tavern and crossing the river; turn right and follow directions above.

waterfall, then reaching the entry door to the guest house gives one permission to breathe deeply and leave driving cares far behind. Inside soft light enters sets of casement windows on either side of the doorway and reflects on warm cedar paneling. In the comfortable sitting area a low Japanese futon beckons. On the small table next to windows in the kitchenette appears a bowl of fresh flowers and a basket filled with, most likely, chocolate truffle muffins, the kinds that melt in your mouth.

You open the cupboard doors and see an array of teas. The coffee maker on the counter is at the ready with freshly ground gourmet coffee. The atmosphere, however, seems rather desiring of an herbal or exotic tea. Or perhaps glasses of pink champagne may be appropriate for the occasion. The coffee can wait until morning. You slip into a kimono and slippers and curl up with a romantic video selection such as, perhaps, *Casablanca, Roman Holiday, Love is a Many Splendored Thing*, or *Continental Divide*.

Later you pad up the narrow carpeted stairway that leads to the sleeping loft. Here a heavenly feather bed with a down comforter and pure cotton sheets invites deep rest and relaxation. The small window offers a view of your miniature water garden. There is no glare from city lights here. On the mountain night falls as dark as India ink. The only sounds you hear may be the gentle waterfall, the nearby creek, or the alto "whoo" of an owl in the tall fir trees. You sleep like a log.

Morning brings light through the windows, the morning newspaper at your door, the pungent smell of fir and cedar, and a gourmet breakfast prepared by Jan. This is delivered to your table by the window on the main level. Your meal may include savory brioche or scrapple, homemade cream waffles, freshly sliced berries and whipped cream, maple syrup, muesli, roasted potatoes, and an onion omelet. Hot truffle muffins often baked with cherries and almond may be presented for dessert. The coffee maker bubbles with gourmet coffee aromas. It is difficult to leave this special place.

What's Nearby

Nearby Lolo Pass offers great hiking, biking, bird watching, cross-country skiing, and scenic panoramas of Mount Hood. A complete fitness center and pool is located in nearby Mount Hood Village. Also see What's Nearby Welches on page 145 and What's Nearby Government Camp on page 111.

Maple-River Bed & Breakfast

20525 East Mountain Country Lane
P.O. Box 339
Brightwood, OR 97011
Phone: (503) 622–6273

Innkeepers: Barbara and Jim Dybvig
Rooms: 2 rooms with fireplaces and private baths; 1 suite in separate barn-style cottage
Extras: Outdoor hot tub overlooking river; robes and sandals; fly-fishing packages suitable for beginners; data ports for business travelers
On the grounds: Salmon River borders rear of property; two small landscaped ponds in front
Smoking? Outdoors only
Visiting pets? No; 2 friendly resident Lakeland terriers, Josie and Bogie
Credit cards: Visa, MasterCard
Rates: $$–$$$
How to get there: From Wemme continue west on Highway 26 1 mile to the Brightwood turnoff; turn right and continue approximately 1 mile passing Mount Hood Coffee Roasters and residences to "Y." Turn left and proceed 2 blocks to Mountain Country Lane, just before the bridge; turn left onto the narrow lane. The inn's mailbox and driveway are located on the right. From the Portland-Gresham area take Highway 26 through Sandy and continue 12 miles to the Brightwood turn-off, turning right off the highway and proceeding just across the bridge to Mountain Country Lane; turn right a few yards to the inn's mailbox and driveway, on the right.

"**B**ecause of our location right on the banks of the Salmon River," says Barbara, "we're finding that many guests are interested in fly-fishing." The Dybvigs have arranged with local fly fishing aficionado John Jones to offer equipment and lessons that are especially geared for beginning fly fishermen. But even those who aren't into fishing enjoy walking the path down to the river and sitting on the boardwalk that Jim has constructed over a section of the river. On warm days guests can dangle their feet in the clear, cold water or simply sit and munch sweet rolls, sandwiches, or sip cups of hot coffee while watching the shallow river chortle past on its way to joining the nearby Sandy River.

Another fine view of the Salmon River can be savored while enjoying a warm soak in the outdoor hot tub located just a few steps from the guest rooms. The hot tub is arranged on a covered raised deck and is surrounded with hanging baskets of greenery and colorful perennials such as ferns, fuchsias, and geraniums. Two well-appointed guest rooms are located on this ground level, both with views of the river. St. Andrews Suite, decorated in muted Scottish plaids, offers a large sitting room with a wood-burning fireplace, TV/VCR and CD tape deck, game table, sofa, chairs, and reading lamps. The queen bed is tucked into a romantic alcove. Northwoods Room, decorated in soft blues and creams, is smaller in size but also features a queen bed along with a gas fireplace, wicker chair, and reading lamps. Bear, moose, and fishing memorabilia complete the decor. A charming barn-style cottage suite is located a few steps from the main house and near two small landscaped ponds.

Breakfast is served upstairs in the dining area next to the large country kitchen. Before the morning meal guests often relax over cups of coffee in the adjacent reading room with its view of the river. This cozy room is done in English country style with colorful chintzes, plump pillows, and soft sitting places. Breakfast often consists of Barbara's Wakeup Casserole with sausage, eggs, cheese, mushrooms, and croutons bubbling in a pleasant tasting combination. Or the fare might be Swedish pancakes with fresh berries or Dutch babies with apple slices sautéed in brown sugar, honey, and cinnamon.

What's Nearby

See What's Nearby Welches on page 145 and What's Nearby Government Camp on page 111.

Other Recommended B&B Nearby

Brookside Bed & Breakfast, innkeepers Barbara and Jack Brooks offer comfortable home-style accommodations perfect for families; flowers, hummingbirds, friendly goats, shaggy llamas, and colorful peacocks; 45232 SE Paha Loop, Sandy, OR 97055; Telephone: (503) 668–4766.

A Bed and Breakfast on the Green

2515 Southwest Forty-fifth Street
Corvallis, OR 97333
Phone: (541) 757-7321; (888) 757-7321
E-mail: sparks@bandbonthe green.com
Internet site: www.bandbonthe green.com

Innkeepers: Neoma and Herb Sparks
Rooms: 4 rooms, 1 with private bath, 3 with a large compartmentalized-shared bath; terry robes and towels provided for outdoor hot tub
Extras: Private phone lines, fax service, photocopying service, data ports, desks, *Wall Street Journal* and local and regional newspapers, current magazines, soft drinks and snacks; nearby are walking and biking paths
On the grounds: On a private golf course; views of fairways and greens; views of Mary's Peak
Smoking? Outdoors only
Visiting pets? No
Credit cards: Visa, MasterCard, American Express, Discover, Diners Card
Rates: $–$$
How to get there: Take I–5 south of Albany to exit 228 and Highway 34 heading east to Corvallis; at the second traffic signal as you enter town turn left to the Highway 34 bypass (signs will indicate Philomath, Oregon coast, and Eugene). At the second traffic signal via the bypass turn left onto Thirty-fifth Street. After passing schools on the left, take the next right onto Country Club Drive and the first left onto Forty-fifth Street.

A lthough the home is situated on the fourth hole of a private golf course, the Corvallis Country Club, there are several public links nearby where you can swing your golf clubs, such as Trysting Tree and Marysville golf courses. "Guests enjoy relaxing on our large back deck where everyone can critique the passing golfers," chuckles Herb. Neoma notes that so far no golfer has sliced a drive into the yard or been compelled to chip a golf ball from underneath the rhododendrons.

Guests can choose from Neoma's Room, a large room with king bed, oriental carpets, and furnishings from the Far East; Nancy's Room, another large room with king bed, plush carpet, and decorated with Americana; Susan's Room with a queen, pecan sleigh bed, Oriental carpet, birds-eye maple chest, and apple-green and white furnishings; and Blake's Room with a queen, cherry sleigh bed, plush carpet, mini-armoire, gentry crafts, and Teddy bears. The latter two rooms overlook the golf course. Later they can pamper themselves in the secluded outdoor hot tub. The innkeepers furnish plush terry robes and towels; guests bring their own swimsuits.

Breakfast, offered from 7:00 to 9:00 A.M., is served in the formal dining room with fine linens, lovely china, and gleaming crystal. Guests enjoy seasonal fresh fruits in compote, perhaps eggs Benedict, and always the house specialty of ample slices of the couple's homemade pie such as apple, blackberry, or sweet cherry. "It's a real winner," says Herb. Both the Sparks are retired teachers, Herb from nearby Oregon State University, and Neoma from the public school system.

What's Nearby Corvallis

Corvallis is also a college town with numerous year-round activities and sports affairs offered at Oregon State University; the football team, the OSU Beavers, wears the school colors, orange and black. Antiques shopping, fishing, golfing, hiking, biking, and walking are also pleasant pursuits. Ask about Avery Park Rose Garden and about the several vintage covered bridges in the area that can be discovered on a self-guided auto or biking tour. The Corvallis Visitors Information Center is located at 420 NW Second Avenue, Corvallis, OR 97330; Telephone: (541) 757-1544 or (800) 334-8118.

Apple Inn Bed & Breakfast

30697 Kenady Lane
Cottage Grove, OR 97424
Phone: (541) 942-2393; (800) 942-2393
E-mail: appleinn@pond.net
Internet site:
www.pond.net/~bnbassoc/appleinn.html

Innkeepers: Harry and Kathe McIntire
Rooms: 2 rooms with private baths
Extras: Evening snack, often of gingersnap cookies and caramel apples; robes for hot tub; gourmet breakfasts; apple shampoo and conditioner in baths; room for RV parking
On the grounds: Mountain views, 190 acres of family owned fir trees; hot tub on outside deck
Smoking? Outdoors only
Visiting pets? No; two friendly orange tabby cats, Taffy and Butterscotch, not allowed in guest rooms
Credit cards: Discover
Rates: $-$$
How to get there: Take I-5 south of Eugene and continue past the first Cottage Grove exit and take exit 172; turn left at the stop sign following the signs to I-5 South. Turn right onto Latham Road then turn left onto Highway 99 at the railroad tracks; turn right onto Kenday Lane and continue 1⅝ miles to the big red Apple Inn sign. Traveling north on I-5 take exit 170 and proceed 2 miles to Kenady Lane; turn left and continue 1⅝ miles to the inn's red apple sign. Traveling south from downtown Cottage Grove, stay on Highway 99 and continue past the Weyerhaeuser Mill about 2 miles to Kenady Lane; turn right and continue 1⅝ miles to inn's red apple sign.

The large home built by Harry and Kathe in the early 1970s sits comfortably in its forest setting with views of Diamond Peak and Fairview Mountain. "Actually, we're on the edge of our 190 acres of family owned fir trees," explains Kathe. The enterprise is managed by Harry who is not only a professional forester and a friendly co-host at the inn, but also is one who enjoys sharing his knowledge. Guests can arrange an appointment on Sunday afternoons with Harry for a personal tour of the tree farm.

Kathe is a home economist and teaches family and consumer studies at the local middle school. Guests soon discover that she enjoys practicing her profession at home—even the smallest details are attended to. This includes supplies of apple shampoo and conditioner in the private baths, her hand-stenciled apple orchard border in the large suite, and wonderful evening snacks such as home-baked gingersnap cookies and crisp apples with caramel sauce. "Folks usually fall asleep full—and happy," says Kathe. Before tumbling into a comfortable bed and beneath a soft homemade quilt, however, you may want to don a swimsuit and find the hot tub out on the deck. Even if it should be raining, the shake roof provides enough protection, and on clear nights, you can see the stars glittering overhead.

In the morning Kathe offers freshly brewed gourmet coffee, tea, and cocoa about one hour before breakfast is served. Guests congregate in the cozy dining room with its antique table dressed in fine linens, silver, and crystal. Breakfast may consist of fruit sorbet, seasonal fruits, home-baked muffins or scones, and a choice of baked cheese and vegetable omelette with German potato cakes or a French toast casserole with apples and sour cream sauce. "It's rare that anyone would leave the table hungry," says Harry with a chuckle.

What's Nearby Cottage Grove

Travelers can visit old gold mines and more covered bridges, including circa 1925 Currin Bridge, circa 1949 Dorena Bridge, and circa 1920 Mosby Creek bridge. Obtains booklets and maps to the covered bridges and to the Bohemia Mine area at the Cottage Grove Visitors Information Center, 710 Row River Road, Cottage Grove, OR 97424; Telephone: (541) 942-2411. Good eateries here include Torero's, The Cottage, and The Covered Bridge. The local historical society museum is worth a stop as well.

Other Recommended B&Bs Nearby

Lily of the Field Bed & Breakfast, newly built home with meadow and mountain views; innkeeper Suzanne Huebner-Sannes, 35712 Ross Lane, P.O. Box 831, Cottage Grove, OR 97424; Telephone: (541) 942-2049; **Tuckaway Farm Inn,** in nearby Yoncalla, a 1920s farmhouse set in a secluded valley, antiques and family heirlooms, flock of Romney sheep; innkeepers Steve and Rosalind Dix, 7179 Scotts Valley Road, Yoncalla, OR 97499; Telephone: (541) 849-3144.

Wine Country Farm

6855 Breyman Orchards Road
Dayton, OR 97114
Phone: (503) 864-3446; (800) 261-3446
Internet site: www.moriah.com/wcf

Innkeeper: Joan Davenport
Rooms: 6 rooms with private baths in main farmhouse; 1 handicap accessible room with private bath; 2-room suite on second floor of tasting room structure next door
Extras: Wine, soft drinks, homemade cookies; croquet and horse shoes; buggy rides and picnics can be arranged
On the grounds: Panoramic views of Tualatin Valley towns, rolling hills, and mountains; gazebo; vineyard and tasting room; stables; Arabian horses; boarding for visiting horses
Smoking? Outdoors only
Visiting pets? No; 7 resident horses, 2 peacocks, 12 chickens, 2 dogs, 3 cats, all outside animals
Credit cards: Visa, MasterCard
Rates: $-$$$
How to get there: Traveling south on Highway 99W from Portland continue through Newberg toward Dundee. Three miles beyond Dundee near the truck weigh station, turn right onto McDougal; after 1 block turn right onto Breyman Orchards Road and proceed 2 miles to the end of the road at the top of the hill.

"The place looked quite sad and run down when I first bought it," shares Joan. "But we loved the top-of-the-hill views out over the valley and we couldn't resist—we rolled up our sleeves and began the renovation." The farm estate dates back to 1910 and includes thirteen acres of grapes and orchards, along with stunning views of the Cascade Mountains some one hundred miles to the east and of the many surrounding vineyards, wineries, and orchards extending to the south toward Amity and Salem.

The large main house of stucco has a European look about it and offers two separate common areas, each with a fireplace. Guests are invited to browse the extensive library and the video library collection, when they can tear themselves away from the large windows that frame those spectacular views of the valley. Guests invariably find themselves out on the large deck with other travelers, perhaps glasses of wine in hand, enjoying the warm breezes and sharing travel plans.

Joan is widely traveled and enjoys chatting with guests when her farm chores and animal chores permit. She raises and shows Arabian horses, one of which might take you for a buggy ride and picnic. The stable can also accommodate visiting horses. The two resident peacocks strut about the grounds and will often show off their gorgeous iridescent blue tail feathers in a duet of plumed finery. A small tasting room is located next door to the farmhouse, available for private parties or drop-in guests. A romantic two-room suite with a view is located on the second floor of the tasting room. The rooms in the farmhouse are small in size, some offer the great views, and one has a fireplace.

A gourmet country farm breakfast is served in the dining room along with the views; breakfast can also be enjoyed outside on the deck. Guests might lift their forks to warm Belgian waffles with freshly cooked cinnamon apples or pure maple syrup and whipped cream along with scrambled eggs, bacon, sausage, and fresh fruit.

What's Nearby

See What's Nearby Newberg on page 121, What's Nearby McMinnville on page 115, and What's Nearby Portland on page 125.

Other Recommended B&Bs Nearby

The Partridge Farm, a restored Victorian farmhouse located at the edge of Newberg on five landscaped acres including large perennial and vegetable gardens; the resident innkeepers can be reached at 4300 East Portland Road, Newberg, OR 97132; Telephone: (503) 538-2050. **Smith House Bed & Breakfast,** 1904 Victorian home furnished with comfortable antiques, located in quiet Newberg neighborhood; innkeepers Mary and Glen Post, 415 North College Street, Newberg, OR 97132; Telephone: (503) 538-1995.

McGillivray's Log Home Bed & Breakfast

88680 Evers Road
Elmira, OR 97437
Phone: (541) 935-3564

Innkeeper: Evelyn McGillivray
Rooms: 2 rooms with private baths
Extras: Fresh flowers in rooms, quantities of quiet away from freeway noises; TV/VCR and videos; books in living room; wood stove
On the grounds: Five acres at the edge of the Coast Range, tall Douglas fir and pine trees, log-bench swing under trees
Smoking? Outdoors only
Visiting pets? No; visiting deer and visiting pheasants
Credit cards: Visa, MasterCard
Rates: $–$$
How to get there: From downtown Eugene drive west on Eleventh Street leaving the city and continuing on Highway 126 about 8 miles to the small community of Veneta. Turn right onto Territorial Road for 1 mile, then turn left onto Suttle Road for 2 miles; at Evers Road turn right ¼ mile and look for the address; follow tree-lined lane to the log house.

Although the bed and breakfast is located less than 15 miles west of Eugene, guests feel as though they are in the forested Coast Range. They are—almost. Florence on the central coast is just 43 miles west of here. Douglas firs line the drive to the log home built by Evelyn McGillivray and her late husband, Dick. "Before we built our log house in 1982, Dick and I owned and operated a country grocery and gasoline station for many years near the Fern Ridge Reservoir," explains Evelyn.

There are a number of special features in the house such as the "blue and buggy" pine used in the kitchen, the wood light-switch covers, the handmade interior doors, the Midwest prairie pattern fieldstone in the living room, and the massive log beams that reach up to the rafters. All the support logs are of Douglas fir. Much of the pine furniture throughout the home was custom made. Touches of the couple's Scottish ancestry are present, such as the dining room curtains of soft wool woven in the McGillivray tartan.

The small guest room on the main floor has a polished floor of fir, as well as lace curtains and a king bed. Up the handsome log stairway fashioned by hand by Dick and Evelyn is a suite with its own sun deck and king and twin beds. Breakfast, served in the dining room each morning up to 9:30 A.M., is a hearty affair, especially on nippy mornings when Evelyn fires up the vintage wood cookstove. Guests enjoy watching her make "square" buttermilk pancakes using the antique hot-cake griddle her mother bought from a Sears, Roebuck catalog for 29 cents more than sixty years ago. It makes six pancakes at a time. Home grown and processed Concord grape juice may be served along with warm apple or berry oat bake and baked eggs encircled with crisp bacon.

The comfortable living room and shelves full of books are available for guests use. "I'm continuing the tradition that Dick and I started," says Evelyn. "We always wanted people to feel at home and to enjoy staying in a real log house."

What's Nearby

See What's Nearby Eugene on page 103 and What's Nearby Florence on page 35. *Note:* Unless you are into funky, somewhat 1960s hippie-style country fairs, you may want to avoid the Oregon Country Fair in July in the Veneta-Elmira area; Highway 126 is clogged with traffic during this time, making travel difficult. It takes place during the weekend following the Fourth of July.

The Campbell House, A City Inn

252 Pearl Street
Eugene, OR 97401
Phone: (541) 343-1119; (800) 264-2519
E-mail: campbellhouse@campbellhouse.com
Internet site: www.campbellhouse.com

Innkeepers: Myra and Roger Plant; Manager: Lydia Lindsay
Rooms: 14 rooms with private baths; 1 handicap accessible room; some rooms offer gas fireplaces, four-poster beds, views from bay or dormer windows, and claw-foot or jetted tubs; 2 large suites on second floor
Extras: TV/VCRs, honor bars, refrigerators, telephones with data ports; in baths are plush terry robes, curling irons, hair dryers; beverages and cookies available all hours; complimentary wine served in the evening
On the grounds: One-and-one-half acre landscaped gardens, pond, rock grotto; courtyard and gazebo, decks; two blocks to the McKenzie River and to riverside walking and biking paths
Smoking? Outdoors on patios or decks
Visiting pets? No; no resident pets
Credit cards: Visa, MasterCard, American Express
Rates: $-$$$$
How to get there: Take I-5 to Eugene-Springfield and exit 194B west onto I-105 and proceed toward downtown Eugene. Take the Coburg Road exit turning left to City Center and turn onto East Third Street, first street on the right after crossing the McKenzie River; continue to Pearl Street—the inn is located at the corner of Pearl and Third Streets.

One day on a bicycle ride around town you detour through the historic Skinner's Butte district, and you spot the outlines of an old house poking out of a tangle of trees, shrubs, and ivy. You see several gables and a chimney. It looks very intriguing, like a house that would appear in a Nancy Drew mystery. Myra and Roger Plant found this house on such a bike ride back in 1992, some one hundred years after the structure had been built by Eugene timber owner and gold miner, John Cogswell. "Along with family and friends and friends of friends, we worked on weekends for a year and brought the old house back to life as a bed-and-breakfast inn," explains Myra. The house was built for Cogswell's widowed daughter, Idaho Cogswell Frazer, and her daughter, Eva Frazer. Idaho later married Ira Campbell, co-owner and editor of the local newspaper, and the couple had three children—Cogswell, Celeste, and Jackson.

The results of the Plant's restoration of the house are stunning. Fourteen rooms offer travelers comfortable decor, cozy sitting areas, and many amenities. Frazer Room, for example, is decorated in an English fishing lodge theme with the original knotty pine walls. The Cogswell Family room, done in forest green prints and stripes, has a golfing motif. The Skinner Family room, off the courtyard, has an English garden theme with blues and greens in plaids and prints; and, Celeste Room, with gabled and dormer windows, offers an extra-

long queen brass bed, antique claw-foot tub with shower, and is done in shades of peach and green. Other rooms have an English hunting lodge decor, and the ambience of cozy country cottages.

Common areas open to guests include an elegant parlor with picture window views of the city; the library with a selection of antique books; and, the dining room with its long windows and views of the gardens. Breakfast is served from 7:00 to 9:30 A.M. Monday through Saturday and from 8:00 to 10:00 A.M. on Sunday. Coffee and tea room service begins at 6:15 A.M. Breakfast may consist of such delightful offerings as fresh fruit scones, hazelnut-apple malted mini-waffles, German apple pancakes, sour dough hot cakes, or special crepes, blintzes, quiches, and fritatas.

What's Nearby Eugene

Eugene hosts the well-loved Very Little Theatre, offering local players in dramas and comedies. A wide variety of eateries offer informal to fine dining; casual brewpubs and cafes dot the downtown and outlying areas as well. The University of Oregon hosts basketball and football games as well as other sports events and cultural events; there is also a theater on campus that offers dramas and musicals. The Eugene-Springfield area offers good access via Highway 126 and Highway 58 to central Cascade Mountain ski areas, and via Highway 126 west to Florence and other destinations on the central Oregon coast. The Lane County Visitors Association is located at 115 West Eighth Street, Eugene, OR 97401; Telephone: (800) 547-5445.

Kjaer's House in the Woods

814 Lorane Highway
Eugene, OR 97405
Phone: (541) 343-3234; (800) 437-4501

Innkeepers: Eunice and George Kjaer
Rooms: 2 rooms with private baths
Extras: Afternoon tea and snacks, flowers in rooms, restaurant guide, square grand piano, and music library
On the grounds: Landscaped grounds with rhododendrons, azaleas, tall Douglas firs and oaks; porch swing; visiting bird species
Smoking? Outdoors only
Visiting pets? No; visiting deer and other visiting wildlife
Credit cards: None; personal checks accepted
Rates: $-$$
How to get there: Driving north on I-5 take exit 189 and turn left (west) onto 30th Avenue; continue west past Lane Community College to traffic light at Hilyard Street. Continue through this light and curve to next traffic light turning left onto Twenty-ninth Avenue; proceed west to Willamette Street traffic light and continue for several blocks to stop sign. Continue straight ahead directly onto Lorane Highway, which winds a bit; at four-way stop—Lorane Highway, Friendly Street, and Storey Boulevard—continue straight to first driveway on left. The address is on mailbox and on tree at foot of driveway; watch for downhill traffic before turning into paved drive.

The Kjaers have the distinction of being one of the oldest bed and breakfast innkeepers in the Eugene area: not in age, but in length of time they've opened the doors of their large 1910 Craftsman-style home to travelers. "I can't believe it's been since 1984," says Elaine. "One wonders where the time goes!" The couple still enjoys welcoming guests to their wooded haven less than 2 miles from the downtown area. "Back at the turn of the century this was considered way out of town," says George.

Guests enjoy relaxing on the porch swing, a good spot for watching and feeding the birds;

they'll often see visiting deer meander through the spacious yard and disappear around large rhododendrons and clumps of azaleas that border the lawn. These well-known and much loved northwest shrubs offer a kaleidoscope of colorful blooms from April through May. Tall Douglas firs and enormous oaks, also bordering the rolling lawn, offer shade and natural outdoor air conditioning. Back inside, music lovers might enjoy browsing through the extensive music library and playing a piece or two on the rosewood square grand piano that resides in the large common area on the main floor. Many cultural events offer good evening options—ask about the current calendar for the Eugene Symphony Orchestra, Eugene Opera, the local ballet company, and the local concert choir. "Folks often check the performing arts Web site, www.hultcenter.org, for the latest schedule and for ordering tickets ahead," says Eunice. You might ask the couple about the American Music Series offered during the summer and about free concerts in the city parks. Some of the best jazz is heard at Jo Federigo's.

For a good night's sleep far from freeway noises, Maria's Room with its adjoining sitting room overlooks a small garden where colors of the Japanese maples blend nicely with the soft mauve and plum hues used in the room. Upstairs the Ivy Room is furnished with Mission-style oak. In the morning guests convene in the dining room for a delicious breakfast of juice blends, fresh fruit or the house special, Danish fruit soup, along with an egg dish or quiche, or French toast, homemade granola, and scones.

For eating out Café Soriah is known for romantic dinners, the Oregon Electric Station for great appetizers, the Old Texas Steak House for juicy steaks, Ambrosia for Italian cuisine, and Café Zenon for absolutely fabulous desserts.

What's Nearby

See What's Nearby Eugene on page 103.

Maryellen's Guest House

1583 Fircrest Street
Eugene, OR 97403
Phone: (541) 342-7326; (800) 736-1475
E-mail: maryellen@continet.com
Internet site: www.continet.com/blarson

Innkeepers: Maryellen and Bob Larson
Rooms: 2 rooms with private baths
Extras: Fresh flowers, Euphoria chocolates, hot and cold beverages, homebaked cookies and cakes, terry robes
On the grounds: Heated outdoor swimming pool, hot tub just off cedar deck; located on wooded hillside near Hendricks Park Rhododendron Garden
Smoking? Outdoors on deck
Visiting pets? No; no resident pets
Credit cards: Visa, MasterCard
Rates: $–$$
How to get there: Traveling south on I-5 take exit 191 and proceed over the freeway turning back onto I-5 heading north; take exit 192 and proceed onto Franklin Boulevard. Continue through the first traffic light at Walnut Street; at the next intersection turn left onto Orchard Street and then turn left onto Fifteenth Avenue; continue to the second stop sign and turn right onto Fairmount then immediately left onto Birch Street. Continue up hill to Fircrest; the inn is the second house on the left after the stop sign at the top of the hill.

Travelers who are a bit road weary may find this quiet and peaceful haven nestled on the south ridge next to Hendricks Park and its outstanding Rhododendron Garden a welcome stop on their itineraries. The living room sitting area has an open, casual elegance with comfortable sofa and chairs and wide views of the Willamette River during the daytime and of city lights at night. The cozy library is equipped with books, games, and videos; a guest refrigerator holds complimentary soft drinks. Maryellen's love of art and decorating is evident throughout the house. "I was an art history major then went into marketing for ten years," she says with a smile.

Both of the elegant guest suites open onto large cedar decks that lead to the heated swimming pool and hot tub. Swimming a lap or two followed by a soothing soak may sound appealing about now on your trek through the Willamette Valley. The elegant Country French Suite offers both charm and romance reminiscent of the French countryside along with a deep Roman-style soaking tub and tiled walk-in shower for two. The Contemporary Suite has a casual elegance. Both rooms have TV and telephones. The private baths offer soft terry robes, guest soaps and bubble bath, shampoo and conditioner.

You can help yourself to freshly brewed coffee or tea as early as 7:00 A.M. from the buffet area that adjoins the two guest suites. Breakfast is served in the dining room or in your suite at 9:00 A.M. or earlier if you wish. Maryellen serves a bountiful meal of baked German pancakes with lemon, powdered sugar, and pure maple syrup along with fresh fruit and sausage with rosemary. "We love sharing our home with wonderful people from all walks of life," she says.

What's Nearby

See What's Nearby Eugene on page 103.

Falcon's Crest Inn

87287 Government Camp Loop Highway
P.O. Box 185
Government Camp, OR 97028
Phone: (503) 272-3403; (800) 624-7384
E-mail: falconscrest@earthlink.com
Internet site: www.falconscrest.com

Innkeepers: Bob (B. J.) and Melody Johnson
Rooms: 5 rooms with private baths
Extras: Truffles from Oregon Candy Farms; large basket of amenities in baths; with prior reservation European-style fine dining with six-course, fixed price dinners; two-person whirlpool tub in 1 suite
On the grounds: Alpine fir, partial views of nearby Mount Hood Ski Bowl
Smoking? Outdoors only
Visiting pets? No; no resident pets, many resident Teddy bears
Credit cards? Visa, MasterCard, Discover, American Express
Rates: $$-$$$$
How to get there: From Hood River take Highway 35 to the junction of Highway 26, a distance of about 30 miles; turn right (west) and continue to Government Camp turning onto the loop drive that parallels Highway 26. Proceed to the inn at the lower end of the loop drive on the right and directly across from the Mount Hood Brew Pub. From Portland take Highway 26 east, passing through the communities of Sandy Welches, Zig Zag, and Rhododendron. Continue to Government Camp and turn left onto Government Camp Loop; the inn is on the left. Government Camp is approximately 50 miles from Portland.

In addition to quantities of lovable Teddy bears placed in pleasant groupings about the inn; the delicious chocolate truffles from nearby Oregon Candy Farms at the bedside; and the six-course gourmet dinners prepared by chef and co-innkeeper B.J.; the morning tray of coffee and freshly baked minimuffins delivered to your door; the spirited conversations that take place around the comfortable sofas in the Great Room; the massive wood stove that warms the inn; the floor-to-ceiling windows allowing views of tall Alpine fir; and two of the most convivial innkeepers on the mountain, there's not much more that can be said about this fine establishment. "We've been sharing our special brand of mountain hospitality for over ten years," says Melody. "We love it here on the mountain and we love getting the word out to travelers to come and spend quality time here in the Mount Hood Recreation Area."

Melody should definitely know how to get the word out—this woman has the energy of a steam locomotive. She's served as chairperson of many annual events in the area such as Christmas on the Mountain; she's served on the staff of the local chamber of commerce; she's spearheaded a bed-and-breakfast association of Mount Hood and Northern Willamette Valley innkeepers; she's played roles in amateur plays at the mountain; and, she's also involved in charitable endeavors. "She's our one-woman PR person," says a fellow innkeeper on the mountain.

Five guest rooms, one on the lower level, two on the main level, and two on the second level, offer well-appointed havens in which to get comfortable. The Mexicali Suite on the lower level features a two-person whirlpool spa. The Master Suite on the main level offers exclusive use of the small hot tub located on the deck just outside the bath. A soothing soak is especially nice on a frosty night when snow clings to the overhead fir branches. The Safari Suite has access to the front decks through sliding glass doors; on a sunny, warm morning the deck offers a companionable place to sit and enjoy one's first cup of coffee.

Breakfast, served in the Great Room's dining alcove, may include fresh orange juice, creamy scrambled eggs, sausage patties with spicy mustard sauce, and B. J.'s famous pancakes. Reservations for the elegant gourmet dinner may be made ahead. This is a fixed-price affair complete with lighted candles, floral arrangements, china, crystal, and silver. The first couple to reserve for the evening is offered the opportunity to choose the main entree from the current gourmet menu.

What's Nearby

See What's Nearby Government Camp on page 111 and What's Nearby Welches on page 145.

Mount Hood Manor

88900 Government Camp Loop
P.O. Box 369
Government Camp, OR 97028
Phone: (503) 272-3440
E-mail: mt-hood-manor-bb@juno.com

Innkeepers: Mary Swanson and Robert Duncan
Rooms: 4 rooms with private baths
Extras: Ski room for ski equipment storage; clothes dryer; hot tub outside on covered deck; extensive video library
On the grounds: Alpine fir, views of Mount Hood to the immediate northeast
Smoking? Outdoors on porch and deck
Visiting pets? No; no resident pets
Credit cards: Visa, MasterCard, Discover, American Express
Rates: $$–$$$
How to get there: From Hood River take Highway 35 past the community of Mount Hood, Cooper Spur Ski Area, and past Mount Hood Meadows Ski Area to the junction of Highway 26. Turn right (west) onto Highway 26 and continue to the small community of Government Camp turning onto the loop drive that parallels the highway; proceed to the inn on the left. From Portland take Highway 26 heading east to the Mount Hood Recreation Area and proceed to Government Camp 12 miles above Rhododendron. Turn onto Government Camp Loop and proceed to the inn on the right; off-street parking is available.

The English-Tudor-style inn located at the 4,000-foot level in the village of Government Camp was constructed in 1993. "I wanted to develop a bed-and-breakfast inn here at the mountain," says Mary, "with views of the mountain and of the passing seasons." The inn has four large guest rooms on the second floor, each with TV/VCR and a good-sized private bath. A large library of contemporary and classic film videos is available for browsing in the adjoining guest sitting room. This cozy space also offers a fireplace and a small no-host bar.

The Garden Room contains a queen wicker bed and a daybed and offers a grand view of the mountain. The floral country motif in shades of pale green and tea rose gives the room a light and airy feeling. The Oregon

Room done in blues and whites, is comfortably appointed with furniture in dark pine accented with white wicker. The works of Oregon artists adorn the walls. The Americana Room has a double bed with an Ethan Allen cannonball headboard in dark pine. Decorated in shades of jade, mauve, and sand, this room also has a collection of Norman Rockwell figurines. The Alaskan Room, the largest, offers two queen beds and black and gray lacquer furniture combined with red accents. Paintings by Alaskan artists, including one known for polar bear paintings, adorn the walls.

Breakfast is served in the dining room on the main floor from 7:00 to 9:00 A.M., and usually consists of juice, muffins, fresh fruit, and an entree such as French toast, blueberry pancakes, a mushroom-cheese quiche, or breakfast casserole. Tasty homemade biscuits are hot from the oven and may accompany the morning meal.

What's Nearby Government Camp

Winter sports lovers find several nearby ski areas to choose from including Summit, Ski Bowl, Timberline, and Mount Hood Meadows. There are downhill runs and snowboarding runs for every ski level, from beginner to expert. Lighted night skiing is also available. Areas for snowshoeing, cross-country skiing, snow-mobiling and, for the kids, innertubing, are also located nearby. Summer and fall weather brings opportunities for fishing, boating, rafting, hiking, mountain biking, and golf. The Mount Hood Recreation Area Visitors' Center in Wemme can provide information, maps, and current weather conditions; Telephone: (503) 622-4822. *Note:* SnoPark permits are required during winter months.

Lakecliff Estate Bed & Breakfast

3820 Westcliff Drive
P.O. Box 1220
Hood River, OR 97031
Phone: (541) 386-7000
E-mail: lakecliff@linkport.com

Innkeepers: Judy and Bruce Thesenga
Rooms: 4 rooms, 2 with private baths, 3 with native stone fireplaces
Extras: Cozy sun room, large deck overlooking Columbia River; afternoon snacks
On the grounds: Eleven acres of native trees, shrubs, lawn; outdoor shuffleboard court
Smoking? Not allowed
Visiting pets? No; 2 outside cats, Parker and Muffy, and 1 blond Labrador retriever puppy, Truman
Credit cards: No; personal checks or traveler's checks are preferred
Rates: $$
How to get there: Driving east on I-84 from Portland to Hood River, take exit 62 and turn left driving over the interstate and turn right onto Westcliff Drive. Turn into the first driveway on the left and proceed to inn's parking area.

Doesn't everyone have five native-stone fireplaces? Probably not but this summer home, constructed in 1908 on a rocky bluff overlooking the Columbia River, still captivates guests with all five of its original stone hearths. The fireplaces were constructed with basalt, the grayish-colored rock characteristic of ancient volcanic activity that happened eons ago in this section of the northwest. Geologists believe the quantities of lava that solidified in this area probably flowed from two nearby snowy peaks,

Mount Hood, looming to the southwest and Mount Adams, easily recognizable to the north of Hood River in Washington state's central Cascades. Lava flows also came from nearby Larch Mountain.

"The large fireplace in the common room seems always to draw guests," says Judy. "There will often be several folks chatting around the fire, getting acquainted and sharing travel adventures." This room has deep, comfortable sofas and wingback chairs placed close to the hearth. A cozy sun room also beckons at the south end of the common area, accessed through French doors; it is filled with green plants, magazines, books, and wicker furniture. But the wide window at the north end of the room draws rave reviews for its panorama—the Columbia River and dozens of windsurfers scooting back and forth on frothy waves. They launch from the area near Spring Creek Fish Hatchery on the far, Washington side of the river.

The guest rooms all are located on the second floor and three of them offer the vintage stone hearths as well as crackling fires on cold evenings. The largest, Garden Room, has views of the garden and woods. Wendy's Room has views of the river and wooded hills on the opposite shore. A corner room, Lynn's Room, looks out on the woods and the river. Emily's Room, although absent one of the stone hearths, is a pleasant space with twin beds and views of the river.

In the morning coffee lovers can enjoy a cup of brew and crisp biscotti by 7:30 A.M., helping themselves from the antique buffet in the second-floor hallway. Just before 9:00 A.M. guests walk downstairs, eyeing the large mounted heads of an elk and a moose, and gather in the fireplaced dining room for breakfast. Along with those great river views, the morning may include a fresh fruit compote, fresh orange juice, cinnamon-raisin French toast, and Lake-Cliff bacon. "Everyone seems to love this," says Judy. "We bake the fresh bacon in the oven with brown sugar."

What's Nearby Hood River

The area is a mecca for windsurfers who come from around the world with colorful sailboards to ply the big waves on the Columbia River generated by the brisk winds that funnel through the gorge. The well-stocked Hood River Visitors' Center is at the Boat Basin and Marina Park; Telephone: (541) 386-2000. Pick up a copy of the brochure and map for a self-guided tour to nearly two dozen orchards, farms, fruit stands, and country stores. Good restaurants in the vicinity include Pasquale's Italian Ristorante at the historic Hood River Hotel, the Coffee Spot on Oak Street, and Sweet Dreams Bakery & Dream Wakers Espresso on Cascade Street.

Steiger Haus
Bed & Breakfast

360 Wilson Street
McMinnville, OR 97128
Phone: (503) 472-0821

Innkeepers: Susan and Dale DuRette
Rooms: 5 rooms with private baths including 2 suites with either fireplace or soaking tub; 1 additional suite has small kitchen and whirlpool bath
Extras: Snacks and hot or cold beverages available in kitchen-common area; TV/VCR, stereo and CDs available; soaking tub and skylight in second floor suite; fireplace in garden level suite; sun room-studio on main floor
On the grounds: Half-acre English garden and lawn, terraced down to small creek; gardenside decks adjoining three guest rooms
Smoking? Outdoors on decks
Visiting pets? No; one outside cat, Speck, a tortise who is "getting on in years," and several visiting deer who frequent the gardens
Credit cards: Visa, MasterCard, Discover
Rates: $-$$$
How to get there: Take Highway 99W southwest from Portland to McMinnville, about 25 miles, staying on 99W into town—it becomes Adams Street. Turn left on Second Steet for 3 blocks, then turn right on Davis Street for 3 blocks to Wilson Street; the inn is on the corner of Davis and Wilson Streets.

"**G**uests especially love our terraced English garden and seeing the deer in the early morning or at dusk," smiles Susan. "And guests also love being able to walk downtown from here for dinner at Nick's Italian Café." The DuRettes have continued the same fine quality of bed-and-breakfast innkeeping as the former owners who built the spacious inn, Doris and Lynn Steiger. The massive structure combines an elegant contemporary and Old-World European ambience with glass and cedar, large decks and intriguing rooflines, and a lovely terraced garden that borders Cozine Creek.

On the garden level guests find the Fireside Suite, a romantic room with queen bed, fireplace, TV, and deck overlooking the garden. Morningsun Suite offers a cozy sitting area with a small kitchenette, whirlpool bath, and queen bed. On the top floor Treetop Suite has a bay window, queen bed, soaking tub, and views of the garden. Rooftop Suite offers twin beds.

Breakfast is served usually between 8:00 and 9:00 A.M. in the garden dining room on the main level, but can be arranged earlier for business travelers. Coffee and tea are available with the morning newspaper anytime after 7:00 A.M. The sumptuous breakfast may consist of poached fresh pears, bran muffins, puffed apple pancake, and thick sliced bacon. During summer months Susan likes to serve her mixed-berry waffle, which includes fresh blueberries, marionberries, and raspberries along with raspberry syrup," she says.

For evening dining ask about Nick's Italian Café, McMenamin's, Third Street Grill, and Kame (Japanese cuisine). Old Noah's Wine Shop often has live music on Fridays and Saturdays and the Gallery Theater offers local players doing contemporary dramas, comedies, and musicals. Antiques lovers will enjoy the eclectic collection of shops and purveyors in nearby Lafayette, located in the old schoolhouse.

What's Nearby McMinnville

In the surrounding Yamhill and Washington counties, travelers find more than thirty fine vineyards, wineries, and tasting rooms. Many of the wineries, in addition to offering spectacular views of the broad Tualatin Valley and Cascade Mountains, host jazz and classical musicians during summer and fall weekends. Sample Oregon's fine wines such as white Rieslings and pinot noirs; also available are many delicious berry and dessert varieties. For helpful maps and more information, contact the McMinnville Visitors Information Center located at 417 North Adams Street, McMinnville OR, 97128; Telephone: (503) 472-6196.

Other Recommended B&Bs Nearby

Baker Street Bed & Breakfast in downtown McMinnville, a restored 1914 home decorated with Victorian antiques; innkeepers Cheryl and John Collins, 129 South Baker Street, McMinnville, OR 97128; Telephone: (503) 472-5575; **Mattey House Bed & Breakfast,** an 1892 Queen Anne Victorian set on a ten-acre vineyard just outside McMinnville; innkeepers Jack and Denise Seed, 10221 Northeast Mattey Lane, McMinnville, OR 97128; Telephone: (503) 434-5058.

Howell House
Bed and Breakfast

212 North Knox Street
Monmouth, OR 97361
Phone: (503) 838–2085; (800) 368–2085
Internet site: www.moriah.com/howell

Innkeepers: Clint and Sandra Boylan
Rooms: 4 rooms including 2 suites; 3 baths
Extras: Guest refrigerator in suites; bathrobes provided; resident VCR and vintage movies; close by are tennis courts, track, and swimming pool
On the grounds: Heritage roses; enclosed Oriental-style hot tub; gazebo
Smoking? Outdoors only
Visiting pets: No
Credit cards: None at this time; personal checks accepted
Rates: $–$$
How to get there: From I-5 exit at Salem and take Highway 22 west to Highway 99W; turn south to Monmouth turning right at J's Restaurant onto Jackson Street; the inn is at the corner of Jackson and Knox Streets. Monmouth is approximately 15 miles from Salem.

"In 1984 the structure was condemned for demolition—it looked very sad," explains Sandy. "But when Clint and I and our four boys went through the old house—it was built in 1891—we decided to restore it and turn it into a bed-and-breakfast inn." Now, with a soft yellow coat of paint and windows that no longer sag and a new front porch, the house sparkles with renewed life and a genuine sense of vintage charm. In the front parlor a small grandfather clock ticks, measuring time as it sits on Sandy's antique parlor piano. A classical pianist, she has been known to serenade guests at breakfast with a Chopin nocturne or two. Sandy also collects vintage clothing so you'll often see a lacy blouse and pleated skirt or graceful floor-length gown edged with lace dressed on mannequins placed about the inn. "The vintage fashions are such fun to wear," she says with a smile.

The Boylans named their guest rooms to remember those early days when three generations of the Howell family rented to students attending the Oregon Normal School (now Western Oregon University). You might choose Housemothers Suite with sitting room and private bath, the new Seniors Guest Suite, Juniors Guest Room, or Alumni's Parlor Room. Framed photographs of many of those college students adorn the walls here and there along with other nostalgic memorabilia such as an old ticket to a football game or a dried rose corsage. "Some of the former students, now adults and even seniors, often stop by when they're in town," adds Clint. The Boylans are members of the American Rose Society and on the grounds of the inn grow some eighty heritage and contemporary roses. When you step out to the backyard to the gazebo or to the enclosed Oriental hot tub, you might see Reine de Violettes, a large and fragrant purple hybrid tea rose; Voo Doo, a flamboyant orange newer variety; and Lavender Lassie, a special heritage rose. While you're outdoors, talk Clint into showing off his restored 1929 dark green Model A Ford pickup.

Breakfast served at the round table in the dining room may include such specials as chocolate-kahlua pancakes or Belgian buttermilk waffles with strawberries and cream. Or you could be served Howell's Spectacular Breakfast Pie, which includes a freshly grated hash brown crust and a scrambled egg filling of eggs, cream cheese, diced ham, minced green onion, and cheddar cheese.

What's Nearby

Being a college town, there are numerous activities offered year round at the Rice Performing Arts Center, which is part of the Western Oregon University complex. Touring some eighteen nearby wineries and shopping for antiques are popular pursuits as well. There are several good restaurants close by including one restaurant with excellent Mexican cuisine. See also What's Nearby Salem on page 141.

Mount Hood Hamlet
Bed & Breakfast

6741 Highway 35
Mount Hood, OR 97041
Phone: (541) 352-3574; (800) 407-0570
E-mail: hoodhamlet@linkport.com
Internet site:
www.site-works.com/hoodhamlet

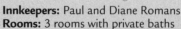

Innkeepers: Paul and Diane Romans
Rooms: 3 rooms with private baths
Extras: Guest refrigerator stocked with juices and soft drinks; large-screen TV, VCR in fireplace great room; outdoor hot tub next to garden sun room
On the grounds: Vegetable and flower gardens; views of Mount Hood; close to cross-country and alpine ski areas
Smoking? Outdoors only
Visiting pets? No; no resident pets
Credit cards: Visa, MasterCard, American Express, Discover
Rates: $$–$$$
How to get there: 60 miles east from Portland via I-84, take exit 64 at Hood River and proceed south on Highway 35 for 15 miles to the small community of Mount Hood; the inn's small sign is located at the driveway entrance at the outskirts of town on the left. The house is not visible from the highway.

Nestled on nearly ten acres of farmland, Douglas fir, hemlock, and cedar, and with Mount Hood looming some 11,235 feet to the immediate southwest, the newly constructed house brings an eighteenth century, New England feeling to this section of the high Cascades. The clean lines of the colonial exterior contrast well with the shaggy forests and craggy mountain peaks. "The property belonged to Paul's family for about 50 years," explains Diane. "He grew up here." Upon arrival guests usually gather in the fireplaced Great Room where a wood-burning fire might be crackling from the red brick hearth. This hearth also opens to the cozy library room. Diane and Paul may offer hot coffee or tea while everyone chats and gets acquainted. Later you could decide to take a starlight soak in the outdoor hot tub. Mount Hood seems ever so intimidating over your shoulder. The hot tub is located just beyond the garden sun room; this cozy room is outfitted with green plants, a comfy chaise lounge, and extra towels. "We decided to have the garden room floor heated," says Paul, "so that walking back indoors is a bit more comfortable for bare or stockinged feet."

The rooms are good-sized, comfortable, and have private baths. In Vista Ridge Room a large window frames snowy Mount Hood, a gas fire burns warmly on the brick hearth, and the queen bed and a whirlpool tub await. Japanese terrycloth washcloths are featured in the baths— extra long for scrubbing one's back. From the king bed in Cloud Cap Room you could awaken to a great view of Mount Hood, and from the cozy corner of Klickitat Room, guests look out to a panorama of forested hills, distant farms, and the top of Mount Adams on the horizon to the north. Breakfast is served between 7:30 and 10:00 A.M. in the dining area next to the Great Room, with coffee and tea available beforehand. Guests enjoy such heart-healthy treats as ginger-peach French toast and lean sausage, or a western omelet with seven vegetables, pear-oatmeal muffins, and grapefruit with caramel-spice pear butter, or cinnamon-apple pancakes with apple compote and huckleberry and maple syrups.

What's Nearby

Winter gets rave reviews here due to several accessible ski areas, including nearby Cooper Spur Ski Area, especially good for families with young children, and Mount Hood Meadows with its numerous runs for all ability levels. Good areas for cross-country skiing, snowshoeing, and snowmobiling are located within easy driving distances. Late spring, summer, and fall bring warm days, blossom festivals, fruit harvests, and activities such as golf, lake fishing, hiking, and biking. Also see What's Nearby Hood River on page 113.

Other Recommended B&Bs Nearby

Avalon Bed & Breakfast, a turn-of-the-century farmhouse near Hood River with views of Mount Adams; innkeepers Jim and Dorothy Tollen, 3444 Avalon Drive, Hood River, OR 97031; Telephone: (541) 386-2560. **The Columbia House Bed & Breakfast,** a rambling 1940s style bungalow overlooking the Columbia River; contact innkeeper Mavis Starnes, 525 East Seventh Street, The Dalles, OR 97058; Telephone: (541) 298-4686. **The Williams House Bed & Breakfast Inn,** a late 1890s gingerbread-trimmed Victorian with fine landscaped grounds; 608 West Sixth Street, The Dalles, OR 97058; Telephone: (541) 296-2889.

Springbrook Hazelnut Farm

30295 North Highway 99W
Newberg, OR 97132
Phone: (503) 538–4606; (800) 793–8528
E-mail: springbr@sprynet.com
Internet site: www.nutfarm.com

Innkeepers: Ellen and Chuck McClure
Rooms: 4 rooms with shared baths in the main house; Carriage House and Rose Cottage on the grounds, each with private bath, kitchenette, and sitting areas
Extras: Carriage House and Rose Cottage both have stocked refrigerators; fresh flowers and packages of hazelnuts in rooms; private-label glycerin soaps, bubble bath, robes, and fresh flowers in baths
On the grounds: Tennis court, solar heated swimming pool, heritage roses, sixty-acre hazelnut orchard, wildflower meadow, pond, vegetable garden, large trees; small fruit tree orchard near tennis court
Smoking? Outdoors only
Visiting pets? No; two resident spaniels, Ghillie and Duffy
Credit cards: None at this time; personal checks accepted
Rates: $$–$$$$
How to get there: From Portland take Highway 99W 14 miles south toward Newberg; just beyond milepost 21 look for the entrance to the inn at the bottom of Rex Hill on the right; the inn is next door to the Rex Hill Vineyards.

"I always have the sense that I'm at a retreat," says one recently returning guest. Even though the house and grounds are close to old Highway 99W, upon entering the tree-shaded drive one has the sense that city cares have been left far behind. The lush greenness of tall trees, flowering shrubs, and some sixty acres of compact hazelnut trees provide fairly good insulation

from automobile noise. Being a native Oregonian I have always thought one of the coolest places to hide on a very hot day is in the center of a shady hazelnut orchard.

Once you get settled into your cozy guest room in the main house or in the Carriage

House or Rose Cottage, what's there to do here? For starters you can sit a spell at the large pond near the wildflower meadow. "We have about eight pair of redwing blackbirds who live here now," says Ellen, "and several great blue heron that cruise through as well . . . it's wonderful to see them!"

You might play a game of tennis on the resident court or take a leisurely swim in the swimming pool; it's heated by solar energy. You could inspect Chuck's extensive vegetable garden or sniff the collection of lovely heritage roses. The small fruit tree orchard includes varieties of cherry, fig, weeping plum, peach, apricot, and apple. Be sure to ask the innkeepers for a very special and private tour of the barn near Rose Cottage.

After a good night's rest beneath down comforters, make your way to the sun room for breakfast. Extending across a front section of the large Craftsman-style house and filled with windows, the light airy room sets a cheerful tone with its blue-and-white-checkerboard floor, bright orange seat cushions on white wicker furniture, fireplace, and hanging baskets. Seasonal flowers like nasturtiums in shades of orange and yellow might be blooming or spilling from vases on the wicker tables.

You may enjoy homemade hazelnut granola with fresh fruit and yogurt, and fresh orange juice along with croissants, muffins, or scones and homemade jam. Ellen's gourmet main course might be crepes with ham and asparagus or a zucchini frittata or a salmon quiche with artichokes.

For evening dining out ask about Tina's, Rex Hills, and Joel Palmer House, all located in the Newberg-Dundee environs.

What's Nearby Newberg

The Rex Hill Winery and Tasting Room are located next door to the inn; musical events are offered in its outdoor amphitheater during summer and fall. Hot-air ballooning, antiquing, and winery touring are other popular activities offered in the Newberg area. See also What's Nearby McMinnville on page 115 and What's Nearby Portland on page 125.

The Clinkerbrick House
Bed & Breakfast

2311 Northeast Schuyler Street
Portland, OR 97212
Phone: (503) 281-2533
Internet site: www.obbg.org

Innkeepers: Peggie and Bob Irvine
Rooms: 3 rooms, 1 with private bath
Extras: Fresh flowers in rooms; separate common area on second floor has guest refrigerator, microwave, TV, Northwest books and magazines; complimentary soft drinks; one room has a private deck
On the grounds: Tree-lined street in one of the city's well-established neighborhoods
Smoking? Outdoors only
Visiting pets? No; resident Llasa
Credit cards: Visa, MasterCard
Rates: $-$$
How to get there: Traveling north or south on I-5 through Portland take exit 302 A, Rose Quarter, and turn east onto Weidler Street; proceed to Twenty-first Avenue turning left to Schuyler. Turn right 1½ blocks to red brick house on left.

In this 1908 Dutch Colonial constructed with clinker bricks and amid Peggie's delightful collections—including antiques, quilts, and strawberries—guests find a comfortable home away from home, especially after a busy day of sightseeing at Mount Hood or golfing at nearby Glendoveer, Rose City, Broadmoor, or Colwood International golf courses. "We can also suggest good places for eating dinner," says Peggie. "Our ever changing local restaurant list is popular—Portland is really a great restaurant town."

The amply sized guest rooms are located on the second floor where there is also a cozy common area for guests to use with both a refrigerator stocked with soft drinks and a microwave for popping a bowl of popcorn or heating food items. Handy reading materials include a large collection of regional travel guides and numerous books about the Northwest. In the Rose Room pink roses and white wicker along with a queen iron bed give this room a soft, romantic feeling. In Strawberry Room Peggie has stenciled one of her favorite strawberry designs on the walls; a handcrafted pencil-post queen canopy bed offers a good night's sleep. Garden Room, the largest with its own small deck, offers a canopied queen bed and a comfy wicker chaise lounge. This room gets the morning sun as well.

Peggie's gourmet breakfasts are the kind one writes home about. In the large dining room on the main floor, guests might take their forks and knives to gingerbread waffles with fresh pears, yogurt, and orange syrup, or perhaps spinach-egg bake with fresh tomatoes, a fresh fruit compote, rosemary potatoes, and brown-sugar muffins. She has also been known to bake an apricot breakfast roll, an Oregon plum cobbler cake, and luscious cinnamon rolls. During warm weather breakfast is often served outdoors on the brick patio. "Guests usually leave the table very full and very happy," Bob says with a grin.

What's Nearby

See What's Nearby Portland on page 125.

Other Recommended B&Bs Nearby

Portland Guest House, a small Victorian in the Historic Irvington district on east side, close to Convention Center and Rose Quarter sports center; innkeeper Susan Gisvold, 1720 Northeast Fifteenth Avenue, Portland, OR 97212; Telephone: (503) 282–1402. **Portland White House,** with its classic columns, circular drive, grand staircase, and period furnishings, looks like its namesake; innkeepers Lanning and Steve, 1914 Northeast Twenty-second Avenue, Portland, OR 97212; Telephone: (503) 287–7131.

General Hooker's Bed & Breakfast

125 Southwest Hooker Street
Portland, OR 97201
Phone: (503) 222-4435
E-mail: ghbandb@teleport.com
Internet site: www.teleport.com/~ghbandb

Innkeeper: Lori Hall
Rooms: 4 rooms, 2 with private baths
Extras: Complimentary cold beverages; extensive travel and video library; innkeeper is "film freak and vegetarian"; guest passes available to nearby Metro YMCA; excellent jogging paths nearby; 2 neighborhood parks; close to downtown cultural centers, performing arts centers, museums, universities, and libraries
On the grounds: Views of downtown and of distant mountains from roof deck
Smoking? Outside on roof deck
Visiting pets? No; resident Abyssinian cat and greeter, Happy Hooker, not allowed in guest rooms
Credit cards: Visa, MasterCard, American Express
Rates: $-$$
How to get there: From points south of Portland take I-5 to exit 298 near downtown Portland, the Corbett-Johns Landing exit, and turn left onto Corbett Street. Proceed for 1 mile where Corbett ends with an underpass that emerges at SW First Avenue; turn left at the third intersection onto Hooker Street. Coming from any other direction, including the airport, contact the innkeeper for brochure detailing specific directions.

The inn is the quintessential city stop, close to everything that downtown Portland has to offer. There are very few questions about the city that this innkeeper, a fourth-generation Portlander and history lover, can't address. Lori also maintains an extensive collection of restaurant reviews, maps, directions, Oregon and northwest travel videos, and suggestions for travelers. "Be sure to pack your swimsuit, gym gear, and running shoes," suggests Lori. "We're close to the well-equipped Metro YMCA and to great downtown running areas."

She explains that the immediate area, Caruther's Addition, was platted in 1875, and all the streets named for Civil War generals. This included one "Fighting Joe" Hooker, a Union general from Hadley, Massachusetts. His name lives on because of his business-like handling of female camp followers, known then as "Hooker's Second Army." "This phrase was later shortened to its current usage," says Lori. Did General Hooker ever sleep here? "Well, no," she says, "but I named my cat and my inn in his honor."

City guests find four comfortable guest rooms and an extensive library of classic videos and travel videos. All of the rooms are equipped with TVs and VCRs, clock radios, telephones and dataports, hair dryers, and robes. The lower level room, Dandelion, has two loft-style beds, well-filled bookshelves, and its own small refrigerator. On the second floor, Rose Room has an extravagant 7-foot-long king bed, a skylight, and glass doors leading onto the roof deck with its comfortable patio furniture and views of downtown lights. Daisy Room, also on the second floor, is decorated in a charming Victorian style with a queen bed, view, and shared bath.

Downstairs in the front parlor comfortable sitting areas flank a cozy gas fireplace and local and national newspapers are on the couch for browsing. Travel reference materials, a restaurant scrapbook, and helpful list of in-house videos all are within easy reach in the parlor.

After a generous continental-style breakfast, including fresh fruit, homemade granolas, and fresh baked goods, guests often enjoy a walk in the historic neighborhood. Later folks often stop for espresso or lattes at the refurbished Lair Hill Market on First Avenue, just around the corner from the inn. The market dates back to the turn of the century when it was a Jewish grocery store. Close by is the historic John's Landing area close to the Willamette River, and an eclectic group of shops housed in a renovated furniture factory below the old water tower.

What's Nearby Portland

Portland caters to a wide range of interests and lifestyles. Here are the Performing Arts Center, Civic Auditorium, and Arlene Schnitzer Concert Hall, the Portland Art Museum, and the Oregon History Center. There's also Portland State University and the Oregon Health Sciences University Hospital as well as trendy RiverPlace Marina on the Willamette River and a host of downtown shops, restaurants, nightclubs, cinemas, cafes, and delis. The Portland Area Visitors Information Center is located at 26 SW Salmon Street, Portland, OR 97204; Telephone: (503) 222-2223 or (800) 345-3214.

Georgian House
Bed & Breakfast

1828 Northeast Siskiyou Street
Portland, OR 97212
Phone: (503) 281-2250; (888) 282-2250

Innkeeper: Willie Ackley
Rooms: 4 rooms, 2 with private baths
Extras: Vintage claw-foot tub in one bath; guest refrigerator
On the grounds: Deck, gazebo, English rose garden
Smoking? Outdoors only
Visiting pets? No; visiting neighborhood squirrel, Herbie
Credit cards: Visa, MasterCard
Rates: $-$$
How to get there: Traveling from the south or north on I-5 in Portland take exit 302A, Rose Quarter, and turn east onto Weidler Street. Proceed to Fifteenth Avenue and turn left (north) traveling about 9 blocks to Siskiyou Street; turn right and proceed to the inn located between Eighteenth and Nineteenth Avenues.

The impressive brick Georgian-Colonial-style house, standing squarely behind its black wrought-iron fence, looks like the sort of residence one would find in Colonial Williamsburg. And it also wouldn't be difficult to imagine Martha Washington emerging from the front door, skirts swirling, on her way out to the rose garden to snip a bouquet for the dining room table. "Actually," says Willie, "it is reported that there are only three true Georgian colonial homes in Portland—this home was built in 1922 by George Schneider. And for good luck he placed several gold coins in the foundation."

Guests often congregate in the living room with its fireplace and inspect a small-scale train set up in the large coffee table. Or someone will ease into the solarium and curl up on the sofa with a novel along with views of the garden and of the birds that chatter at the feeder. A TV and VCR are also available in this comfy room. The guest rooms, some reached by a spiral staircase, are comfortable havens. East Lake Room offers a sunny southern exposure and its own private veranda with chaise, chairs, umbrella, and view of the rose and rock garden, and gazebo. Other amenities include a Victorian East Lake queen bed, marble-top dresser, French windows, lace curtains, oak floors, and English wardrobe.

Pettygrove Room offers a relaxing country style with old German pine beds and a hand-made quilt that matches the shades of forest green used in this room's decor. Lovejoy Suite, with a small sitting room, has an antique queen bed with a canopy, oak floors, an antique chaise, a writing table, TV, and ceiling fan. This room commands a view of the grounds and Willie's extraordinary rose garden; it was once featured in *Better Homes & Gardens*.

Breakfast is served in the light and airy dining room with its built-in corner china cabinets and views of the grounds; this view often includes Herbie, the neighborhood squirrel who usually eats his breakfast just outside the windows. Because Willie loves to garden, her tasty breakfasts often feature her fresh raspberries, blueberries, and strawberries. These may be found on hot waffles along with dabs of whipped cream. Other entrees might include omelets, French toast with marionberry glaze, or crepes with fresh raspberries.

What's Nearby

See What's Nearby Portland on page 125.

Heron Haus

2545 Northwest Westover Road
Portland, OR 97210
Phone: (503) 274–1846
E-mail: hhaus@europa.com
Internet site: www.europa.com/~hhaus

Innkeeper: Julie Keppeler
Rooms: 6 rooms with private baths
Extras: All rooms feature gas fireplaces, telephones and data ports, alarm/radios, work areas, sitting areas, Hawaiian original art prints; large two-person whirlpool spa in enclosed second-floor spa room with wide northeast views of the city; outdoor unheated swimming pool; extensive library of Northwest history, geology, and fiction
On the grounds: Views of the city and of distant Cascade Mountain peaks to east, north
Smoking? Outdoors only
Visiting pets? No; no resident pets
Credit cards: Visa, MasterCard
Rates: $$–$$$$
How to get there: From downtown Portland take West Burnside Street to Twenty-third Avenue; turn right onto Twenty-third and proceed to Johnson turning left to intersection of Johnson, Twenty-fifth, and Westover. Continue uphill 1 short block on Westover to inn's address sign at base of driveway; proceed up narrow driveway to parking area near entry.

"When I purchased the house in 1985," says Julie, "I knew that it just needed some tender loving care in order to become a wonderful city bed and breakfast." And that it has. With Julie at the helm, nearly all 10,000 square feet of the three-story, 1904 English Tudor house was totally refurbished with light colors, new carpeting, new window treatments, updated baths, and new furnishings. "I also wanted to use my family heirlooms so these pieces are in the mahogany library on the main floor," she explains. This includes a large, glass-topped coffee table, comfortable upholstered chairs, and an extensive library of classics as well as newer titles all tucked on shelves behind their glass doors.

The guest rooms were given names reminiscent of the years that Julie lived in the Hawaiian Islands. Second-floor rooms are called Kanui (John), Kulia (to desire), and Ko (sugar); third-floor rooms are called Manu (bird), Makua (elder), and Mahina (moonlight). New gas fire-places, cozy sitting and work areas, and spacious baths combine with queen or king beds, down comforters, pillows, and books and magazines to make each room a haven for the discriminating business or vacation traveler. Guests often linger on the large second-floor landing to inspect Julie's extensive informal gallery of framed black-and-white and color photos and snapshots depicting those years in Hawaii raising her four children.

A continental breakfast is served from 8:00 to 9:00 A.M. in the fireplaced dining room at small tables; the original oak parquet flooring gleams in the morning light. Fresh-cut fruit such as honeydew melon and cantaloupe combine nicely with pastries, granolas, and freshly brewed coffee or hot teas. Just adjacent is a cozy TV room, and, through an archway to the front of the house, the enclosed plant-filled sun room overlooks the small swimming pool and the dis-tant mountains to the east. Within walking distance are the eclectic Nob Hill shops, bou-tiques, cafes, delis, and restaurants; they range along Northwest Twenty-third and Twenty-first Avenues for several blocks between West Burn-side and Pettygrove Streets. In a mix of cultures and lifestyles, congenial neighborhood dwellers and shopkeepers mix with townsfolk and out-of-town visitors.

What's Nearby

In the immediate area are the International Rose Test Gardens and the renowned Japanese Gar-den, both at Washington Park, with wide-angle views of the city and mountains to the east. Also nearby are Forest Park with its extensive network of hiking paths and world-class arboretum, and the Portland Municipal Zoo, the World Forestry Center, and the Vietnam Memorial. Also see What's Nearby Portland on page 125.

The Lion and The Rose
Bed & Breakfast

1810 NE Fifteenth Avenue (street address)
1517 Northeast Schuyler Street (mailing
address)
Portland, OR 97212
Phone: (503) 287-9245; (800) 955-1647
E-mail: lionrose@ix.netcom.com
Internet site: www.lionrose.com

Innkeepers: Kay Peffer, Kevin Spanier, Sharon Weil
Rooms: 6 rooms, 5 with private baths; 1 bath with whirlpool tub
Extras: Complimentary soft drinks and juices; TV available on request; afternoon dessert tea served in elegant parlor
On the grounds: English-style flower garden, landscaped yard with brick walkways, fountain, bird baths, and gazebo
Smoking? Outdoors only
Visiting pets? No; 1 resident cocker spaniel, Cuccina, not allowed in guest areas
Credit cards: Visa, MasterCard, American Express
Rates: $$-$$$
How to get there: From I-5 in Portland take exit 302A, Rose Quarter, and turn right (east) onto Weidler Street; proceed to NE Fifteenth and turn left. The inn is 2 blocks north at the corner of NE Fifteenth Avenue and Schuyler Street.

"We invite guests into our lovely Victorian parlor to enjoy a traditional dessert tea served every afternoon from 4:00 to 6:00 P.M.," says Kay. The majestic Queen Anne structure was built in 1906 for Gustav E. Freiwald, a onetime owner of the Star Brewery and an early Portland real estate speculator. An ornate cupola and extensive architectural detailing on the third floor display distinctive classic Greek styling. Short and sturdy Ionic columns support the deep wraparound porch on the entry level; and there are examples of oriel windows and of ornate decorative plasterwork reflecting a style popular at the turn of the century.

The guest rooms are done up in lush colors, romantic fabrics, antique furnishings, full window treatments, and extravagant canopies. Lavonna Room, in the round cupola on the top floor, is decorated in soft cream with accents of lavender and green. It features an ornate wrought-iron king bed with a draped canopy and white wicker settee and chair in the sitting area. Starina Room is done in rich shades of green, rust, and gold and features an 1870 high-back Edwardian bed with matching accessories.

Escapade Room has a king bed draped in sheer organza cascading from a high wrought-iron canopy frame; the sheers can be pulled to entirely enclose the bed for the romantic ambience of a sultan's tent. Shades of plum, raspberry, and ivy green are used in the decor. Rose Room, very Victorian and with a view of the English flower garden, gazebo, and brick walkways, features a light-oak sleigh bed and other antique oak furnishings, period wall coverings, and plush shades of plum, green, and dusty rose.

Early morning coffee is available at 6:30 A.M. The chef arrives at 7:00 A.M. to prepare a sumptuous breakfast, served from 8:30 to 9:30 A.M., that may include sour cream/chocolate chip muffins, fresh fruit plate, strawberry-banana baked French toast, and baked eggs with new potatoes. In-room service is available on request.

What's Nearby

Plan a walking tour of the historic Irvington District where this and several other bed-and-breakfasts are located. On nearby Northeast Broadway, take in trendy crafts and gifts shops, boutiques, galleries, flower shops, cafes, restaurants, and cinemas extending on both sides of the street from Tenth Avenue east to Twentieth Avenue. Also see What's Nearby Portland on page 125.

Sauvie Island
Bed & Breakfast

26504 Northwest Reeder Road
Portland, OR 97231
Phone: (503) 621–3216

Innkeepers: Marie and John Colasurdo
Rooms: 2 rooms, 1 with private bath
Extras: Morning newspaper, dinner can be arranged for extra cost
On the grounds: Sandy beach and Columbia River; decks facing river; outdoor hot tub on private deck facing river
Smoking? Not allowed
Visiting pets? No; resident Dalmatian, Max
Credit cards: No; checks preferred
Rates: $–$$
How to get there: From either I-5 or I-405 follow signs for U.S. Highway 30 West and proceed through the waterside industrial area. Continue past the St. Johns bridge and travel 5 miles to take the Sauvie Island Bridge crossing this and loop underneath onto Gillihan Road; continue 6⅜ miles to Reeder Road. Turn right and proceed 1⅛ miles passing Reeder Beach sign to mailbox and driveway on the right.

"**O**ur house sits on the sandy banks of the Columbia River," explains Marie. We look out to the decks that face the river and watch a low-slung freighter cruise by on its way to the Port of Portland berths about 10 miles from here. To the east some 80 miles farther, Mount Hood rises like an ice cream cone in the Cascade Mountain Range. "The sunrises over the mountain are quite spectacular," comments John. A. J., as he is most often called, is a semi-retired dentist who loves to tend his organic garden and the rambling Italian-style gardens that grow in happy profusion on the grounds.

Two comfortable guest rooms in a separate wing of the house offer cozy havens. River Room has a queen bed, view of the river, private bath, and its own private entry to the riverside deck and to the hot tub. Sunset Room includes a double bed and half bath. The inn is also smoke-free and pets are not allowed. The resident Dalmatian, Max, loves to snoop from his perch in the kitchen—"He really enjoys the guests," says Marie with a smile. Once in a while Max will join guests when they come into the common area and gather around the floor-to-ceiling stone fireplace.

But there are other animals and fowl in evidence here including a few sheep and a much-prized flock of Araucana chickens, which lay pastel-colored eggs. These special eggs, collected fresh by A. J., will often be included in guests breakfast fare, Egg Soufflé. This also contains cheese, mushrooms, red pepper, and ham. It is a heavenly dish that might be served with warm cinnamon rolls from Delphina's Bakery and steaming hot Barista Blend coffee from Boyd's Red Wagon Coffee; both are located in Portland.

Each season brings different pastimes for island visitors and rural residents. In summer folks harvest U-pick fruits and flowers including blueberries, peaches, and colorful zinnias. September heralds the start of pumpkin season. From October 1 through March the great migration of birds along the Pacific Flyway brings more than 8,000 avid hunters and their rifles to hunt ducks at Sturgeon and Steelman lakes near Oak Island on the Sauvie Island Wildlife Area. From spring through the end of September, birdwatchers, photographers, and hikers also can enjoy the wildlife areas and a wonderful nature trail on Oak Island; there is a $3.00 per day parking fee.

What's Nearby

See What's Nearby Sauvie Island on page 137. There are several public beaches on the island along the Columbia River; one beach is clothing-optional. The Sauvie Island Wildlife Area office (503–621–3488) is located at 18330 Northwest Sauvie Island Road, 2³⁄₁₀ miles north of the island bridge; helpful information panels explain how the north section of the island is managed year-round for wildlife and its habitat. The staff can assist with maps and information about seasonal birding spots; some offer picnic areas. Note: No gasoline is available on the island.

Sullivan's Gulch
Bed & Breakfast

1744 Northeast Clackamas Street
Portland, OR 97232
Phone: (503) 331-1104
E-mail: thegulch@teleport.com
Internet site: www.teleport.com/~thegulch/

Innkeepers: Skip Rognlien and Jack Robinson
Rooms: 4 rooms, 2 with private baths
Extras: Ceiling fans, guest refrigerator, small sitting rooms
On the grounds: Garden, decks, Eastside city location
Smoking? Outdoors only
Visiting pets? Ask innkeeper's permission if you have a small, well-behaved pet; resident dog
Credit cards: Visa, MasterCard, American Express
Rates: $–$$
How to get there: From I-5 in Portland take exit 302A, Rose Quarter, and turn right onto Weidler Street; proceed to Sixteenth Avenue and turn right. Turn left onto Clackamas Street; the inn is in the middle of the block.

In a comfortable eastside bed and breakfast decorated with Native American paintings, sculpture, and artifacts, the two gentlemen innkeepers explain emphatically that, "We are definitely not Laura Ashley." The circa 1907 Craftsman-style house sits comfortably in a well established and quiet neighborhood, Sullivan's Gulch, just a few blocks east of the Lloyd Center mall shops and Lloyd Cinema, the Holladay Market shops, and the trendy Northeast Broadway shops and eateries. This section of Portland is termed eastside because it expands from the east shore of the Willamette River 10 to 15 miles toward Troutdale, Fairview, Gresham, and the Cascade foothills. The broad river bisects the city near the downtown area and is spanned by a number of bridges; it then empties into the mighty Columbia River 10 miles northwest of the downtown area. The two waterways carry long cargo ships to and from ports of call around the world.

The innkeepers come from a background of interior decorating in New York and from the theater. "We also are pleased to celebrate and welcome at our bed and breakfast a diversity of both lifestyles and cultures," explains Skip. They also like to provide guests with traditional Western-style comfort along with all the modern conveniences available in a large city. Northwest Room and Montana Room share a bath with tub/shower. The Red Suite and Green Suite each have cozy sitting rooms and private baths with showers.

A light continental breakfast is served around 8:30 A.M., and consists of fresh fruit such as sliced oranges, bananas, cantaloupe, honeydew, or grapefruit along with croissants from a local bakery. Freshly ground coffee bubbles and brews close by, sending delicious morning aromas throughout the house.

What's Nearby

See What's Nearby Portland on page 125.

Westland's River Edge Bed & Breakfast

22502 Northwest Gillihan Road
Portland, OR 97231
Phone: (503) 621–9856
E-mail: rivers-edge1@juno.com
Internet site: www.riversedge-bb.com

Innkeepers: Beverley and Wes Westlund
Rooms: 2 rooms, 1 bath; entire guest suite is often rented by families or friends traveling together
Extras: One room has special mattress that is adjustable for firmness with dual controls; private patio facing the river and access to private beach; kitchenette with stocked refrigerator; wood stove in common area; TV/VCR; phone and modem hookup; wheelchair accessible
On the grounds: Views of Columbia River and boating and shipping traffic; private sandy beach along river; lawn and shaded picnic area
Smoking? Outdoors on patio
Visiting pets? No; no resident pets
Credit cards: No; personal checks accepted
Rates: $, or $$$ for entire guest suite
How to get there: Traveling north on I-5 take exit 302B, St. Helens, and cross over the Fremont Bridge; take exit 3, St.Helens/Industrial Area, and proceed northwest on Yeon Street and onto St. Helens Road, U.S. Highway 30. Travel 9 miles to the Sauvie Island Bridge crossing this bridge and looping underneath onto Gillihan Road; continue 5¼ miles east and north to large white house on right.

"Our bridge is short and it's a bit narrow," says Beverly, "but it connects us with the mainland and also offers travelers a way to enjoy our pastoral island near the city." Sauvie Island and its 24,000 acres offers a rural retreat not only to travelers but also to wildlife. A good-sized section of the island comprises the Sauvie Island Wildlife Area and serves as a rest stop for two to three million migratory wildfowl and as the winter home for more than 150,000 ducks and geese. Tundra swans and sandhill cranes visit during the fall, and great blue herons, wood ducks, beavers, and red foxes live at the refuge

year-round. "Guests who want to visit the wildlife area can use our annual parking permit to do so," explains Wes.

The large guest suite, located on the lower level, has two bedrooms and a comfortable common area. This is often reserved by families or by friends traveling together. The bath, kitchenette, and common area are shared. Kindling and wood are provided for the wood stove, a special treat on chilly mornings. Those traveling with laptop computers will find an extra phone hookup for a modem. But when you see the views, you may decide to leave the laptop in its case. Low-slung freighters navigate right under your nose—if you were any closer you'd be standing on their fore or aft decks.

The freighters ply the Columbia River channel on their way to Portland, as well as nearby Longview on the Washington side of the river. They pass by the inn's wide windows and decks again on their return trips to the port of Astoria on the north coast, about 60 miles downriver.

In addition to the enormous freighters, guests will often see large sailboats, good-sized motorboats, and small runabouts. Canoes, kayaks, and rowboats paddle close to shore, well away from the river's main current. "Our nearby Multnomah Channel is a good place to canoe," says Beverly, "but folks need to bring their own canoes—there are no rentals available on the island." The channel is a lovely, quiet body of water away from the main river channel where numerous houseboats reside; it provides a safe place for smaller nonmotorized craft to navigate and better opportunities to spy wildlife.

Guests are served breakfast along with the great river views at the dining table on the main level; Wes and Beverly often join their guests, too. Entrees might include Beverly's Decadent French Toast with fresh applesauce, or hazelnut oatmeal pancakes with raspberry syrup along with egg and sausage scramble. For dining out travelers can pop into the St. Johns section of North Portland via the St. Johns bridge to find McMenamin's Pub and Eatery and other cafes and restaurants. You could also use the on-premise barbeque in the picnic area by the river. *Note:* No gasoline is available on the island.

What's Nearby Sauvie Island

Flat country roads that encircle the island are great for bicycling or auto touring and they lead to U-pick flower farms and seasonal fruit and vegetable stands at several family farms. The historic Bybee-Howell House on the island is open for tours from June through Labor Day; it's part of an 1856 farmstead that also includes a small orchard, a collection of old roses, and a display of old farm implements in the restored barn. Bring your own canoe and paddle along quiet Multnomah Channel. Also see What's Nearby Portland on page 125.

Cottonwood Cottage
Bed & Breakfast

960 E Street Northeast
Salem, OR 97301
Phone: (503) 362–3979; (800) 349–3979
E-mail: ctnwdctg@open.org
Internet site: www.open.org/ctnwdctg

Innkeepers: Bill and Donna Wickman
Rooms: 2 rooms with shared bath—glass enclosed tub and shower
Extras: Beverages on arrival; cable TV in rooms; computer terminal and telephone line; bathrobes; fireplace and music system in common room; two cats to pet
On the grounds: Garden, gazebo, and large deck in back yard
Smoking? Outdoors and in a closed-off room
Visiting pets? No; two cats, Willyum and Merry
Credits cards: Visa, MasterCard, Discover
Rates: $
How to get there: Traveling south on I–5 take the North Salem exit 258 and proceed 3 miles to E Street. Turn left onto E Street; the inn is between Summer and Capitol Streets. Traveling from the south on I–5 take the Market Street exit 256 turning left (west) onto Market Street; proceed to Summer Street and turn left 2 blocks to E Street.

Located on a quiet shaded street, the charming English-style cottage looks as though it could just as easily be nestled in a small forest where Hansel and Gretel might dwell. Bill and Donna haven't traveled to mythical woods but they have visited the British Isles, Ireland, the European continent, Japan, Canada, and much of the U.S. "We've slept in a lot of feather beds, met some wonderful people, and have been well treated," says Bill. "We decided that we wanted to fashion our home into a welcoming bed and breakfast and treat our guests in the same way."

Two cozy rooms are offered to travelers, one with a queen bed and the other with twin beds. Down comforters provide warmth on chilly autumn and winter nights; air conditioning cools the guest rooms on overheated spring and summer days. Guests often gather in the common room, a comfortable spot on the main floor decorated in colors of pale cream, off whites, and oyster. Deep upholstered sofas flank the fireplace and sunlight filters through wide bay windows.

Breakfast is served at a time convenient to guests schedules at Bill and Donna's antique dining table set with colorful linens, fresh flow-ers, fine china, and vintage silver. The morning fare might be Dutch babies, Puffed Eggs Mon-terey, or a special quiche along with bakery breads, fresh fruit, link sausage, hash browns. Plenty of hot coffee and tea are available as well.

What's Nearby

See What's Nearby Salem on page 141.

Marquee House
Bed & Breakfast

333 Wyatt Court N.E.
Salem, OR 97301
Phone: (503) 391–0837; (800) 949–0837
Internet site: www.oregonlink.com/marquee/

Innkeeper: Rickie Hart
Rooms: 5 rooms, 3 with private baths
Extras: Complimentary juices, sodas, tea; candy dishes in each guest room; "Butler's Basket" in each bath has a variety of travel amenities; nightly film showing in living room complete with popcorn and snacks
On the grounds: Mill Creek at lawn's edge can be viewed from outdoor veranda; flowering shrubs and flowers
Smoking? Outdoors only
Visiting pets? No
Credit cards: Visa, MasterCard, Discover
Rates: $–$$
How to get there: Traveling south on I-5 take exit 256, Market Street, and turn right onto this thoroughfare; travel west about 1 mile to Seventeenth Street and turn left (south); proceed two stoplights on Seventeenth and turn right onto Center Street looking for Wyatt Court about ¾ block beyond on the left. This small street looks like a driveway so watch closely; there is ample parking in front of the inn.

Garden lovers will enjoy visiting Salem and vintage-movie lovers will enjoy this lovely Mount Vernon Colonial-style inn. One of the much-loved traditions at Marquee House is the nightly showing of a vintage black-and-white or color movie, "complete with a bottomless bowls of popcorn, snacks, and soft drinks," Rickie says with a chuckle. Among the old movies are names the innkeeper has given to her guest rooms, located on the second floor of the inn— *Auntie Mame, Blazing Saddles, Pillow Talk, Christmas in Connecticut,* and *Topper.* Each room captures the ambience of the particular film with both memorabilia and decor.

The living room, aptly named *Harvey,* also serves as the nightly screening room. Recently redecorated and updated, with fireplace and views of nearby Mill Creek, this comfortable room offers a plush loveseat and divan along with Colonial period chairs and coffee tables. You'll find charming rabbits tucked here and there, reminiscent of the movie starring Jimmy Stewart. "Guests seem to enjoy our movie marathons," says Rickie.

Through the archway and into the adjoining dining room guests gather in the morning between 8:00 and 9:30 A.M. for a sumptuous breakfast. They may be served hazelnut waffles with cranberry butter, poached pears with berry sauce, oatmeal custard, chicken strata, herbed potatoes, and rhubarb coffeecake along with fresh juices and plenty of steaming hot coffee or tea.

Ask the innkeeper for suggestions for evening dining—there are a number of good restaurants located nearby. Pack extra film for the cameras and save at least one day to visit notable historic homes and gardens like the Asahel Bush House and Bush House Gardens with its heritage rose collection. Adjacent is the six-acre Historic Deepwood Estate with its fine collection of perennials and lovely garden rooms. Other gardens, Willson Park and Capitol Park, are located on the state capitol grounds; and at nearby Willamette University, travelers enjoy the Martha Springer Botanical Garden, Rose Garden, and Fuller Japanese Garden.

What's Nearby Salem

The Oregon State capitol and grounds offer self-guided walking tours, and Mission Mill Village along Mill Creek allows a step back in time to the 1890s. Here visitors can see and tour the old Thomas Kay Woolen Mill and visit the Jason Lee Home and Methodist Parsonage. The latter two structures date back to 1841, before the first wagon train crossed the Oregon Trail. Browse through the Marion County Museum's fine gift shop, snoop into other crafts shops and boutiques, and bring a picnic or find a cafe and coffee shop on the grounds. Visitors can tour the Historic Elsinore Theatre, a Tudor-Gothic movie palace dating to the mid-twenties; tours can include a brief organ recital on the newly restored 1924 Parks/Murdock Mighty Wurlitzer Organ with 4,000 pipes. The Salem Visitors Association and Visitors Center can provide maps and information about dozens of nurseries, tree farms, berry farms, iris fields, bulb farms, and fruit and nut orchards located in the lush Willamette Valley environs; the center is located at 1313 Mill Street Southeast, Salem, OR 97301; Telephone: (503) 581–4325 or (800) 874–7012.

McKenzie View,
A Riverside Bed & Breakfast

34922 McKenzie View Drive
Springfield, OR 97478
Phone: (541) 726-3887; (888) 625-8439
E-mail: mckenzieview@worldnet.att.net
Internet site:
www.design-web.com/mckenzieview/

Innkeepers: Scott and Roberta Bolling
Rooms: 4 rooms with private baths
Extras: Bottomless cookie jar; soft drinks and juice in guest refrigerator; afternoon appetizer; bathrobes, shampoo, lotion, hair dryers in baths
On the grounds: The inn is situated on six acres with 625 feet of frontage on McKenzie River; large cutting garden and arbor; deck and gazebo near river;
Smoking? Outdoors only
Visiting pets? No; no resident pets
Credit cards: Visa, MasterCard
Rates: $$-$$$$
How to get there: From I-5 traveling south toward Eugene, take exit 199 turning right toward Coburg; turn left onto Coburg Road continuing to McKenzie View Drive. Turn left just before the bridge and continue 4⅞ miles to the inn; driveway is on the right. From I-5 traveling north, take exit 195B to Beltline (sign will say JUNCTION CITY/FLORENCE) and exit at Coburg Road; turn right onto Coburg Road continuing to McKenzie View Drive; follow directions above.

Situated along 625 feet of the north bank of the McKenzie River, the inn is bathed in sunlight from the south all afternoon. The small tributary chortles and bubbles as it flows several miles farther west where it empties into the larger Willamette River. The Willamette then gains in breadth and depth as it flows north, passing Corvallis and Albany. From here it rushes to Portland and its final destination,

the mighty Columbia River. Long a favorite with fishermen and -women and with river rafters, the small McKenzie River is accessible in many places along its length and also drops over basalt ledges into several frothy waterfalls in its upper section above the small communities of Blue River and McKenzie Bridge.

"Transforming this lovely place from a private home to a bed and breakfast was a pleasant job," says Roberta, who is also a registered nurse. Scott worked for Proctor & Gamble for many years; his family was in the restaurant business in Chicago. Current plans include adding a deck overlooking the river and a gazebo at the edge of the garden path. The couple maintains a large cutting garden of colorful annuals and perennials.

The four guest rooms are spacious, elegantly comfortable, and most have views of the river and gardens. The Woodland Suite has a queen bed, deep upholstered chairs, antique armoire, gas fireplace, and French doors opening to a private porch. The Moonlight Suite on the second floor is furnished with antiques and offers panoramic views of the river, woods, pasture, and hillside. The Riverbend Room and The Coburg Room are smaller but equally inviting.

In the morning coffee is ready by 6:00 A.M., and, weather permitting, can be enjoyed on the large deck that extends along the back of the inn and faces the river. "I usually am up by 5:30 A.M.," says Roberta, "to bake a special fresh pastry." Guests enjoy poppyseed bread, cinnamon rolls, poached pears with cranberry juice, egg scramble and sliced tomato, and sausage biscuits.

What's Nearby

The small community of Coburg offers several antiques shops and good eateries. See also What's Nearby Eugene on page 103.

Other Recommended B&B Nearby

Marjon Bed & Breakfast Inn, on the McKenzie River, 15 miles east of Eugene-Springfield via Highway 126, two acres of rhododendrons and azaleas, elegant contemporary home with two guest rooms; innkeeper Margie Haas, 44975 Leaburg Dam Road, Leaburg, OR 97489; Telephone: (541) 896–3145.

Doublegate Inn
Bed & Breakfast

26711 East Welches Road
Welches, OR 97067
Phone: (503) 622–4859
E-mail: dgatebnb@teleportcom
Internet site: www.mthoodlodging.com

Innkeepers: Charlene and Gary Poston
Rooms: 3 rooms with private baths; 2 rooms have spa tubs with hand-held shower, 1 room has a soaking tub with separate shower
Extras: Guest lounge on second floor offers snacks and beverages in guest refrigerator, TV/VCR and video library, extensive collection of Oregon Trail history-related books and travel guidebooks, current magazines and country decorating books; cassette players and relaxing tapes in guest rooms
On the grounds: Salmon River, herb garden, courtyard, small pond with waterfall
Smoking? Outdoors only
Visiting pets? No; no resident pets
Credit cards: Visa, MasterCard, American Express, Discover
Rates: $$
How to get there: From Highway 26 at Welches, turn south at the stoplight at Welches Road and proceed about 1 mile to the inn on the right.

The 1920s vernacular house, lovingly restored by Gary and Charlene, nestles on a small knoll near the banks of the Salmon River. "We wanted to design the kind of inn that provided a special feeling of romance and restoration for couples," says Charlene. The large common area on the main floor offers a wood-burning fireplace and inviting sitting places where couples can meet and share travel plans and adventures. Early in the evening Gary lights a crackling fire in the fireplace. Someone might wind up the

vintage phonograph and play a 78 record, perhaps a Bing Crosby or Perry Como love song from the 1930s or 1940s. Someone else might strum the guitar or play a tune on the piano. Everyone may decide to watch a vintage video like *Casablanca,* or a couple might curl up with a glass of wine and a book or magazine by the fire.

On the second floor, Bit O Country Room is decorated with Americana collectibles and features an antique bed with a blue calico quilt. A deck just outside the French doors overlooks the Salmon River. A jetted tub waits in the private bath. In English Cottage Suite shades of sage green, ecru, rose, and yellows combine with sunlight or moonlight coming through the windows to create a romantic feeling. This spacious room features a queen bed, cozy wicker sitting places, ample reading lamps, and a two-person soaking tub. The Victorian Suite, perhaps the most romantic, features a lavish half-canopied queen bed dressed with lace pillows and a heritage quilt. The room's small parlor offers a love seat of soft green fabric, a Victorian floor lamp, floral wallpaper, lace curtains, an antique dresser and round table, and small French provincial chair.

Breakfast is served from 8:00 to 9:30 A.M. in the fireplaced dining room on the main floor. Honeymooners are always offered breakfast delivered to their room. The morning repast may include Good Morning Parfaits garnished with pansy blossoms, shrimp and broccoli quiche, warm caramel cinnamon rolls, and a choice of juice, coffee, tea, and hot chocolate. "On request we also are happy to deliver a tray of coffee to guests rooms earlier in the morning," says Charlene. For evening dining the innkeepers recommend several good eateries nearby—Rendezvous Grill, Don Guido's, Resort at the Mountain, rustic Zig Zag Inn, and the dining room up at Timberline Lodge at the 6,000-foot level on Mount Hood. This requires a 12-mile drive up to Government Camp, at a 4,000-foot elevation, and another 6 miles up to the lodge. To really experience the panoramic mountain vistas, however, plan to make this trip during the daytime on a clear day and have lunch with Mount Hood peering over your shoulders.

What's Nearby Welches

The Mount Hood Recreation Area Visitors' Information Center offers a wide array of maps and information about the area, (503) 622-3017. The center is located on Highway 26 at Mount Hood Village near Wemme and Brightwood. Nearby Resort at the Mountain offers twenty-seven holes of golf, pro lessons, and a golf shop. A number of good restaurants, cafes, bakeries, delis, coffee shops, and gift shops are in the immediate area between Rhododendron, Zig Zag, and Welches. During winter months this area, which is above 1,500 feet, often gets snow. The ranger station at Zig Zag, (503) 622-3191, can provide helpful year-round weather information as well as maps and information about ski areas, designated snowmobile areas, snowshoeing areas, hiking trails, lake and stream fishing, and mountain biking. Also see What's Nearby Government Camp on page 111.

Old Welches Inn
Bed & Breakfast

26401 East Welches Road
Welches, OR 97067
Phone: (503) 622-3754
Internet site:
www.innsandouts.com/property/old_
welches_inn.html

Innkeepers: Judith and Ted Mondun
Rooms: 3 rooms with private baths; separate cottage with 2 bedrooms
Extras: Fresh flowers in rooms; refreshments on arrival; custom-made robes in rooms; sweets on pillows at night
On the grounds: Gardens, gazebo, Salmon River, outdoor sitting areas
Smoking? Outdoors only
Visiting pets? Yes, at the cottage with fenced yard; 1 resident Akita/shepard mix, Sadie
Credit cards: Visa, MasterCard, Discover, American Express
Rates: $$–$$$
How to get there: From Government Camp drive down the mountain about 15 miles passing the communities of Rhododendron and Zig Zag to the community of Welches. At the stoplight turn left and proceed to the inn located about ½ mile beyond The Resort at the Mountain; the inn is directly across from the original first hole of the resort's golf course. From Portland take I-84 to exit 16A, turn right (south) to Burnside Street then left (east) continuing to the junction of Highway 26. Proceed on Highway 26 through the community of Sandy and on to Welches, approximately 20 miles. Turn right at the stoplight at Welches Road and proceed to the inn.

The small sign at the edge of the driveway reads "Old Welches Inn, 1890." The Salmon River bubbles along quietly at the lower end of the property to the rear of the house. The structure was built by Samuel Welch and his son Billy and was operated by the family until the late 1930s, first as a summer hotel and campground, and later with cabins added on a nearby knoll as a small resort and golf course. "Families would come up from Portland, but before the turn of the century they traveled via horse and buggy," says Judi. "The trip took two days with an overnight stop, usually in the community of Sandy just 10 miles or so above Gresham." Moms and the kids would stay several weeks camping, fishing, and picking gallons of juicy native blackberries and native huckleberries. Later the first gasoline-powered automobiles chugged up to the mountain. Folks have flocked here ever since making the Mount Hood Recreation Area one of the most popular year-round destinations in the state.

Now travelers can stay at the historic Colonial-style inn, which has been completely restored and refurbished by Judi and Ted, transplants from Florida. "The place was a pretty sorry sight when we first saw it back in 1986," says Ted. "Time and weather and transient renters had taken their toll on the house." The couple's hard work is evident and the large house and its grounds have been brought back to life. Light streams through wide expanses of windows and colors gleam from new chintzes and soft carpeting. Guests have their choice of well-appointed guest rooms and a well-stocked library lounge on the second floor—Trillum, Sweet Briar, and Columbine. The rooms are named for native wildflowers, all of which grow and bloom in the extensive perennial beds that Judi has planted around the house and throughout the grounds.

One room has a queen sleigh bed and English chintzes, another offers an ornate wrought-iron double bed, and in another is a vintage cannon-ball-style bed and views of the river. For the adventurous negotiating two flights of steep stairs to Forget-Me-Not suite is appealing—this snug hideaway on the third floor has twin beds, a sitting area, and views of the river and mountaintops. Lutie's Cottage, just next door, has two bedrooms, a kitchen, and a comfortable living-dining area with a river-rock fireplace. Children are welcome in the cottage.

On the inn's main floor two cozy common areas offer comfortable couches, overstuffed chairs, and footstools along with books, magazines, and games. Breakfast is served in the light and airy dining area adjacent to Judi's large open kitchen and with a view of the rear grounds and Salmon River. If the inn and the cottage next door are full, an expansive breakfast might include sunset fruit compote, garden zucchini pie, sausage cheese casserole, cheese grits, croissants, Danish sweet rolls, mimosas, orange juice, and coffee and tea. "Then I always have fresh coffee and sweets on a tray upstairs at 6:30 or 7:00 A.M. for early risers," says Judi. "Everyone seems to love whatever is under the cake dome!" Sadie, the friendly resident canine, thumps her tail in enthusiastic agreement.

What's Nearby

See What's Nearby Welches on page 145 and What's Nearby Government Camp on page 111.

Suite River Bed & Breakfast

69437 East Vine Maple Drive
P.O. Box 530
Welches, OR 97067
Phone: (503) 622–3547; (888) 886–6820
E-mail: suiterbb@jps.net

I f you visit during early spring months, say May and June, you'll get to see a profusion of blooms on the rhododendron and azaleas that grow in lush groupings about the house and grounds. "We have many colors," says Pat, "including deep pinks, scarlets, pale pink, and creamy whites." Rising like sentinels protecting the edges of the property are stands of tall Douglas fir and Western red cedar so character-istic of the Northwest. The swift-running Sandy River borders the property to the north. The couple has constructed a path that leads from

Innkeepers: Pat Dutmers and Steve Rickeard
Rooms: 1 suite with private bath
Extras: European chocolate truffles at the bedside; fresh flowers; chocolate mints in candy jar; roman-tic breakfast served with china, crystal, silver, lace, and fresh flowers; bathrobes, thick towels, hair dryer and ample supply of toiletries in bath
On the grounds: Native perennial beds, large rhododendrons, tall Douglas fir, path down to Sandy River, bank areas for trout fishing; many visiting bird species
Smoking? Not allowed
Visiting pets? No; friendly resident German short-hair, Ariel, and young beagle, Scoobee
Credit cards: Visa, MasterCard, American Express
Rates: $$
How to get there: Driving east from the Portland-Gresham area take Highway 26 about 15 miles through Sandy continuing about 17 miles farther to Wemme-Welches, the start of the Mount Hood Recreation Area. At Woodsey Way, near milepost marker 41, turn left (Lion's Club will be on the right) and proceed to fork and DEAD END sign. Veer right onto Vine Maple, an unmarked one-lane gravel road. Continue ½ block to the inn on the left; park in graveled area in front of garage and take path to front door.

the guest suite deck down through the cotton-wood trees to the river. Here you can bask in the sun on large round rocks at the shoreline or on other large rocks in the water close to shore. A pleasant way to spend a sunny afternoon is to head down along the river with a picnic, a fishing pole or a novel to read, and a couple of folding chairs or an old blanket and a couple of pillows. Scoobee, the young beagle, or Ariel, the German shorthair might be persuaded to accompany you, but only if you desire canine company.

The Marie Frances Suite is named for Pat's beloved aunt who rambled about the West in her automobile during the 1930s and 1940s. "She traveled on those old corduroy or mud roads of the day," says Pat. "I have her scrapbook of wonderful old postcards." The roomy suite is outfitted with a queen bed with antique white crocheted coverlet, a cozy sitting area with a cream-colored loveseat, rose-patterned footstool, rose-patterned curtains, and a two-person whirlpool bath. Aunt Marie crocheted the lacy coverlet in the mid-1940s as a wedding gift for Pat's parents. Guests also are welcome to watch TV in the family room or use the cozy TV nook located down a set of spiral stairs to the garden level. This space is outfitted with a small sofa, reading lamps, VCR, and video library of contemporary comedies and romances.

Breakfast is an elegant affair served in the dining room generally between 7:00 and 10:30 A.M.; guests may choose the time. Pat sets the table with Aunt Marie's lace tablecloth and one of several sets of fine china. You might be served on patterns called Spring Moire, Trousseau, Floradora, or, on the oldest pattern, a gift from Pat's sister, Royal Pinxton Roses. You could ask for a particular pattern from one of these if you like. The decor is completed with crystal, silver, lighted candles, and fresh flowers. Guests can let Pat know what they would like for breakfast from the menu. They might order cran-raspberry juice, caramel pecan rolls, a cheese-mushroom omelet, and crisp bacon or turkey sausage. Freshly brewed cups of coffee are readily available too, of course.

What's Nearby

See What's Nearby Government Camp on page 111 and What's Nearby Welches on page 145.

Westfir Lodge
Bed & Breakfast Inn

47365 First Street
Westfir, OR 97492
Phone: (541) 782-3103

Innkeepers: Ken Symons and Gerry Chamberlain
Rooms: 8 rooms with private baths; 1 handicap accessible room
Extras: Fresh flowers, guest robes
On the grounds: Perennial beds, garden, and gazebo; the inn is located directly across from the longest covered bridge in Oregon; near North Fork of the Willamette River
Smoking? Outdoors only
Visiting pets? Yes, with restrictions; no resident pets
Credit cards: None; personal checks accepted
Rates: $-$$
How to get there: From I-5 near Eugene take exit 189 and proceed east on Highway 58 toward Oakridge. In 35 miles take the Westfir exit and travel 3 miles to Westfir; the inn is located 3 miles below Oakridge and directly across from the covered bridge.

You are deep in the heart of the Willamette National Forest, within shouting distance of the mountains of the central Cascades, and close to where the region's rivers begin. You're also in the heart of Oregon's covered bridge country. The conifers dominate the landscape in every direction—Douglas fir, western red cedar, and hemlock—tall, majestic sentinels of the past, the present, and the future. The crystal clear, bubbling mountain creeks, streams, and rivers originate as tiny rivulets thawing and dripping at winter's end from the high country snow-pack. These empty into other creeks and streams and ultimately join the grand Willamette and mighty Columbia rivers. Final destination: the Pacific Ocean.

"Beginning in the 1920s and lasting until the early 1960s, our inn was the company office for the several different lumber companies that came and went from Westfir," explains Ken. But the structure doesn't look like an office—it has a cozy, Craftsman-style look about it, including a graceful mini-archway at the main door. A charming picket fence encloses the yard and its beds of colorful roses and perennials. Just across the road guests can inspect the 180-foot-long covered Office Bridge; it dates back to 1944. It was fully restored in 1993 and has the distinction of being the longest covered bridge in the state. It is also the only bridge in the state with an attached covered pedestrian walkway. For a handy map showing the location of twenty covered bridges in this part of the Willamette Valley, guests can pick up "A Guide to Covered Bridges in Lane County, Oregon," which is usually available at the inn.

Is Westfir a ghost town? Well not entirely but the lumber companies are gone and the resident mill has closed. Guests go for drives; the Aufderheide National Scenic Byway is one of the best drives in this part of the state. The self-guided auto tour begins in Westfir and you can borrow a cassette tape of the tour from the Oakridge Ranger Station located nearby. Take a picnic and

beverages along and make a day of it—you'll find many hiking trails, picnic areas, creeks, old growth groves, campgrounds, even a horse camp and the outer environs of two wilderness areas, Three Sisters Wilderness and Waldo Lake Wilderness. The ranger station can provide additional information and hiking maps.

Back at the inn, enjoy a fire in the fireplace or in the wood stove, watch a video like *The Bridges of Madison County,* and hunker down for the evening. I think it's safe to say that most guests have no trouble getting a great night's sleep in this mountain haven close to all those giant trees and the chortling sounds of North Fork of the Willamette River, which the covered bridge spans. In the morning enticing breakfast smells include freshly made coffee and, often, an English-style breakfast of eggs, banger sausage, broiled tomatoes, scones, muffins, and fresh fruit.

What's Nearby

The small community of Oakridge offers several cafes, restaurants, service stations, and grocery stores. Services are available related to river and stream fishing, fly fishing, and also services for winter activities such as snowmobiling and skiing; Snow Park permits are required during winter months. The Oakridge Pioneer Museum on Pine Street is open on Saturdays from 1:00 to 4:00 P.M. Highway 58, the main thoroughfare, continues up to the 5,128-foot summit, Willamette Pass, where one of the state's oldest ski areas is located; it dates back to the mid-1940s. The highway continues east past Odell Lake, the trees change from fir to pine, and travelers connect with Highway 97 near Crescent, entering the high desert region of Central Oregon. The Oakridge-Westfir Visitors Information Center has a booth at Greenwaters Park at the east edge of Oakridge; Telephone: (541) 782-4146 or (541) 782-3733 (Westfir City Hall).

Swift Shore Chalet

1190 Swift Shore Circle
West Linn, OR 97068
Phone: (503) 650-3853

Innkeepers: Nancy and Horace Duke
Rooms: 2 rooms, 1 bath and a half bath available; can sleep up to seven for a family using the entire suite
Extras: Welcome basket of snacks, bathrobes, and fresh flowers; large Western-style den-common area with wood stove, indoor swing settee, TV/VCR, and guest refrigerator
On the grounds: Extensive terraced and landscaped gardens including pond, footbridge, teahouse, and swing
Smoking? Outdoors only
Visiting pets? No; resident cockapoo, Cricket
Credit cards: Visa, MasterCard
Rates: $$
How to get there: From I-205 heading north or south take exit 6, the Tenth Street exit, near West Linn and turn south toward the Chevron station to Willamette Falls Drive; turn right and proceed approximately ½ mile to Swift Shore Drive. Turn left, then immediately left again onto Swift Shore Circle; the house is on the right, gray with dark green trim.

Perched on a bluff in an upscale neighborhood near the historic district of Willamette in West Linn, the elegant chalet-style bed and breakfast overlooks both an array of landscaped terraces as well as the nearby Tualatin River. The Tualatin flows into the Willamette River within a mile of here, near the city park. "We've always loved gardening," says Nancy. "It took us quite a while to finish this project but we are pleased that guests enjoy our outdoor haven." The results are stunning, to say the least. A koi pond and its charming bridge invite walking and looking. A willow swing invites sitting. A small teahouse invites quiet meditation. Flowering trees, fragrant shrubs, native grasses, and large beds of annuals and perennials invite reveling in spring, summer, and fall colors and textures.

On the garden level are the cozy Meadow Room and Homestead Room that offer feather beds in which to disappear for a comfy night's sleep. Or one could hole up with a great read on a chilly evening in the common area decorated in a comfortable and rustic Western style. The wood stove will be burning cheerily and offering warmth, of course.

In the morning guests navigate upstairs to the main level for breakfast in the dining area with its wide expanse of windows that offer views of the deck, gardens, and river. If you are celebrating a very special occasion, however, you can request breakfast in bed; this will be served on a large wicker tray at a civilized hour of your choosing. Nancy offers many breakfast selections including Belgian waffles, seafood quiche, Elegant French toast, and fresh fruit sorbets along with her tasty mandarin orange scones and jams and jellies homemade from Northwest fruits and berries. Warm mornings often find guests taking their plates outside to tables on the wide deck to eat breakfast in the company of water sounds, birdcalls, and the stunning terraced garden.

What's Nearby West Linn

You can investigate the little shops in the historic old town Willamette, visit the city park where the Tualatin converges with the larger Willamette River, or drive a couple of miles over to historic Oregon City, where you can visit the historic John McLoughlin House, the Oregon Trail Interpretive Center, and the Willamette Falls Locks. The Oregon City Municipal Elevator gives vertical rides from downtown up to the promenade, a walkway along the top of the basalt bluff; this offers a grand panorama of the city, the river, and its falls. The locks were constructed in the late 1800s because the falls obstructed the flow of river traffic. The Oregon City Visitors Center is located at 1795 Washington Street, Oregon City, OR 97045; Telephone: (503) 656-1619. Also see What's Nearby Portland on page 125.

Other Recommended B&B Nearby

Captain Ainsworth House, 1851 Greek Revival restored and furnished with period antiques, in Oregon City; innkeeper Claire Met, 19130 Lot Whitcomb Drive, Oregon City, OR 97045; Telephone: (503) 655-5172.

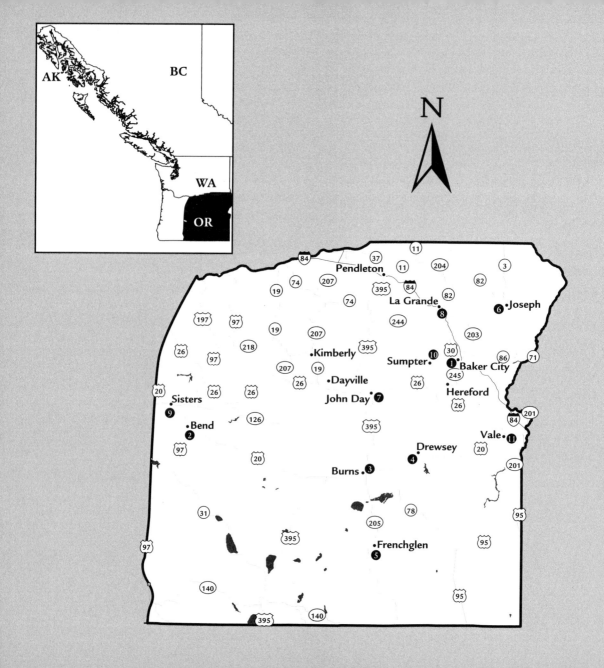

Central and Eastern Oregon

Numbers on map refer to towns numbered below.

Juniper Acres Bed & Breakfast

65220 Smokey Ridge Road
Bend, OR 97701
Phone: (541) 389-2193
E-mail: verndella@prodigy.net
Internet site: www.moriah.com/juniper/

Innkeepers: Della and Vern Bjerk
Rooms: 2 rooms with private baths
Extras: Sun decks, private high-desert country setting
On the grounds: Ten acres of young and old growth juniper; views of Mount Washington, Mount Jefferson, the Three Sisters, Brokentop, and Mount Bachelor
Smoking? Outdoors only
Visiting pets? No; resident deer, rabbits, and 2 visiting golden labs
Credit cards: No; personal checks accepted
Rates: $
How to get there: From Sisters drive east on Highway 20 turning left (north) onto Smokey Ridge Road about ¼ mile past milepost 12; the driveway is next to the inn's sign. From Bend drive 6 miles northwest on Highway 20 and turn right onto Smokey Ridge Road.

"**W**e built our log home as a bed and breakfast in 1991," says Vern. "The large logs—12, 14, and 16 inches—were cut and assembled in Canada." This is called a full-scribed log house, the Cadillac of log homes. "We like the central Oregon high desert area with its wide-open spaces and with its sagebrush, juniper, and tall ponderosa," says Della. Aromatic juniper and pungent sagebrush as well as bitterbrush grow on the couple's ten acres. The house faces south and east with an expanse of floor-to-ceiling windows framing great views of the major volcanic peaks in the Cascade Range including Mount Washington, Mount Jefferson, the Three Sisters, Brokentop, and Mount Bachelor. Guests, particularly those from the East Coast, are just as impressed by the commanding panorama as those of us who have lived with these snowy peaks all our lives. But we don't take them for granted; we're always gasping and ogling just like everyone who visits the Northwest. "Actually I don't think I could ever be a city person again," says Vern with a grin.

We're sitting on the comfortable sofa and chairs in the large common area enjoying conversation and cups of hot coffee and Della's warm caramel-nut rolls. The cheery wood stove burns brightly. The log walls gleam in the late afternoon light and several snowy peaks look as though they might walk right through the tall windows and join our party. It's early January and there is a decided nip in the air. "It could snow tonight," says Vern, "but I keep our road plowed out to the highway."

Not to worry when one can curl up in a queen log bed beneath a thick down comforter, turn on the reading lamp next to the bed, and start a vintage novel such as *Call of the Wild* by Jack London. As in the rest of the house, guests can appreciate the log walls in the two guest rooms and the creamy white chinking that was done to them a year or so after the logs had settled.

The next morning we waken to 8 inches of powdery snow and the welcome aroma of freshly brewing coffee. The innkeepers often serve breakfast outside on the sundeck during the summer; everyone agrees that breakfast indoors will work nicely today, served in the dining alcove next to the great room. The log walls hold the warmth from the wood stove as couples sip tasty Pineappe-Guava-Raspberry Juliuses and work on second cups of coffee. This is followed by baked pears with a sweet-butter, brown-sugar cream sauce, a delicious egg-cheese-broccoli soufflé, fresh baked coffeecake, and orange muffins. "Guests would need to stay longer than a week to have any breakfast repeated," says Della with a smile.

What's Nearby Bend

At an elevation of over 3,000 feet the area often gets snow during winter months and enjoys long hot days during summer months. Mount Bachelor offers premier downhill and cross-country ski facilities, from beginner to advanced. There are opportunities in the area for snowshoeing and snow camping as well. Visitors to the area include on their itineraries the Oregon High Desert Museum, Lava Butte and Lava Cast Forest, Lava River Caves, Cascade Lakes Highway Scenic Drive, and to the south, Diamond Lake and magnificent Crater Lake National Park. There are fine museums, restaurants, cafes, bakeries, and good shopping facilities in Bend, Redmond, and Sisters. Maps and additional information for hiking, biking, golfing, cave touring, lake fishing, and winter sports can be obtained from the Central Oregon Visitors' Center; Telephone: (541) 389-8799; Internet site: www.empnet.com/cova.

Lara House Bed & Breakfast

640 Northwest Congress Street
Bend, OR 97701
Phone: (541) 388-4064; for reservations,
(800) 766-4064

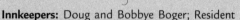

Innkeepers: Doug and Bobbye Boger; Resident Manager: Maryse Vrambout
Rooms: 6 rooms with private baths
Extras: Afternoon snack such as orange muffins, coffeecake, hot apple cider, coffee, teas
On the grounds: Sun room overlooking Drake Park, Mirror Pond, and inn's gardens; outdoor hot tub on south deck
Smoking? Outdoors only
Visiting pets? No; resident Yorkshire terrier, Sasha, and Scottish terrier, Jessie
Credit cards: Visa, MasterCard, Discover
Rates: $–$$$
How to get there: From Highway 97 traveling south to Bend, turn west onto Franklin Avenue and proceed through two traffic lights; take a sharp left turn onto Louisiana Street—the inn is on the corner of Louisiana and Congress Streets.

Located directly across from Drake Park and Mirror Pond in downtown Bend, the Craftsman-style house was built by A. M. Lara, a pioneer Bend merchant in 1910. "It's another of those wonderful old houses that transition so nicely into bed-and-breakfast inns," says Bobbye. And well it should with over 5,500 square feet of space on three floors. On the main level a spacious common area invites travelers to curl up in front of a large brick fireplace, especially on a snowy winter night. Off this area a bright and cheerful sun room with large windows overlooks the landscaped grounds. Several tall pon-

derosa pine trees grow nearby. The quacking sounds of duck families over on Mirror Pond can often be heard as they paddle about the lovely pond; canoers often paddle on the quiet water as well. The pond is actually a widened portion of the Deschutes River that flows through town.

Located on the main floor of the inn, Bachelor Room (formerly the library) has walnut paneling, dark green carpeting, and soft tones of light blue, soft rose, and eggshell. The room is outfitted with a king bed, walnut armoire, and, in the bath a large claw-foot tub with shower. On the second floor Drake Room is done in burgundy, browns, and dark green and is accented, quite appropriately, with ducks and fishing memorabilia. The queen bed has a pine headboard and the cozy sitting area offers a corner sectional sofa, small desk, and ample reading lamps. The Deschutes Room is decorated in a garden theme and features wicker furniture in the sitting area. The romantic Shevlin Room is done in soft taupe, gold, and peach also sporting the dark green carpeting along with a comfortable Queen Anne–style sofa and lady's chair, both in soft seafoam green.

The Cascade Room features handsome striped wallpaper of black, beige, and maroon, a nostalgic 1940s round-mirrored dresser and bed set, cafe curtains of burgundy, and floral comforter in beige, maroon, gold, and a touch of purple. In the sitting area with its oversized love seat with a footrest for two, one would almost expect to see young Katharine Hepburn curled up and chatting with Spencer Tracy over dry martinis. On the top floor the amply sized Summit Room features high peaked and sloping ceilings, a king bed with seafoam green spread, rattan chair, and Berber carpet of soft maroon and blue with a touch of green. The large sitting area contains a cozy futon, pillows, writing desk, and reading lamps. The large bath comes with a tub and shower combination.

Early morning coffee is always available and breakfast is served in the main floor dining room, in the large sun room, or outside on the deck. Breakfast is served between 8:00 and 9:00 A.M. with an earlier get-up-and-go option during winter months for skiers. The menu may consist of puffy pancakes with fruit, Chile egg puff with orange muffins and fruit, French toast stuffed with cream cheese and fruit and topped with warmed fruit sauce, or one of Maryse's specialties, croissant with a delectable apricot glaze.

What's Nearby

See What's Nearby Bend on page 157 and What's Nearby Sisters on page 175.

Other Recommended B&B Nearby

DiamondStone Guest Lodge, a peaceful and romantic retreat and art gallery hidden away from city lights about thirty minutes south of Bend and near the LaPine Recreation Area; innkeepers Doug and Gloria Watt, 16693 Sprague Loop, La Pine, OR 97739 (mailing address: P.O. Box 4584, Sunriver, OR 97701); Telephone: (541) 536–6263.

The Sather House Bed & Breakfast

7 Northwest Tumalo Avenue
Bend, OR 97701
Phone: (541) 388–1065

Innkeeper: Robbie Giamboi
Rooms: 4 rooms, 2 with private baths, and 2 with shared bath
Extras: Afternoon tea served from 4:00 to 5:00 P.M. at fireside during winter months including complimentary wine, teas, and pastries; lemonade and soft drinks served on the veranda during summer months
On the grounds: Wraparound porch with wicker furniture; close to Drake Park, Mirror Pond, and downtown shops
Smoking? Outdoors only
Visiting pets? No; no resident pets
Credit cards: Visa, MasterCard, Discover
Rates: $–$$
How to get there: From the Sisters area take Highway 20 then Highway 97 driving south Bend; turn right onto Franklin Street then left onto Broadway. The inn is located at the corner of Broadway and Tumalo Streets.

Internet site: www.moriah.com/sather

Robbie tells guests that the large, two-story Craftsman home was built at the turn of the century in 1911, and was occupied by the Sather family for seventy-five years. "We're in a neighborhood of older historical homes," she says, "and this house is featured on the cover of our walking tour guide." The Deschutes River, Drake Park, and lovely Mirror Pond are located just three blocks away as are downtown shops, cafes, delis, and restaurants. "Most guests enjoy planning at least one dinner at the Pine Tavern Restaurant," says Robbie. This historic eatery on Mirror Pond features two ponderosa pine trees growing through the roof of the garden room section of the establishment. Guests can also try two other award-winning eateries, Alpenglow on nearby Bond Street offering exceptional lunches, and Westside Bakery near Drake Park with wonderful pastries.

Guests are offered four well-appointed rooms, all with Victorian wallpapers and lovely fabrics. Women cater to the Victorian Room, especially when its white wrought-iron queen bed is dressed in pink a satin coverlet; other times the bed is covered with a creamy white-and-blue quilt. Wallpaper in a soft floral print; French provincial bureau, lady's chair, and bed-side tables; and velvet and lace window treat-ment complete the decor. The private bath features a large 1910 claw-foot tub and is won-derful for a long soak in the late evening. The men appreciate the English Room with navy print wallpaper, dark wood furnishings, framed English hunt prints, and richly colored paisley spread on the queen bed. The Garden Room has a green wrought-iron king bed dressed in an ivory Battenberg coverlet and down comforter with double sheeting. This spacious room with four windows dressed in Battenberg lace cur-tains features seafoam green carpeting, an ivory rocker, pecan-and-glass coffee table, side table, and dresser along with a green wrought-iron bird cage filled with flowers.

The upstairs landing has raspberry carpet-ing, wallpaper of raspberry and taupe, blue vel-vet chairs, a table, reading lamp, chandelier, and small library of reading materials. There is a guest telephone here as well. Breakfast is served in the formal dining room on the main floor between 8:00 and 9:00 A.M. The delicious repast may consist of banana pancakes with either caramelized apples with pecans or homemade lemon syrup; cheese strata with fresh fruit; or French toast with vanilla yogurt and fresh berries. "I notice that guests always manage to clean their plates," says Robbie with a grin.

What's Nearby

See What's Nearby Bend on page 157 and What's Nearby Sisters on page 175.

Sage Country Inn

351-½ West Monroe Street
P.O. Box 227
Burns, OR 97720
Phone: (541) 573-7243
E-mail: pstick@ptinet.net
Internet site: www.ptinet.net/~pstick

Innkeepers: Susan Pielstick, Georgia Marshall, and Carole Temple
Rooms: 4 rooms, 3 with private baths
Extras: Refreshments on arrival or after dinner; beverages in guest refrigerator; gourmet breakfast fare; fresh flowers in rooms; sandalwood shampoo and soap in baths
On the grounds: Landscaped grounds, perennial beds, lawn swing, and croquet
Smoking? Outdoors only
Visiting pets? No; no resident pets
Credit cards: Visa, MasterCard
Rates: $–$$
How to get there: From Bend proceed east and south on Highway 20 to Burns, a distance of 130 miles; (Note: refuel in Bend; there are minimal services along this route). Travelers could also enter from the John Day-Canyon City region by proceeding south on scenic Highway 395 to Burns, a distance of 70 miles. From Boise, Idaho, go west via Highway 20/26 through Nyssa and Vale and continue west on Highway 20 to Burns, a total distance of about 177 miles. The inn is located ½ block off of Highway 20 between Diamond and Court Avenues.

"Some people still can't believe that three women were able to pick out wallpaper together," says Susan with a grin. But indeed they did, as well as work together scraping layers of old paint from the woodwork and tearing worn linoleum from the now gleaming fir floors. The renovated and redecorated Victorian farmhouse, with its wide front porch supported by dainty columns, was ready to open its doors to bed-and-breakfast travelers in May 1996. The three lifelong friends—Susan,

Georgia, and Carole—take turns minding the inn—they divide the duties and make schedules months in advance. One of the three is always there to greet guests and to prepare breakfast in the morning.

Four guest rooms, each with a different theme, provide comfortable quarters for anyone visiting the Burns area. Cattle Baron Room honors Harney County's Western history and features an ornate black wrought-iron queen bed fit for a cattle king and his bride. Western memorabilia, inviting antiques, and collection of books on local history along with reading lamps and sitting places invite guests to curl up and read for a spell. Kathreen's Room is a delight in soft pinks, green, oyster, and burgundy as well as Victorian wallpaper and a stunning window treatment. Another room has twin beds, and the Dormer Room is outfitted with an antique brass double bed with a floral comforter and matching pillow shams. The bath for this room is located downstairs.

Breakfast is served in the large dining room on the main level usually between 7:00 and 9:00 A.M. This is an elegant affair and the enticing food might be raspberry compote topped with crème fraîche and homemade granola along with banana-stuffed French toast with whipped banana cream and sugar cured ham. On another day guests might be served peaches in amaretto sauce sprinkled with pecans along with a pork and apple-sausage frittata and orange scones topped with orange butter. The gourmet repast begins with the inn's personalized blend of juices, Vienna blend coffee, and a selection of teas. There are a number of good eateries in town including Pine Room Café, Highlander Restaurant, Mazatlan Mexican Restaurant, Apple Peddler, RJ's, and Linda's Thai Room.

What's Nearby Burns

The area is a good jumping-off point for those who want to visit the renowned 193,000-acre Malheur National Wildlife Refuge (541-493-2612) located 25 miles south of Burns. The refuge is the transient home to hundreds of thousands of birds navigating the Pacific flyway north and south. Early spring and fall are good times to view the wildlife and hear the sounds that permeate the air when species of geese, ducks, cranes, pelicans, and herons visit the area's two large lakes. Nearby Steens Mountain offers a scenic drive up to an elevation of nearly 10,000 feet that has a panoramic view of the Alvord Desert to the southeast. The entire area is well used by river and stream fishermen, fly fishermen, birdwatchers, hikers, runners, mountain bikers, hunters, and wilderness lovers. Contact the Harney County Visitors Information Center, 76 East Washington Street, Burns, OR 97720; Telephone: (541) 573-2636. Internet site: www. harneycounty.com.

Blue Bucket Inn
at 3 E Ranch

HC68–536
Drewsey, OR 97904
Phone: (541) 493–2375 or (541) 493–2525
Internet site: www.inns@moriah.com

Innkeepers: Judy Ahmann; Ranch Managers: Sam and Maria Sanchez
Rooms: 5 rooms, 1 room is wheelchair accessible with accessible shared bath; 2 rooms on the second floor have private baths
Extras: Light snacks and beverages on arrival; the entire original ranch house is for guests use
On the grounds: Central fork of Malheur River, meadows, lawn, view of Battle Mountain
Smoking? Outdoors only
Visiting pets? No; about 400 head of cattle
Credit cards: No; personal checks accepted
Rates: $–$$
How to get there: From Burns take Highway 20 east for 39 miles to the Drewsey turn-off, then turn north and proceed through Drewsey; after crossing the Malheur River bear to the left on the paved Drewsey-Van road and continue for 13 miles to Forest Service Road #14—the inn's sign is on the mailbox shelter at this intersection; turn right and proceed about 1½ miles crossing two cattle guards then enter the first drive on the left (look for the ranch and inn sign). If you start up the hill, you've missed the turn.

In a remote location in the state's far southeast corner, the Blue Bucket Inn at the 3E Ranch is just outside the small ranching community of Drewsey. Judy says, "Our motto is 'come enjoy the Oregon outback.'" You can't get much farther into the hinterlands unless you're on a horse and heading east across sagebrush and rangeland country toward the Idaho border. Adventurous bed-and-breakfast travelers who desire a Northwest ranching experience quite distant from the hustle-bustle of city sounds and city lights will do well to call ahead and arrange a trek into this historic cattle and ranch country.

Guests can relax under the wide skies, hike in designated areas of the ranch, try fly fishing on the Malheur River, inspect remnants of historic ranch buildings, and learn about the workings of a real cattle ranch. About 400 head of cattle are ranged here showing the rocking 3E brand on their right hindquarters. The large common room is a comfortable place in which to hole up—the L-shaped sofa has a southwest Indian print slipcover, a pair of club chairs is upholstered in soft teal. The room also has a fireplace with an insert stove, an upright piano, and large windows that look out on the lawn, meadows, and rangeland. Through French doors the adjacent library offers shelves of books for choosing and reading, cozy chairs, and reading lamps. The kitchen is equipped with an island electric stove, refrigerator, basic supplies, and an old-fashioned wood stove as well. On the second floor two guest rooms with private baths have queen beds with juniper headboards and warm down comforters, comfy reading chairs, and reading lamps.

Two similarly appointed guest rooms on the main floor share a bath.

In the morning coffee is ready by 8:00 A.M. and breakfast is served about 8:30 A.M. in the dining room. Hearty ranch fare may include oatcakes, Dutch babies, stuffed French toast, waffles, or cheese egg strata. Homemade muffins and breads along with bacon, sausage, or ham will also accompany the meal. For evening meals the Drewsey Café in nearby Drewsey is a great place to eat and meet some of the local ranchers and buckaroos. With plenty of advance notice, Judy can arrange to have dinner prepared for guests at about $10 per person. You can also bring provisions for lunch and dinner, shopping in Burns before heading out to the ranch.

What's Nearby

See What's Nearby Burns on page 163.

Other Recommended B&Bs Nearby

Frenchglen Hotel, south of Burns, offers small rooms, baths down the hall, and family-style dinners, in a 1916 building; Highway 205, Frenchglen, OR 97736; Telephone: (541) 493–2825. **McCoy Creek Inn,** a working ranch located south of Burns, offers three rooms in the main house or a cozy bunkhouse next door along with gourmet breakfasts; contact the family of innkeepers at HC72, Box 11, Diamond, OR 97722; Telephone: (541) 493–2131 days and (541) 493–2440 evenings. **Sears, Roebuck Home Bed & Breakfast,** an elegant Victorian ordered in 1900 from the company's catalog (from which its name comes), located not too far from the Red Garter Ice Cream Saloon, 484 North Tenth, Vale, OR 97918; Telephone: (541) 473–9636.

George Hyatt House Bed & Breakfast

200 East Greenwood Street
Enterprise, OR 97828
Phone: (541) 426-0241; (800) 954-9288
Internet site: www.moriah.com/hyatt/

Innkeepers: Members of the extended Driver family
Rooms: 4 rooms with private baths
Extras: Victorian ambience in 1898 classic Queen Anne Victorian; library featuring local history and books by regional authors; regional and national newspapers.
On the grounds: Extensive English-style landscaped grounds and gardens; hot tub outdoors near carriage house
Smoking? Outside only
Visiting pets? No; no resident pets
Credit cards: Visa, MasterCard
Rates: $$; inquire about off-season rates
How to get there: Traveling via I-84 east beyond The Dalles and Pendleton, continue over Meacham Pass to LaGrande, a distance of 178 miles; take Highway 82 northeast through Elgin, Wallowa, and Lostine, and continue to Enterprise, a distance of about 78 miles. Upon entering Enterprise turn right onto River Street passing the courthouse and turning left onto Greenwood Street; the inn is 1 block farther on the right. The Enterprise Airport serves small private aircraft (541–426–3502).

The Hyatt House was built in 1898 for the city's founding father and early entrepreneur, George Wilson Hyatt. His later business efforts proved failures, however, and in 1928 the house was sold at a sheriff's auction on the nearby courthouse steps. "The buyer paid a total of $23.50 for this wonderful house," says a member of the Driver family. Following its use as a doctor's office in the 1980s, the house was renovated and redecorated as a bed and breakfast. The creamy white Queen Anne Victorian with dark green trim sits like a regal dowager behind a refined white picket fence. An immaculate lawn and lush flowering perennial beds surround the house; an herb garden grows next to the rear patio. When guests enter the house they get a light, airy feeling—sunlight streams through large windows in the parlor and library, and some windows are surrounded with trim of lovely stained glass. This comfortable common area contains a collection of books by regional authors and local histories.

The four guest rooms feature luxurious queen beds dressed in fine linens and down comforters. Every room has an adjoining private bath with pedestal sink, ornate brass fixtures, and old-fashioned sconce lighting. Two of the rooms offer the original, restored claw-foot tubs. Another room features an elegant bath in the restored Queen Anne tower. In this room one looks through stained-glass windows onto the flower garden. In the Cottage Room a set of Victorian cottage–style furniture offers a charming and nostalgic ambience. All rooms are decorated in the luxurious fabrics and wallpapers of the era.

Mornings at Hyatt House are gracious and genteel with freshly brewed coffee and tea appearing on the sideboard in the dining room for self-service about a half-hour before breakfast is served. The morning repast often begins with fresh fruit compote of layered local berries and melons with homemade granola hiding at the bottom; the whole delicious affair may be topped with blueberry cream. The next course bring Egg Soufflé Adrienne, a Finnish dish topped with freshly made blue plum sauce. Local farm-fresh brown eggs are used in the preparation of all morning fare.

What's Nearby Enterprise

The Wallowa County Visitors Information Center is located at 107 SW First Street, P.O. Box 427, Enterprise, OR 97323; Telephone: (541) 426-4622; Internet site: www.wallowa@eoni.com.

Other Recommended B&Bs Nearby

Stang Manor, a Georgian Colonial mansion built by a lumber baron offers large comfortable rooms, sweeping grounds; innkeepers Pat and Marjorie McClure, 1612 Walnut Street, La Grande, OR 97850; Telephone: (541) 963-2400. In Enterprise find **Tickled Trout Bed & Breakfast,** a renovated English-style century-old farmhouse, one guest room has a step-up feather bed, imported English teas; innkeepers Martha and Dale Wietzel, 507 South River Street, Enterprise, OR 97828; Telephone: (541) 426-6039.

Pine Valley Lodge Bed & Breakfast

163 North Main Street
P.O. Box 712
Halfway, OR 97834
Phone: (541) 742–2027
Internet site:
www.neoregon.net/pinevalleylodge/

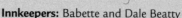

Innkeepers: Babette and Dale Beatty
Rooms: 3 rooms in the main lodge, 2 with shared bath and 1 suite with a private bath; in The Blue Dog cottage next door 4 rooms with shared baths or these rooms combined into 2 suites, with private baths
Extras: The innkeepers' gourmet bakery, restaurant, and lounge, The Olde Church, located across the street from the main lodge offers world class cuisine
On the grounds: Extensive gardens including sunflowers
Smoking? Outside only
Visiting pets? No; resident chickens that provide fresh eggs
Credit cards: Visa, MasterCard
Rates: $–$$
How to get there: From Baker City, detour from I-84 onto Highway 86 heading northeast over Flagstaff Summit and passing the Oregon Trail Interpretive Center to Halfway, a distance of approximately 50 miles. The inn is located on Main Street.

When you think of Halfway, think of a small Western town set in a small rural valley and surrounded by the craggy, Swiss-like Wallowa Mountains and their foothills. Main Street looks like a cross between a movie set from *High Noon,* trendy Carmel on the mid-California coast, and funky N.W. Twenty-third Avenue in uptown Portland. Into this intriguing mix is an immigrant innkeeper, Babette Beatty, who in the early 1960s graced the cover of *Sports Illustrated* magazine, and her husband and co-innkeeper, Dale, who makes custom fishing rods. He is also the one responsible for skinning the pine logs to create furniture and the massive beams that support wide porches connected to the main lodge. Metal corrugated roofs help shed snows that blanket the area during winter months.

Two rooms on the second floor offer comfortable beds with fine linens and eiderdown duvets and a shared bath. Another room, a suite with private bath, is located on the main floor. You might choose the room that has the feather hat collection on the wall, or the room with green walls on which artist Babette has hand-painted tropical flowers. Another room offers an enormous four-poster pine bed made by Dale. Carved and painted impressionistic ducks appear to be flying straight out, one from each upper corner post at the foot of the bed. The Blue Dog Cottage next door offers four rooms and a rustic Western parlor with comfortable sofa, reading lamps, TV, VCR, and kitchenette.

Breakfast, served between 8:00 and 9:30 A.M., often includes fresh items from the inn's bakery—hand-crafted European breads, pastries, chewy New York–style bagels, and steaming espresso. Dining on mismatched fine china seems quite appropriate here.

What's Nearby Halfway and What's Nearby Baker City

During mid-autumn or late spring (May is perfect), drive from Halfway up the narrow winding road that skirts the Snake River down to Hells Canyon Dam (at road's end), a roundtrip distance of 132 miles. On the way back to civilization via Highway 86, plan a stop at the fine Oregon Trail Interpretive Center located at Flagstaff Summit, 30 miles east of Baker City. Dim remains of actual pioneer wagon ruts can be seen here. The well-stocked Baker County Visitors Center is located at 490 Campbell Street, Baker City, OR 97814; Telephone: (541) 523-3356; Internet site: www.neoregon.com/vistbaker.

Other Recommended B&Bs Nearby

Clearcreek Farm Bed & Breakfast Inn offers ponds, wildlife, resident bison, orchard, perennial gardens and old-fashioned rose garden, cozy rooms in the main farmhouse and romantic starlight rooms in the renovated barn and granary; innkeepers Mike and Rose Curless, Clearcreek Road, P.O. Box 676, Halfway, OR 97834; Telephone: (541) 742-5175. **A Demain Bed & Breakfast** (à demain is French for "until tomorrow") offers candlelight breakfasts and feather-bed Victorian rooms; innkeepers Pat and Kristi Flanagan, 1790 Fourth Street, Baker City, OR 97814; Telephone: (541) 523-2509.

Chandler's Bed, Bread & Trail Inn

700 South Main Street
Joseph, OR 97846
Phone: (541) 432-9765; (800) 452-3785
E-mail: chanbbti@eoni.com
Internet site:
www.eoni.com/~chanbbti/inn.html

Innkeepers: Ethel and Jim Chandler; manager: Crystal Sanchez
Rooms: 5 rooms, 3 with private baths and 2 with shared bath
Extras: Freshly baked cookies, coffee and teas on arrival; robes and hair dryers in baths; well-stocked library of regional travel material
On the grounds: Two-story gazebo with hot tub on its upper level; lush plantings and flowering perennials; views of nearby Chief Joseph Mountain, Ruby Peak, Mount Howard
Smoking? Outdoors only
Visiting pets? No; no resident pets
Credit cards: Visa, MasterCard
Rates: $-$$
How to get there: At the city of LaGrande turn northeast from I-84 onto Highway 82 proceeding through the small communities of Elgin, Wallowa, and Lostine toward Enterprise; continue 5 miles farther to Joseph and drive to the east end of Main Street turning left at the inn's sign and into the off-street parking area.

This large lodge, built of post-and-beam construction, offers a convenient home base and jumping-off point for Wallowa Lake, the Wallowa Mountains, and the Eagle Cap Wilderness. "Lots of folks bring their mountain bikes during summer months," says Ethel. "And their skis and snowshoes and snowmobiles during winter," adds Jim. This active couple can often be seen walking or bicycling the 2-mile round-trip to Wallowa Lake and back, and their guests enjoy pursuing the same activities. In the evening couples who are ready to unwind from the day's adventures soon find the bubbling hot tub located on the second level of the outdoor gazebo. Later guests may dispatch to nearby downtown Joseph to try local cuisine at Embers Restaurant, Old Town Café, The Outlaw Restaurant, or Maria's. Microbrew lovers may want to try one of the local amber brews such as Terminal Gravity.

The inn offers several comfortable common areas. One is on the main level near the light and airy kitchen. Magazines abound as do helpful regional travel books, brochures, and maps. Comfortable well-worn sofas, plump pillows, and easy chairs await, and the innkeepers' antiques are placed in pleasant groupings—a copper boiler, an early treadle sewing machine, an antique bathtub, and family quilts. Jim and Ethel are happy to answer questions about the history of Wallowa County and also about what to see and do while visiting this vast area of Swiss-like mountains and pristine lakes.

Three guest rooms located on the second floor are large and outfitted with comfortable beds and sitting areas. The east wing has two additional guest rooms that share one and a half baths, a cozy sitting area, and adjoining deck with views of the nearby mountain peaks. Children over the age of 12 are welcome.

Coffee aromas waft upstairs beginning around 6:00 A.M. Breakfast is served between 7:00 and 9:00 A.M. with the first course often fresh fruit and six-grain cereal with homemade granola sprinkled on top. This may be followed by eggs Benedict, a special quiche, cheese strata, and apple babies. Local honey and jams are also served at the inn.

What's Nearby

Art lovers and antiques buffs can browse in nearby galleries and shops including several renowned bronze foundries. The Eagle Cap Wilderness and Hells Canyon Recreation Area provide areas for hiking, fishing, lama trekking, horse packing, white water rafting, and during winter months alpine skiing and outback hut-to-hut skiing in the wilderness areas. One of the best high altitude views is from atop 8,000-foot Mount Howard. Easily accessed via the Wallowa Tramway, this fifteen-minute ride in two-person gondolas ascends 3,800 feet up the mountain. For additional information check the internet site: www.wallow@eoni.com. For back-country wilderness information contact the Wallowa-Whitman National Forest headquarters in Baker City; Telephone: (541) 523-6391.

Strawberry Mountain Inn

HCR 77, Box 940 Highway 26E
Prairie City, OR 97869
Phone: (541) 820-4522; (800) 545-6913
E-mail: linda@eoni.com
Internet site: www.moriah.com/strawberry

At an elevation of 3,535 feet in the John Day Valley near the meandering John Day River and the John Day fossil beds, Linda and Bill Harrington welcome travelers to their 1911 inn, especially those who delight in getting way off the beaten path. "Because of our crisp clear nights, and because we're so far away from city lights, guests are quite taken by the millions of stars crowded into the nighttime sky here," says Linda. The canopy of glittery constellations is indeed almost overwhelming. A walk through

Innkeepers: Linda and Bill Harrington
Rooms: 5 rooms, 1 with private bath, other rooms share 2 baths
Extras: Library, game room with billiards, CD music and video library; guests can arrange for private gourmet dinners and special anniversary or honeymoon gifts; canoe available to rent by pre-reservation; outdoor hot tub
On the grounds: 100-year-old apple trees, flower gardens; John Day River nearby; facilities for boarding and pasturing horses; children's outdoor play area
Smoking? Outdoors only
Visiting pets? Yes, facilities in barn only, please notify in advance; visiting deer, resident chickens; standard silver poodle, Deja; two Maine coon cats, Duke and Duchess; 1 large quarterhorse in pasture, Shiloh, who loves apples
Credit cards: Visa, MasterCard, American Express, Discover
Rates: $-$$
How to get there: At Redmond north of Bend, turn east off Highway 97 onto Highway 26E traveling to Prineville; continue on Highway 26E approximately 110 miles passing through Mitchell and Dayville to John Day. Continue east on this Journey Through Time tour route 13 miles to Prairie City; the inn is located ¼ mile east of town. There are municipal airports in both Redmond and Boise serving commuter size aircraft; the John Day State Airport located 13 miles west of Prairie City serves small private aircraft and has a refueling facility (541-575-1151).

the hundred-year-old apple orchard followed by a soothing soak in the hot tub, also outdoors under all those stars, is lovely.

The Harringtons offer five rooms on the second floor that are outfitted with an elegant mixture of Victorian and traditional Queen Anne furnishings. The original master bedroom features a bay window with a view of 9,000-foot Strawberry Mountain, a generous sitting area with an antique writing desk, a king bed and a trundle daybed, and a private bath. Another room decorated in warm earth tones offers a king bed, reading area and antique writing desk, and has the original leaded-glass window headers that date from 1910. This room shares a bath and has a view of the orchard and garden. Another delight-

fully romantic room offers a black wrought-iron canopied queen bed, draped with floral garlands, and views of the mountains to the south and of rolling farmland to the east.

Awaken to the aroma of coffee and sound of soft classical music wafting up the stairs. Before 7:30 A.M. breakfast may consist of waffles with fresh fruit. Breakfast served between 8:00 and 9:30 A.M. will be more gourmet in style and consist of perhaps cinnamon-apple pancakes with crisp bacon or a bacon-onion-vegetable quiche with sausage. Cheese blintzes, eggs Florentine, or eggs Benedict with homemade bread and hot-from-the-oven coffeecake may be served on weekend. For evening meals there are restaurants in nearby John Day and Canyon City.

What's Nearby Prairie City and John Day

This is a large wilderness area. Enjoy the Kam Wah Chung Chinese Museum, the DeWitt Museum depicting life in the valley between 1891 and 1947, and the Oxbow Trade Company Museum featuring a collection of horse-drawn vehicles, a resident buggy maker and a resident wheelwright. The John Day Fossil Beds National Monument is located nearby. The Grant County Visitors Center is located at 281 West Main Street in John Day; Telephone: (541) 575-0547.

Other Recommended B&Bs Nearby

Fish House Bed & Breakfast offers three guest rooms in the main house, a 1908 bungalow, and a small cottage, located near the John Day River in Dayville; innkeepers Mike and Denise Smith, P.O. Box 143, Dayville, OR 97825; Telephone: (541) 987-2124. **Fort Reading Bed & Breakfast**, a working cattle ranch near the community of Hereford; innkeeper Barbara Hawes, HCR86, Box 140, Hereford, OR 97837; Telephone: (541) 446-3478.

Conklin's Guest House

69013 Camp Polk Road
Sisters, OR 97759
Phone: (541) 549-0123; (800) 549-4262
Internet site: www.informat.com/bz/conklins

Innkeepers: Frank and Marie Conklin
Rooms: 5 rooms with private baths including 1 wheelchair accessible room and 1 dormitory-style room with queen bed and 5 single beds
Extras: Three rooms feature large claw-foot tubs; breakfast served in sunny poolside solarium; reunion and wedding parties welcome
On the grounds: Heated swimming pool; large pond stocked with trout, catch and release; large gazebo extends over pond area; views of snow-capped mountains
Smoking? Outdoors only
Visiting pets? No; 3 outside cats
Credit cards: No; personal checks accepted
Rates: $$–$$$
How to get there: From Salem and the Willamette Valley region proceed over 4,800-foot Santiam Pass via Highway 22 approximately 75 miles to the Sisters area. Drive through Sisters to eastern edge of town turning left onto Camp Polk Road near the two public schools; proceed about ¼ mile to the inn located on the left.

Situated at the edge of Sisters, the bed and breakfast commands a panoramic view of snow-capped mountains, Three Sisters. In addition to the mountains, the focal point of the inn is a large pond that is stocked with catch-and-release trout. Expanses of lawn surround the pond and a deck and large gazebo extend over a section of the water. A heated swimming pool with sunning and picnic areas is located closer to the house.

The guest rooms are filled with comfortable furniture, light and airy floral prints and colors, skylights, wicker, and reading lamps.

Columbine Room features a cozy wicker sitting area with skylight and a queen bed. Forget-Me-Not Room has a fireplace and queen bed along with an outdoor deck and view of the mountains. Morning Glory Suite has a magnificent view and spacious accommodations. These three rooms have handsome wrought-iron flat-top canopies and also large claw-foot tubs that have been restored by Frank. In Morning Glory guests can soak with a view of the snowy peaks.

Lattice Room is wheelchair-accessible and Heather Room offers a dormitory-style arrangement with a queen bed and five single beds. Children 12 years and older may accompany their parents to the inn.

Evening refreshments and early morning coffee are served in the comfortable common area on the main floor. Freshly brewed coffee arrives around 7:00 A.M. and breakfast follows at 9:00 A.M. served in the poolside solarium that also offers views of the Three Sisters. On small glass-topped tables stemmed glasses hold fresh orange juice, fresh flowers bloom from glass vases, condiments await in small cut-glass dishes. The main entree is served on lovely china and the day's selection could be special French toast with Grand Marnier, creamy scrambled eggs with pesto, and baked sausage links. The innkeepers can offer suggestions for good eateries in the area, for midday and evening dining.

What's Nearby Sisters

This is horse and rodeo country. You'll see horses of every size, breed, and color and well-worn cowboy and cowgirl boots, jeans, and wide-brimmed hats. The Western town of Sisters is a shopper's mecca with an eclectic mix of charming boutiques, gift shops, coffee shops, crafts shops, Western shops, and antiques shops. The town also hosts a lively Jazz Festival and a Quilt Show each year. The local Ranger Station and the Sisters Area Visitors Information Center (541–549-0251), can provide helpful information for all-season outdoor recreation. There are more than twenty public golf courses in the area. The small Sisters Airport can accommodate small private aircraft. Also see What's Nearby Bend on page 157.

Other Recommended B&Bs Nearby

Cozy and friendly **Bear Pond Bed & Breakfast** is near Sisters, with innkeepers Gary and Rhonda Sneva, 16584 Highway 126, Sisters, OR 97759; Telephone: (541) 549-1974. **Rags to Walker Guest Ranch,** offers casual elegance, stocked ponds, mountain views on a seventy-five-acre Tennessee Walking–horse ranch about 6 miles east of Sisters; energetic innkeepers Bonnie Jacobs-Halousek and Neal Halousek, 17045 Farthing Lane, Sisters, OR 97759; Telephone: (541) 548-7000.

Sumpter Bed & Breakfast

344 North Columbia Street,
P.O. Box 40
Sumpter, OR 97877
Phone: (541) 894-0048; (800) 640-3184

Innkeepers: Barbara and Jay Phillips
Rooms: 6 rooms with 3 shared baths
Extras: Historic location, gold mines, several ghost towns
On the grounds: Tall ponderosa pine; winter snowmobiling trails begin at the inn's door
Smoking? Outdoors only, guests may smoke on porches
Visiting pets? No; no resident pets
Credit cards: Visa; personal checks accepted
Rates: $–$$
How to get there: From John Day-Prairie City continue northeast on Highway 26 driving over 5,279-foot Dixie Summit to Austin Junction; from here continue on Highway 7 to Sumpter, a total distance of 37 miles. Just before the Stage Stop Gas Station in Sumpter turn right onto Columbia Street uphill 1 block to the inn.

Deep in the heart of the region's historic gold mining country at an elevation of 4,400 feet, innkeepers Jay and Barbara Phillips welcome bed-and-breakfast travelers to their inn, originally a small hospital. Guests climb the stairs to the front porch and enter through a pair of glass doors set in the center of the building. Stairs to the second floor hug the wall to the left and to the right you step onto a Victorian carpet of soft pinks, blues, and greens and into the common area. Arranged near the side bay window, a late 1920s sofa invites guests to sit and rest a bit. Dark wood gleams from a pair of Federal-style chairs whose upholstered seats are done in a hunter-green and wine floral fabric. The windows are dressed in lace with an ivy design and with stylistic cabbage roses attached at the upper corners. The walls are pale bisque color with wainscoting of hunter green striped wallpaper embellished with a 10-inch border of a rose garland design just below the handsome crown molding.

An oak roll-top desk sits in a nearby alcove and guests usually inspect the vintage oak cash register that sits atop 4-foot carved oak legs; it reportedly came from San Francisco. Rocking chairs sit in a cozy grouping around the fireplace. Barbara explains that the entire downstairs area contained the original thirty-two-bed ward. With the renovation completed, an open kitchen and two good-sized dining areas extend beyond the common area to the rear of the structure—the near section contains a square five-legged oak table on the refinished fir floor. The rear dining section, through a small archway, contains two additional antique oak tables.

Up the open stairway to the second floor there are six rooms that share three full baths, two with showers and one with a large claw-foot tub. The small rooms are furnished with com-fortable double beds of iron or brass, soft Victorian floral fabrics, and antique dressing tables. One room, at the front of the inn, has access to the balcony that extends above the first-floor porch and is supported by four sturdy columns.

Breakfast is served to most guests between 7:00 and 9:00 A.M. "When the snow plow crews and road crews come through," says Barbara, "we serve them at 5:00 A.M.!" You may eat in the company of bikers, hikers, history buffs, and, during the winter months, enthusiastic snowmo-biling buffs and both downhill and cross-country skiers. Jay and Barbara team up to prepare the morning fare that may consist of huckleberry pancakes with warm maple syrup, link sausages, homemade biscuits with sausage gravy, or a fluffy egg dish with garden herbs, bacon, ham, tomatoes, and a mild salsa. The couple serves a boldly flavored coffee called Nine to Five as well as a selection of teas and hot chocolate.

What's Nearby Sumpter

This area is ripe with old gold mines, gold dredges, vintage trains, even reported ghost trains, and several old ghost towns. The eateries and establishments in town have names like Sumpter Nugget Restaurant, Gold Post Grocery, and Stage Stop Gas Station. The historic Sumpter gold dredge has recently undergone restoration and is now open as Sumpter Valley Dredge State Heritage Area. The restored narrow-gauge Sumpter Valley Railroad operates on weekends from Memorial Day through September with depots in Sumpter and at McEwen Railroad Park off Highway 7. Additional information can be obtained from the regional Visitors Information Center in Baker City; Telephone: (541) 523-3356. Road conditions for the major mountain passes in the state of Oregon; Telephone: (503) 976-7277.

II. Washington

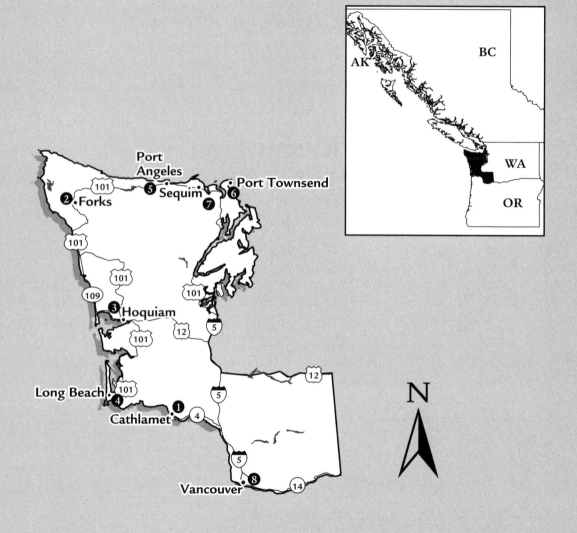

Southwest, Long Beach Peninsula, and Olympic Peninsula

Numbers on map refer to towns numbered below.

The Bradley House
Bed & Breakfast

61 Main Street
Cathlamet, WA 98612
Phone: (360) 795-3030; (800) 551-1691
E-mail: bradleyhouse@transport.com

Innkeepers: Barbara and Tony West
Rooms: 4 rooms, 2 with private baths, and 2 with shared bath
Extras: 1907 Eastlake home built for a lumber baron
On the grounds: Views of the Columbia River and Puget Island
Smoking? Outdoors only
Visiting pets? No; one large tabby cat, Mooch
Credit cards: Visa, MasterCard
Rates: $-$$
How to get there: From Portland take I-5 north to Longview, Washington, and turn west on Highway 4 to Cathlamet, a total distance of 72 miles. Turn left onto Main Street (Highway 409) and continue 1½ blocks to the inn, located across from the courthouse. Alternatively from Portland travel west on Highway 30 on the Oregon side of the Columbia River to Westport, a distance of 74 miles; from here board the Wahkiakum County Ferry, which crosses hourly to Puget Island. Proceed 3 miles across the island to the bridge that connects to Cathlamet on the Washington side of the river.

With names like Rose Room, Monet Room, Garden Room, and Blue Room, The Bradley House may have travelers thinking they are sleeping in garden bowers. In addition to the light and airy rooms and their comfortable queen or king beds, the inn's windows overlook the small town of Cathlamet and out to the Columbia River and small Puget Island. One large room has corner window seats and these offer prime views. Long-legged blue herons might fly over, gulls often sweep low looking for tasty tidbits, and bald eagles are seen now and then—taking daily cruises from Sauvie Island, near Portland, down to the coast.

The small riverside community of Cathlamet offers small antiques shops, gift boutiques, and historic sites to explore. "It's a fun place to explore on foot," says Barbara. Small cafes, delis, and espresso shops offer cozy spots to stop for snacks and beverages. Those looking for athletic pursuits will find bicycling, fishing, sailing, canoeing, kayaking, and windsurfing. Back at the inn guests are invited use two comfortable parlors where ample supplies of books, games, and puzzles await as well as a vintage piano, sheet music, TV, and a music system. The innkeepers thoughtfully provide a self-service beverage sideboard including coffee, tea, hot chocolate, cider, sherry, and port.

A full breakfast is served at 8:30 A.M. in the formal dining room that once seated the family of a local lumber baron. The Eastlake home was constructed for them in 1907. The woodwork gleams as it did then, morning light peeks through vintage stained-glass windows, and the table is set for bed-and-breakfast guests with lace, silver, china, crystal, and fresh flowers. The morning meal may consist of fresh squeezed orange juice, a cheesy herb soufflé, tasty sausages, fresh fruit in season, and poppyseed muffins warm from the oven. For evening dining ask about eateries in Cathlamet and about The Berry Patch Restaurant, (503) 455-0204, in nearby Westport, reached by the Wahkiakum County Ferry that crosses hourly from Puget Island to the Oregon side of the river.

What's Nearby Cathlamet

The wide Columbia River and nearby Puget Island are the major natural attractions here with an abundance of prime wildlife viewing. The Julia Butler Hansen Columbia White-tailed Deer Refuge is located just northwest of Cathlamet via Highway 4. A short distance farther travelers find the River Life Interpretive Center, situated in an 1894 schoolhouse within Skamakawa National Historic District; the center offers natural and human history on the Columbia River Estuary. The Grays River Valley Covered Bridge, the only remaining working covered bridge in Washington state, is also easily discovered nearby. To view the bald eagles up close and personal, journey on the Oregon side of the Columbia River to the Twilight Eagle Sanctuary; proceed west on Highway 30 toward Astoria to reach the sanctuary.

Cooney Mansion
Bed & Breakfast Inn

1705 Fifth Street

P.O. Box 54

Cosmopolis, Wa 98537

Phone: (360) 533-0602;

reservation number: (800) 9–SPRUCE

E-mail: cooney@techline.com

Internet site: www.techline.com/~cooney/

Innkeepers: Judi and Jim Lohr
Rooms: 8 rooms, 5 with private baths
Extras: TVs in some rooms, VCR in master suite, radios and clocks in all rooms; fireplace and player piano in living room; two parlors and an exercise room; ballroom with large TV/VCR; tennis and golf nearby
On the grounds: Landscaped lawns and plantings; the inn overlooks a public golf course
Smoking? Outdoors only
Visiting pets? No; resident 9-year-old Welsh terrier, Mali; 7-year-old "pound pup," Pookey
Credit cards: Visa, MasterCard, American Express
Rates: $–$$$$
How to get there: From the Long Beach Peninsula area drive north on Highway 101 through South Bend and Raymond to Cosmopolis. From Olympia proceed west on Highway 8 through McCleary and Montesano to the Cosmopolis-Aberdeen area. Entering town on First Street proceed to C Street; turn right and go to Fifth Street. Turn left and drive to the top of the hill; a circular driveway leads to the inn's covered portico.

It may seem odd that a 10,000-square-foot residence built and owned by a bachelor lumber baron was once called a cottage, but, indeed, says Judi, "Mr. Neil Cooney's mansion was originally known as The Spruce Cottage!" Built in 1908 the house, its abundance of gleaming woodwork and its early 1900s Arts & Crafts furniture, has been restored as a sumptuous bed and breakfast. The inn in a woodsy setting with landscaped grounds is adjacent to Mill Creek Park and also overlooks the Highland Public Golf Course. The south lawn is framed by a lovely rose garden surrounded with lacy clematis, lilacs, and peonies. The north lawn is home to a grove of mature rhododendrons. Tall pines edge the property.

The guest rooms are spacious, airy havens in which to relax and rest one's travel weary body. Five rooms have private baths with claw-foot tubs and access to a sun deck that overlooks the golf course and rose garden. Some rooms have TV and all rooms are equipped with ample-sized bathrobes. Outfitted for the most discriminating traveler, the largest room, Cooney Suite, offers an oak four-poster king bed, a fireplace, an antique parlor sofa and chair, and TV/VCR; there's a cozy wicker settee on its enclosed sitting porch. This spacious suite is done in shades of mauve and soft pinks.

Another room overlooking the park and golf course offers a queen sleigh bed, vintage dresser, and antique trunk; this room is done in shades of blue.

In the morning early-bird coffee and tea are generally out by 7:00 A.M. Breakfast served at bachelor Cooney's original wood table of Sitka spruce in the formal dining room may consist of Belgian waffles with fruit topping, *Pannekoeken* with fruit filling, or buttermilk pancakes with sausage, and Judi and Jim's famous Lumber Baron Potatoes.

What's Nearby Cosmopolis

There are easy routes to ocean beaches, oyster farms, cranberry bogs, rain forests, a historic seaport, and a nautical museum as well as numerous antiques shops, farmers' markets, and cafes and restaurants. For further information: Westport/Grayland Visitor's Information, telephone: (800) 345-6223; Tourism Grays Harbor, Telephone: (800) 621-9625; Internet site: www.graysharbor.com. Continuing north on Highway 101 takes travelers into the heart of the Olympic Peninsula including rugged coastal areas, the Pacific Ocean and Puget Sound, the Olympic Mountains, and the primeval old-growth rain forests.

Boreas Bed & Breakfast

607 North Boulevard
P.O. Box 1344
Long Beach, WA 98631
Phone: (360) 642–8069; (888) 642–8069
E-mail: boreas@boreasinn.com
Internet site: www.boreasinn.com

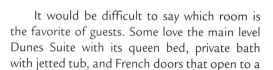

Innkeepers: Susie Goldsmith and Bill Verner
Rooms: 5 rooms with private baths
Extras: Chocolates, brownies; assistance with ordering roses or balloons; sweeping views of Pacific Ocean from 2 rooms on second level; fireplace and baby grand piano in common area
On the grounds: Enclosed gazebo with therapeutic spa; path to beach and ocean; landscaped grounds for strolling or sitting
Smoking? Outdoors only
Visiting pets? No, but seeing-eye dogs are allowed; resident pets in innkeepers quarters—female Rottweiler-chow, Dee-O-Gee; portly tabby, Nikki, and long-haired grey cat, Davidson
Credit cards: Visa, MasterCard, American Express
Rates: $$–$$$
How to get there: From Portland drive northwest on Highway 30 to Astoria taking the Astoria-Megler Bridge to the Washington side and onto Highway 101; proceed north to Long Beach and continue through two traffic lights to Sixth Street. Turn left here for 1 block and turn right onto North Boulevard. From Seattle-Tacoma, drive south on I-5 to Olympia; proceed west on Highway 8 to Montesano and follow signs to Highway 101 South. Proceed south through Raymond and South Bend to Long Beach. The inn is about two hours from Portland and about three hours from Seattle.

"We named the inn for the Greek god of the North Wind," explains Susie, "because he reportedly brings crisp, clear weather!" The restored 1920s-style beach house sits near the sand dunes and sea grasses that edge the Pacific Ocean. The narrow Long Beach peninsula extends north and ends with a small hook near Leadbetter State Park.

It would be difficult to say which room is the favorite of guests. Some love the main level Dunes Suite with its queen bed, private bath with jetted tub, and French doors that open to a private deck within earshot of the surf. In this airy suite a special feature is a mural of North Head lighthouse and dunes painted by a local artist. For other guests two large suites on the second level are favorites because of their sweeping ocean views. Spectacular sunsets often color the western horizon in hues of pink and magenta. Both rooms have vaulted ceilings, one is decorated in blues and whites, the other in neutral tones with lace.

Breakfast is a lively event with guests gathering in the dining area for delectable treats—roasted Washington pears stuffed with pecans, dried cranberries, cinnamon, and brown sugar; peach kuchen baked in custard; scones made with white-chocolate, apricot, and toasted walnut; a three-mushroom fritatta sautéed with sherry; and, fresh roasted organic coffee. For dining out ask about The Ark Restaurant in Willapa Bay and about the innkeepers' favorite local spot, Cheri Walker's 42nd Street Café.

What's Nearby Long Beach

The 28-mile-long peninsula is home to small villages, oyster farms, rhododendron nurseries, sandy beaches, wildlife refuges, and a world-famous Kite Museum. For current information browse the Internet site, www.visitors@funbeach.com, or call the visitors center, (360) 642-2400. Nearby Ocean Park also has an Internet site: www.willapabay.org/~opchamber. The annual Washington State International Kite Festival is held on the peninsula during mid-August.

Other Recommended B&Bs Nearby:

Caswell's On The Bay, an elegant Queen Anne Victorian on three acres at the edge of Willapa Bay; contact innkeepers Bob and Marilyn Caswell, 25204 Sandridge Road, Ocean Park, WA 98640; Telephone: (360) 665-6535. **Scandinavian Gardens Inn Bed & Breakfast,** special pampering with a touch of Scandinavia and a five-course gourmet breakfast; contact innkeepers Rod and Marilyn Dakan, 1610 California Avenue SW, Long Beach, WA 98631; Telephone: (360) 642-8877. **The Shelburne Country Inn,** a restored 1896 coastal inn, offers 15 rooms decorated with antique furniture; the inn's restaurant and pub feature art nouveau stained-glass windows; contact innkeepers David Campiche and Laurie Anderson, 4415 Pacific Way, P.O. Box 250, Seaview, WA 98644; Telephone: (360) 642-2442.

Bear Creek Homestead
Bed & Breakfast

2094 Bear Creek Road
Port Angeles, WA 98363
Phone: (360) 327-3699
E-mail: baysnger@olypen.com
Internet site: www.northolympic.com/bch

Innkeepers: Sherry and Larry Baysinger
Rooms: 2 rooms with private baths; 1 bath has original claw-foot tub and polished plank floors
Extras: Homesteaded in 1891; basket of fruit, muffins, pastries, and cookies in each room on arrival
On the grounds: 16 acres of meadow and surrounded by forested mountains in the heart of the Sol Duc River Valley and near the Olympic rain forests and rugged ocean beaches
Smoking? Outdoors only
Visiting pets? No; resident animals: black-and-white Manx barn cat, Hopper; female blue heeler, Misty; laid-back male Rottweiler, Sam; 2 llamas, Ody and Idy; 2 pygmy goats, Joey and Jimmy; and several horses—Taz, Ribbon, Willy, Tiger Rose, Goldy, and Drifter
Credit cards: Visa, MasterCard
Rates: $$
How to get there: Take Highway 101 from Port Angeles west passing Lake Crescent and continuing toward Forks. At mile 206, located 30 miles west of Port Angeles and 15 miles northeast of Forks, turn onto Bear Creek Road and follow the double yellow lines 2 miles to the end of the road and the inn's driveway.

Those with a sense of adventure and a love of solitude will appreciate this off-the-beaten-path part of the Olympic Peninsula. They will find all types of weather including the blustery rainstorms of late fall and winter as well as the sunny warm days of late spring and summer. Couples and families may visit moss-draped rain forests with walking trails through old growth trees, gaze at frothy waterfalls, or walk a planked trail out to a rugged ocean beach.

In the common area, guests can sink into the overstuffed sofa to enjoy lemon muffins and beverages. Afternoon light streams in from ample-sized windows throughout the renovated house. You might be tempted to play the piano, strum the guitar that stands nearby, or even pluck a tune on the old-fashioned banjo. Those who amble about the pastoral homestead often sight Roosevelt elk and bald eagles.

Two light and spacious guest rooms have queen beds with warm quilts, Northwest art, and cozy sitting places. If you can pull yourself from your warm nest, you'll find the coffee and tea tray waiting downstairs and the breakfast table set with a lovely lace tablecloth, an arrangement of fresh flowers, and country-style dishes. The morning fare might be a salmon omelet with bacon or apple Dutch oven cakes with link sausage, a fruit dish, and home-baked yeast rolls or muffins or biscuits.

What's Nearby

Take Highway 112 out to Clallam Bay, Sekiu, and Neah Bay. Cape Flattery, a few miles from Neah Bay, provides nearly 360-degree views of the ocean and rugged cliffs as well as seabirds, often whales, and the coast of British Columbia. The Makah Cultural and Research Center's museum, on Bayview Avenue in Neah Bay, offers Native American and natural history of the region; call (360) 645-2711 for hours and information about archaeological digs. A nearby detour takes travelers to Lake Ozette and to a planked trail toward rugged beaches. The Hoh Rain Forest offers trail loops and the Forks Timber Museum is worth a visit; (360) 374-9663. The Forks Web site, www.northolympic.com/forks, can provide helpful information and links to Olympic National Park sites. Call the Forks Visitor's Center at (800) 443-6757 for maps, and tide tables. Highway 101 from Forks leads to Kalaloch, Quinault and Lake Quinault, Humptulips and on to the Grays Harbor, Hoquiam, Aberdeen, and Cosmopolis regions of southeastern Washington. Also see What's Nearby Port Angeles on page 193.

Other Recommended B&Bs Nearby

At **Miller Tree Inn,** new innkeepers Susan and Bill Brager run the large 1914 farmhouse; contact them at 654 East Division Street, Forks, OR 98331; Telephone: (360) 374-6806. At **Misty Valley Inn Bed & Breakfast,** Rachel and Jim Bennett offer restful pastoral views and marvelous gourmet breakfasts just off Highway 101 at mile marker 195; contact them at RR1, Box 5407, Forks, WA 98331; Telephone: (360) 374-9389.

Domaine Madeleine
Bed & Breakfast

146 Wildflower Lane
Port Angeles, WA 98362
Phone: (360) 457-4174
E-mail: romance@domainemadeleine.com
Internet site: www.domainemadeleine.com

It would be difficult to imagine a more secluded and romantic setting with wide views of the Strait of Juan De Fuca, the Canadian Cascades, and Victoria, British Columbia, at the tip of Vancouver Island. "At night the lights of Victoria sparkle in the distance like a diamond necklace," says Madeleine. Her voice hints of a French accent and indeed the innkeeper speaks not only French but also Spanish and Farsi.

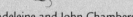

Innkeepers: Madeleine and John Chambers
Rooms: 5 rooms including a separate cottage, all with fireplaces, private baths and whirlpool tubs for two; 3 rooms have refrigerators, coffee makers, and microwave ovens; all the beds have feather beds atop firm mattresses
Extras: Five-course gourmet breakfasts; romantic and secluded; his-and-hers designer bath robes; telephones, TV/VCRs and stereos with selection of romantic CDs; harpsichord; outdoor games such as croquet, boules, badminton, volleyball, and horseshoes
On the grounds: Views of Strait of Juan De Fuca and lights of Victoria, B.C.; nature trails nearby; rose and clematis covered arches in garden area; visiting deer and visiting bird species
Smoking? Outdoors only
Visiting pets? No; pet boarding facilities are located nearby
Credit cards: Visa, MasterCard, American Express, Discover
Rates: $$$–$$$$
How to get there: Continue from Sequim 3 miles west on Highway 101 toward Port Angeles; at Carlsborg Road (flashing yellow light) turn right and proceed 1⅛ miles to Old Olympic Highway. Turn left here and proceed for 3⁷⁄₁₀ miles to Matson Street; turn right and continue for ⅞ mile to Finn Hall. Turn left here and continue 1 mile to the inn's sign at Wildflower Lane.

Guests can disappear into several lovely rooms. One occupies the entire top floor of the main house and has its own 30-foot balcony.

The sumptuous queen bed faces the wide expanse of windows. Another room, on the garden level, has a fireplace, queen bed, sitting area, and glass door out to the yard. Both of these rooms have views across the water to distant Vancouver Island. The equally romantic cottage is light and airy and offers cozy sitting and sleeping spaces and a whirlpool tub for two. Guests who choose the Renoir Room in the main house also have private use in the evening of the large common room with its fireplace and window views of the strait.

Morning brings an unforgettable *petit déjeuner* in the dining area next to the kitchen, a repast that includes favorites from Madeleine's eclectic European menus. Freshly brewed rich coffee and teas, artistic arrays of fruit, and fresh-baked petite baguettes and croissants are served with an assortment of exotic cheeses and jams for the first courses. Entrees may include such fare as baked salmon Florentine with artichoke hearts; chicken crepes accompanied by fresh asparagus; or spanakopita complemented by roasted tomatoes stuffed with turkey sausage and rice. A light dessert completes the meal. For guests who need to depart early for the ferry to Victoria, a bountiful "breakfast on the go" can be provided. You also may arrange to have breakfast served in your guest room.

What's Nearby

Ask the innkeepers about performances at the Port Angeles Symphony and Port Angeles Light Opera Company; theater and performances are also offered at Peninsula College and at the Port Angeles High School. The forty-five-minute drive up to 5,200-foot Hurricane Ridge is popular for hiking, bird watching, alpine wildflower viewing, picnicking and, during the winter months, cross-country skiing and guided snowshoeing treks. For current information and maps including applicable fees, call the Olympic National Park headquarters in Port Angeles, (360) 452-0330. The Port Angeles Museum offers a collection of early logging memorabilia. Also see What's Nearby Sequim on page 203 and What's Nearby Port Angeles on page 193.

Tudor Inn Bed & Breakfast

1108 South Oak Street
Port Angeles, WA 98362
Phone: (360) 452-3138
E-mail: info@tudorinn.com
Internet site: www.tudorinn.com

Innkeeper: Jane Glass
Rooms: 5 rooms with private baths, 1 room offers a fireplace and private balcony
Extras: Tea and freshly baked cookies served each afternoon; within walking distance of downtown Port Angeles shops, cafes, waterfront, and ferry dock
On the grounds: Landscaped rear grounds and gazebo
Smoking? Outdoors only
Visiting pets? No; resident chinchilla Persian cat, Stanley
Credit cards: Visa, MasterCard, American Express, Discover
Rates: $$–$$$
How to get there: From Sequim via Highway 101, turn left in Port Angeles onto Lincoln Street and proceed to Eleventh Street. Turn right on Eleventh for 2 blocks to Oak Street; the inn is located at the corner of Eleventh and Oak streets. Off-street parking is available at the rear of the inn.

As guests enter the 1910 English Tudor house and walk into the common area, they see the handsome fireplace with its raised hearth, dark polished furniture, and a restored 1856 John Broadwood grand piano; a fringed paisley cloth may be draped over its side and the floor lamp turned low. There may be fresh flowers in a crystal vase sitting next to a silver tea set on the glass-and-wood coffee table. Guests may also see Stanley, the resident silver Persian cat, who often reclines near the sumptuous rose velvet sofa. His imperious look seems to imply, "You may enjoy this lovely room with me and you may pet me, too, if you're quite careful not to muss my silky hair." Jane, a seasoned innkeeper for more than fifteen years at her home here in Port Angeles, serves tea and freshly baked cookies to guests between 3:00 and 6:00 P.M. Stanley often joins the festivities.

The five guest rooms are richly appointed with private baths and cozy sitting areas. One of the most sumptuous rooms, located on the second floor, has a fireplace and its own balcony. Softly muted wallpapers evoke images of an English countryside or of an English garden. The comfortable double or queen beds may have carved headboards and footboards, soft down comforters encased in duvets, and an ample supply of soft pillows. Antique reading lamps grace the bedsides on small antique tables. There may be stained-glass accents in your room as well. Several rooms overlook the rear garden and gazebo.

Guests are invited to use the main common area or the small intimate library with its rock fireplace. A wood fire often crackles cheerfully here on cold evenings. A TV/VCR is also available. In the morning breakfast is served in the formal dining room with guests sitting together at Jane's long table that seats ten. Fresh fruit or a fruit compote may begin the meal followed by buttermilk waffles or blueberry pancakes and berry syrup along with bacon or sausage. On special weekends Jane prepares caramel-apple baked French toast or eggs Florentine.

What's Nearby Port Angeles

Port Angeles is the main metropolitan area for the northern Olympic Peninsula and also the terminus for ferry service to and from this section of the peninsula to Victoria, British Columbia. Two ferries make several crossings each day; check current information via the Internet at www.northolympic.com/coho, and also at the Port Angeles Visitors Information Center, 121 Railroad Avenue, Port Angeles, WA 98362; Telephone: (360) 452-2363. The Olympic National Park headquarters is located here as well; its Internet site, www.nps.gov/olym, offers helpful information and links to the Olympic National Forest and the Olympic Park Institute. For current information, maps, and information about fees within sections of the national park, call (360) 452-0330. A tour of the U.S. Coast Guard cutter *Active* can be arranged when the ship is in port; Telephone: (360) 452-2342. Visitors can climb the observation tower at the end of the pier or, even better, stroll the Waterfront Trail that extends about 1 mile east of the pier. Also see What's Nearby Sequim on page 203.

Other Recommended B&B Nearby

BJ's Garden Gate Bed & Breakfast, a newly constructed Victorian-style inn with water views, gardens, and French-style furnishings; contact innkeepers BJ and Frank Paton at 397 Monterra Drive, Port Angeles, WA 98362; Telephone: (360) 452-2322.

Ann Starrett Mansion
Victorian Bed & Breakfast Inn

744 Clay Street
Port Townsend, WA 98368
Phone: (360) 385-3205; (800) 321-0644
Internet site: www.olympus.net/starrett

Innkeepers: Edel and Bob Sokol
Rooms: 11 rooms with private baths
Extras: Historic Victorian architecture with 3-story octagonal entry; spiral staircase to second floor; renovated frescoes in tower cupola and on ceilings in several of the common rooms
On the grounds: Separate cottage next door offers two large suites; children are welcome in the cottage suites
Smoking? Outdoors only
Visiting pets? No; no resident pets
Credit cards: Visa, MasterCard, American Express, Discover
Rates: $$-$$$$; inquire about winter and summer rates
How to get there: From downtown Port Townsend take Kearney Street uphill to Lawrence Street; turn right and proceed to Adams Street; turn right 1 block to Clay Street. The inn is located at the corner of Adams and Clay streets.

In this historic seaport town many of its ostentatious mansions were built in the late 1800s by sea captains, prominent businessmen, and shipping magnates. Edel relates that in 1889 George Starrett, a wealthy contractor, built this ornate Victorian mansion for his bride, Ann. Inside the cupola that caps the octagonal three-story entry section, George is reported to have painted the frescoes himself for his bride that depicted the Four Seasons and the Four Virtues. Walk up the free-hung spiral staircase to the tower to inspect these frescoes; they were painstakingly restored by Edel and Bob in the mid-1980s. "Actually the nymph in the Winter panel is reported to have caused quite a flurry during Victorian days," says Edel. "This chubby little character was apparently too scantily dressed for some of the more conservative town matrons!"

The mansion is a marvel of Victorian design and decor, including elaborate moldings that feature carved lions, doves, and ferns. Literally every surface inside and outside the mansion was carefully repaired, restored, repainted, rewallpapered, and authentically redecorated under the direction of Edel and Bob Sokol. For their efforts the mansion won an honorable mention in the National Trust for Historic Preservation's 1996 Great American Home Awards in the special category of bed and breakfast.

Lavishly appointed guest rooms on the top floor, second floor, and carriage-house level welcome travelers. You might nest in a two-room suite under the gables on the top floor where you can see oceangoing ships, the mountains, the sparkling waters of Admiralty Inlet, and colorful sunrises. This room offers a king bed and a round soaking tub for two. The private bath has a hand-held shower. In another suite on the second floor, a magnificent canopy double bed looks as though it could have been on the set of a Valentino or Clark Gable movie. In its lovely sitting alcove a Victorian fainting couch offers a cozy reclining spot. Another suite has an antique tin soaking tub painted with cherubs. On the garden level the Carriage Room offers 1920s antiques, a double sleigh bed, and the original brick walls and authentic carriage doors adorned with antique horse-and-carriage tack and memorabilia.

Breakfast is served in the formal dining room on the main level, the antique dining table placed beneath one of the restored frescoed ceilings. Guests can enjoy such treats as German apple griddle cakes, New Orleans French Quarter French toast stuffed with cream and strawberries, freshly baked coffeecakes, and the inn's special granola along with steaming hot coffee and teas.

What's Nearby Port Townsend

Once a major port for sailing vessels coming to and from the northwest, the city retains its nautical and seafaring flavor, particularly the old downtown area that extends along the waterfront. Visitors enjoy its many shops, boutiques, galleries, cafes, delis, and fine restaurants. Numerous music festivals are offered year round as are other events such as the Wooden Boat Festival, the Tour of Victorian Homes, and the Victorian Festival. Find maps and current information at the Port Townsend Visitor's Center, 2437 Sims Way, Port Townsend, WA 98368; Telephone: (360) 385-2722 or (888) 365-6978; E-mail: ptchambr@olympus.net; Internet site: www.olympus.net/ptchambr. For current information for Washington State Ferries: (206) 464-6400 or (888) 808-7977 in Washington only; Internet site: www.wsdot.wa.gov/ferries.

The James House

1238 Washington Street
Port Townsend, WA 98368
Phone: (360) 385-1238; (800) 385-1238
E-mail: jameshouse@olypmus.net
Internet site: www.jameshouse.com

Innkeepers: Owner: Carol McGough; Innkeeper: J. R. Terry
Rooms: 13 rooms, 11 with private baths; 1 wheelchair accessible room with private bath; separate Gardener's Cottage has private garden patio
Extras: Fine example of Queen Anne Victorian architecture and original furnishings
On the grounds: Victorian-style gardens, fruit trees; expansive views of Puget Sound, Port Townsend Bay, Olympic Mountains, and Cascades
Smoking? Outdoors only
Visiting pets? No; no resident pets
Credit cards: Visa, MasterCard, American Express
Rates: $-$$$$
How to get there: From downtown Seattle take Bainbridge Island Ferry, then Highway 305 to Poulsbo and Highway 3 to the Hood Canal Bridge; follow Highway 104 and signs to Port Townsend; driving time from Bainbridge is approximately one hour. From points south including Portland and Olympia, take Highway 101 east from Olympia proceeding north to the intersection of Highway 20 at Discovery Bay. Proceed northeast on Highway 20 to Port Townsend. The area can also be reached via the Keystone Ferry from central Whidbey Island. The inn is on the bluff above the downtown area and overlooks the salty waters of Admiralty Inlet.

The James House has the distinction of being one of the first bed-and-breakfast inns to open its doors to travelers in the Pacific Northwest in the early 1980s. At that time the house was owned by Lowell and Barbara Bogart, the couple who initiated the restoration of the fine Queen Anne Victorian on the bluff, which was built in 1889. I first visited the inn in the early 1980s and enjoyed seeing the collection of historic memorabilia from the original owner's family that the Bogarts had displayed in a glass-fronted cabinet in the downstairs parlor. Guests marvel at the finely crafted woodwork through-out the three floors and thirteen guest rooms. It makes one want to know more about Francis W. James, who had the vision to build such a fine home.

One of the most stunning features is the grand staircase to the second and top floors, with its elegant newel posts, spindles, and ban-isters. It was fashioned of native wild cherry and the reddish tones of the polished wood would hardly give one a sense of the passing of so many years since its construction. On the second floor, the Master/Bridal Suite offers a wood-burning fireplace, a sitting room, queen antique bed, private balcony, and views of the bay and mountains. Throughout all the beautifully deco-rated rooms, the rich fabrics, warm carpets, handsome wallpapers, polished dark wood-work, and antique furniture offer a decidedly Victorian ambience.

A full breakfast is served on the main floor between 8:00 and 9:30 A.M. Guests are encour-aged to dine at their leisure on dishes of fresh fruit, freshly baked scones, delicious hot break-fast entrees, and coffee, tea, and juices.

What's Nearby

See What's Nearby Port Townsend on page 195.

Other Recommended B&Bs Nearby

The Commander's House Bed & Breakfast, a restored commander's house at the old Coast Guard station near the historic downtown area; contact innkeepers Pat and Ray Ferschke at 400 Hudson Street, Port Townsend, WA 98368; (360) 385-1778. **Lizzie's Victorian Bed & Breakfast,** an historic Italianate inn; contact the innkeepers at 731 Pierce Street, Port Townsend, WA 98368; (360) 385-4168. **Nantucket Manor,** an elegant beachside retreat in nearby Port Ludlow; contact innkeepers Peggy and Peter Conrardy, 941 Shine Road, Port Ludlow, WA 98365; (360) 437-2676. **Old Consulate Inn,** located on the bluff, offers lavish Victorian ambience and water views in the historic F. W. Hastings House; contact the innkeepers Rob and Joanna Jackson at 313 Walker Street, Port Townsend, WA 98368; (360) 385-6753. **Quimper Inn,** an 1886 sumptuous Victorian; 1306 Franklin Street, Port Townsend, WA 98368; (360) 385-1060.

Ravenscroft Inn
Bed & Breakfast

533 Quincy Street
Port Townsend, WA 98368
Phone: (360) 385-2784; (800) 782-2691
E-mail: ravenscroft@olympus.net
Internet site: www.olympus.net/ravenscroft

Innkeeper: Leah Hammer
Rooms: 8 rooms with private baths; 3 rooms have fireplaces
Extras: Coffee and refreshments on arrival; evening refreshments
On the grounds: Views to the south of Port Townsend Bay, Admiralty Inlet, and the Cascade Mountains
Smoking? Outdoors only
Visiting pets? No; no resident pets
Credit cards: Visa, MasterCard, American Express, Discover
Rates: $-$$$$
How to get there: Go through Port Townsend on Water Street; turn left onto Monroe Street, then turn left onto Clay Street, and left onto Quincey Street and immediately right into the inn's driveway.

Located high on a bluff overlooking old town, Port Townsend Bay, and Admiralty Inlet, the Colonial-style inn also commands views of the Cascade Mountains—they rise to the east and south. Guests will often see the foothills and snowy peaks like Mount Baker and Mount Rainier reflected on the shimmering water. Guests can watch ferries transporting scores of travelers and automobiles back and forth from nearby Whidbey Island as well as sailboats and motorboats of all sizes gliding past. "There is nearly always something to see from our windows," smiles Leah. "It's a veritable feast for the eyes and senses!" Couples will often congregate on the wide verandahs that extend across the front of the inn to get acquainted and to peer out at the water. The colorful scene is often punctuated with the friendly cries of seagulls and whiffs of fresh salt air as the twice-daily tides come in and then recede back toward the

Strait of Juan De Fuca and the Pacific.

The inn's Great Room, with its fireplace and comfortable sofa, is also a place where guests enjoy meeting to share a cup of brew and the day's adventures. A grand piano sits nearby. Soft light streams in from the corner windows and warms the soft tweed carpet of teal, rose, green, and cream. Small glass-topped tables, with teal blue ladderback chairs, are dressed in muted floor-length paisley tablecloths and teal blue or white table toppers. Breakfast is served here in the morning. The Quiet Library, adjacent to the Great Room, offers TV/VCR, selection of videos, and a good supply of books and magazines. Leah, an expert in glass, particularly crystal and fine china, enjoys sharing "glass talk" with interested guests. "My three R's, however," says Leah, "are for guests to have here a place of refuge, romance, and relaxation."

The guest rooms offer supremely comfortable beds, soft bed linens, great pillows, cozy sitting areas, and private baths equipped with baskets of amenities. Your guest room might offer a cozy window alcove, a window seat for two, a fireplace, a soaking tub for one or for two, French doors to the second-level veranda, a king or queen bed—even a four-poster—and good reading lamps. One room offers garden wicker. The two most sumptuous suites are Admiralty Suite and Mount Rainier Suite.

Morning brings luscious aromas wafting from Leah's kitchen—freshly brewed coffee and the amenable sounds of gourmet breakfast preparations. Guests may select their breakfast time. Hot entrees might include au gratin zucchini-mushroom-rice with feta cheese crust and topped with Gruyère along with sun-dried tomato and chicken sausage. Another entree might include baked apples and puff pastry with artichoke hearts, sun-dried tomatoes, and capers—Leah notes that many travelers are looking for vegetarian breakfast options.

What's Nearby

There's live local theater at the Key City Players, cabaret music in numerous clubs and restaurants, and chamber and classical music at the Centrum Center for Performing Arts. The Victorian Festival in March each year offers workshops that showcase restoration, renovation, crafts, hobbies, dances, and design of the Victorian period. The festival also includes gala festivities such as a costume ball, a Victorian fashion show, band concerts, Victorian inn tours and teas, wine tasting and lectures, garden demonstrations, bars and bordellos tour, and maritime heritage ship tours and lectures. Also see What's Nearby Port Townsend on page 195.

Dungeness Panorama
Bed & Breakfast

630 Marine Drive
Sequim, WA 98382
Phone: (360) 683–4503
E-mail: pmpanorama@webtv.com
Internet site:
www.northolympic.com/panorama

Innkeepers: Patricia and John Merritte; Paulette and Roger Ferrari
Rooms: 2 suites separate from the main house, each with private bath, outside decks
Extras: One suite has a gas fireplace and small kitchenette with refrigerator and microwave; second suite has eating area; both have coffee makers, TV (no cable access)
On the grounds: Views of Strait of Juan De Fuca to north and of Olympic Mountains to south; large sunken greenhouse with patio and outdoor furniture; rose garden
Smoking? Outdoors only
Visiting pets? No; no resident pets
Credit cards: None; personal checks accepted
Rates: $$
How to get there: From Highway 101 at Sequim (pronounced "skwim") turn right onto Sequim Avenue and proceed north onto Sequim-Dungeness Way. At the fork when this road angles to the right, stay to the left and continue on East Anderson Road; immediately after crossing the Dungeness River turn right onto Clark Road and then turn left onto Marine Drive to second house from the corner.

The distinctive character of this bed and breakfast by the sea is defined both by France and by the French-speaking family of innkeepers. Patricia Merritte and her husband, John, operate the inn along with assistance from Patricia's parents, Paulette and Roger Ferrari. Originally from Paris, the Ferraris offer French accents as well as interesting extras from Roger's talent as a wood-carver and furniture-maker to Paulette's skill in the kitchen. Roger worked for years in southern California designing and carving furniture for well-known Hollywood personalities.

Roger created the elegant furniture for the main house and two spacious guest suites. One suite is done in shades of green and white; dark woods were chosen for the second suite. In the main house where guests are invited for a French country-style breakfast, Roger designed and built the dining room table, the buffet, and the upholstered chairs of Hungarian walnut. The chair backs in particular show his detailed carving work. A short distance from the wide windows and dining area, the kitchen section is dominated by a circular breakfast table fashioned of red tiles. The table's raised center is an indoor barbecue with an antique brass tent-warmer from Arabia as a covering.

The usual breakfast hour is 9:00 A.M. with room service available by prior arrangement. Breakfast prepared by Paulette and Patricia begins with fruit juice, French roast coffee, teas, and hot chocolate. The second course is often crepes filled with smoked salmon or shrimp, roast turkey, or spinach with cheese. This is followed with homemade breakfast cake surrounded by fresh fruit and fruit sauce along with croissant or brioche. Vegetarian dishes are also available.

Guests enjoy the sunken living room with its brick fireplace that soars 24 feet to the ceiling and Roger's hand-crafted coffee table of wormy chestnut. Ten steps down from the living room, one enters the library, one of its walls entirely filled with bookcases. Two steps down from this guests walk into a large greenhouse and patio filled with lush ornamentals, vegetables, and hanging baskets of flowers. Guests are encouraged to practice their French conversational phrases, too, if they wish.

What's Nearby

For lunch and evening dining ask about Khu Larb Thai Restaurant, The Bella Italia, The Three Crabs, and, in nearby Port Angeles, C'est Si Bon, Bella Italia, Café Garden, and Destiny Seafood & Grill. Garden lovers can discover nearby Cedarbrook Herb Farm and Purple Haze Lavender Farm. Wine lovers can ask directions to nearby Olympic Cellars Winery. There are many historic museums in the area as well. Also see What's Nearby Sequim on page 203.

Other Recommended B&Bs Nearby

Groveland Cottage B&B, located in the historic country market with its completely restored and renovated residence, five rooms, three with private baths; contact owner Simone Nichols 4861 Sequim-Dungeness Way, Sequim, WA 98382; Telephone: (360) 683-3565. **Toad Hall English B&B,** a charming English-style inn; contact innkeepers Linda and Bruce Clark at 12 Jessica Lane, Sequim, WA 98382; Telephone: (360) 681-2534.

Greywolf Inn
Bed & Breakfast

395 Keeler Road
Sequim, WA 98382
Phone: (360) 683-5889; (800) 914-WOLF
E-mail: info@greywolfinn.com
Internet site: www.greywolfinn.com

"We're transplants from North Carolina," says Peggy. "We bring a sense of southern hospitality to our inn here at the top of the Olympic Peninsula." If you travel a little farther north, you can look across the wide Strait of Juan De Fuca and catch glimpses of both the San Juan Islands and of Victoria, British Columbia, at the tip of Vancouver Island. The inn is located on five pastoral acres just south of the Dungeness Spit, a wildlife refuge and longest natural sand spit in the U.S.

Innkeepers: Peggy and Bill Melang
Rooms: 5 rooms with private baths
Extras: Guest rooms have TVs, clock/radios, designer robes, custom embroidered towels and linens, and individually wrapped toiletries; weather permitting, bistro-style breakfast served on outdoor deck
On the grounds: Japanese shoji-style enclosed hot tub and bathhouse on terrace; gazebo and walking paths on the naturally landscaped grounds
Smoking? Outdoors only
Visiting pets? Restrictions, inquire; two friendly outside dogs who enjoy accompanying guests on walks—female black lab, Tar Baby, and male yellow lab, Fred
Credit cards: Visa, MasterCard, American Express, Discover
Rates: $-$$$
How to get there: Follow Highway 101 north and west from Port Townsend and Discovery Bay around the top of the Olympic Peninsula and toward Blyn and Sequim. A short distance west of Sequim Bay State Park and just beyond Happy Valley Road, turn right onto Keeler Road proceeding about ½ mile north to the inn's driveways—the first and second drives on the left.

In addition to the inn's comfortable gathering room—centered around a huge fireplace with the couple's massive collection of reading material and books and the soft music that wafts throughout the inn—perhaps the most memorable features here are the fabulous beds in the guest rooms. Each room is decorated in a theme from around the world. One room has a mahogany four-poster queen bed with a comforter in navy and white—an elegant though understated Oriental design is appliqued and stitched in its center; a small stuffed wolf rests between the two pillows. A second room offers a decidedly Bavarian influence with a massive feather bed—the four tall supporting pine beams at each corner support a lightly carved flat upper canopy. On the richly colored spread another friendly stuffed wolf greets visitors. In a third room another large bed is supported by four wood corner posts attached to a canopy; fabric curtains at each corner can be drawn to entirely enclose the bed and create an intimate sleeping bower. A small stuffed wolf rests on the antique quilt done in shades of cream, russet, gold, and dusty blue.

One reason to leave these sumptuous, havens would be a trek to the outdoor hot tub—this is enclosed in a sky-lighted Japanese shoji bathhouse on the terrace. A soothing and intimate environment is thoughtfully provided for guests. Another reason to depart one's room would be to attend to the Olympian breakfast served in the country French-style dining area with its wide windows that allow pastoral views of pond and pasture. A charming garden mural graces one wall area. Guests dine on fresh fruit in season, warm muffins, juice, and hot beverages followed by a hot entree such as spicy sausage quiche, eggs Benedict, or orange French toast with Grand Marnier sauce. The delicious meal concludes with iced sorbet or a stick of chocolate to stir in one's final cup of coffee.

What's Nearby Sequim

The Dungeness Scenic Loop leads through a lush rural area, past old barns, fences entwined with wild roses and native blackberries, and out to closer views of the Olympic Mountains, the Canadian Cascades, and along the shoreline of the Strait of Juan De Fuca. At the Dungeness National Wildlife Refuge visitors can hike part way or out to the end of the 6-mile sand spit often seeing deer, sea lions, otters, numerous shore birds, and even whales. For maps, tide tables, and current regulations, contact the wildlife refuge headquarters in Port Angeles; Telephone: (360) 457-8451. For further information about the area contact the Sequim-Dungeness Visitor's Information Center, 1192 East Washington Street, Sequim, WA 98382; Telephone: (360) 683-6197; Internet site: www.cityofsequim.com (this Web site also contains good links to the Olympic Peninsula region).

Vintage Inn Bed & Breakfast

310 West Eleventh Street
Vancouver, WA 98660
Phone: (360) 693-6635; (888) 693-6935
E-mail: info@vintage-inn.com
Internet site: www.vintage-inn.com

Innkeepers: Mike and Doris Hale
Rooms: 4 rooms, no private baths; 1 ½ baths with shower and claw-foot tub serve all rooms; 1 room overlooks herb and flower garden
Extras: Fresh flowers, books and magazines in guest rooms; chocolates at the bedside; bathrobes; wake-up beverages outside room doors; 1 room has oak-mantle fireplace
On the grounds: Herb and perennial garden
Smoking? Outdoors only
Visiting pets? No; no resident pets
Credit cards: Visa, MasterCard
Rates: $$
How to get there: From I-5 driving north from Portland across the Columbia River and into Vancouver, take exit 1-C, Mill Plain. Turn west onto Fifteenth Street and proceed to Columbia Street; turn left and proceed 4 blocks turning right onto Eleventh Street.

The house, constructed in 1903, is a particularly fine example of a Craftsman residence with its deep front porch supported by four columns. Once inside visitors marvel at the stunning fireplaces, the gleaming woodwork, softly tinted stained-glass windows, the oak pocket doors, and the polygonal window bays, all features that were influenced by the Colonial Revival architecture of the early 1900s. "We found all sorts of treasures during the restoration process," explains Doris with a smile. "Books, artwork, pieces of antique furniture, and even a bottle of Lydia E. Pinkham's Vegetable Compound!" This liquid was billed in the 1930s as a cure-all for a number of ailments.

Guests enjoy poking into the large butler's pantry next to the kitchen to see the vintage sign that reads VANCOUVER CAB CO., PHONE 8. They learn from the Hales that one of the home's former owners operated a stagecoach business, which eventually became the cab company. Doris also will show guests the "whisper tube," a vintage intercom device that once allowed communication from the master bedroom to the kitchen. Guests can use two inviting parlors, one a sitting-reading-visiting parlor. Its fireplace and distinctive mantel is fashioned of European brick. The other parlor has a TV and VCR, selection of videos, a piano, and a selection of helpful travel literature. A sun room adjacent the dining room also offers cozy sitting places.

Four spacious guest rooms are tastefully furnished with period antiques and queen beds. One room has an antique fainting couch covered in deep royal-blue velvet. The bed features handsome head and footboards with carved accents that match those on the antique scroll-shaped dresser and mirror. The windows are outfitted with ceiling-to-floor lace curtains with a vertical design that complements a similar design in the soft taupe and ivory wallpaper. Another room has a 1930s ambience with deep red carpeting, brass bed, softly hued quilt, and striped wallpaper with a handsome border at the top. Violins, old opera programs, and portraits of composers are displayed. The two polygonal window bays are draped in layers of lace and sheer.

Breakfast is an elegant affair served between 7:00 and 10:00 A.M. Doris uses her antique china, gold flatware, crystal goblets, and cloth napkins arranged on a lace tablecloth. Guests often find a cheery fire burning in the dining room fireplace. The delicious meal may consist of homemade muffins and sweet breads along with a cheese blintz soufflé, special quiche with crispy bacon, or almond-crusted French toast with fresh strawberries. "If we have just a wedding couple staying overnight," says Doris, "I like to add lighted candles on the table."

What's Nearby Vancouver

Visit historical attractions including the Art Deco Kiggins Movie Theater, as well as the Fort Vancouver National Historic Site, Officer's Row, and Pearson Air Museum. At Fort Vancouver, established by the British in 1825, visitors enjoy living history and a walk through the British garden restored in early 1990. Restaurants nearby include Café Augustinos, Thai Orchid, Hidden House, and Sheldon's Café in the historic Grant House on Officer's Row; The Chart House and Who Song & Larry's Mexican Cantina, are located near the Waterfront Trail, a 3½-mile handicap accessible paved walkway along the river. History buffs can arrange a visit to the Clark County Historical Museum, 1511 Main Street, Vancouver, WA 98660; Telephone: (360) 695-4681. The Greater Vancouver Visitors Information Center is located at 404 East Fifteenth Street, Suite 11, Vancouver, WA 98663; Telephone: (360) 694-2588.

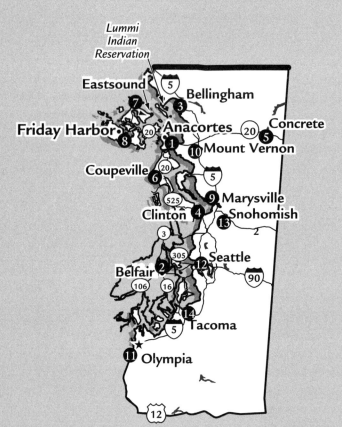

Lummi
Indian
Reservation

Eastsound

Bellingham

Friday Harbor

Anacortes

Concrete

Coupeville

Mount Vernon

Clinton

Marysville

Snohomish

Belfair

Seattle

Tacoma

Olympia

N

AK

BC

WA

OR

Seattle Environs, Kitsap Peninsula, Whidbey Island, North Coast, and San Juan Islands

Numbers on map refer to towns numbered below.

Channel House
Bed & Breakfast

2902 Oakes Street
Anacortes, WA 98221
Phone: (360) 293–9382; (800) 238–4353
E-mail: beds@sos.net
Internet site: www.channel-house.com

Innkeepers: Dennis and Patricia McIntyre
Rooms: 4 rooms with private baths in the main house; 2 rooms in Rose Cottage with fireplaces and whirlpool tubs
Extras: Late afternoon coffee, tea, and Pat's Famous Oatmeal Cookies; morning coffee basket available for guests having late breakfast; Ferry Box of breakfast treats for guests who need to leave for 7:30 A.M. ferry sailing
On the grounds: Hot tub on rear deck; views of Guemes Channel and of Guemes, Cypress, Decatur, and Blakely islands
Smoking? Outdoors only
Visiting pets? No; no resident pets
Credit cards: Visa, MasterCard, American Express, Discover
Rates: $–$$
How to get there: Via Highway 20 from Whidbey Island cross the Deception Pass Bridge and proceed to Anacortes on Fidalgo Island, a distance of approximately 15 miles. From Seattle take I-5 north to Mount Vernon and turn west onto Highway 536; continue on Highway 20 to Anacortes, a total distance of approximately 75 miles. Bear to the right onto Commercial Avenue, the main business street, and turn left at traffic signal (near Chevron station) onto Twelfth Street; this becomes Oakes Avenue. The inn is at the corner of Oakes and Dakota streets, on the right.

After checking in road-weary guests are drawn to comfortable wingback chairs and cozy sofa in the fireplace common area. Afternoon light brightens the stained glass above the French doors that lead to a solarium; from here views west toward the ferry landing and to nearby Guemes Island are noted. Relaxing with steaming vanilla-nut decaf coffee and one of Pat's Famous Oatmeal Cookies, guests brighten considerably and begin discussing dinner options. "Anacortes is blessed with many fine restaurants," says Pat with a smile. SalmonRun Restaurant offers seafood as does Slocum's Restaurant at nearby Skyline Marina. The innkeepers often suggest La Petite, an intimate European-style restaurant located downtown. On warm evenings outdoor dining with live entertainment at Compass Rose might appeal.

Later, a soothing soak in the outdoor hot tub under the stars and with views of Guemes Channel may precede climbing into bed beneath a warm comforter. The comfortable guest room may come with a four-poster queen bed with hand-knotted canopy or a king bed piled high with pillows. In the cottage is a classic four-poster queen bed as well as French doors that open to views of the water and the nearest islands. Guest rooms in the main house come with an antique oval soaking tub with shower, a Victorian fainting couch, a claw-foot soaking tub and shower, a wood-burning fireplace, a cozy window seat, or a garden view.

Morning brings a delicious breakfast served at the community table in the dining room. On chilly mornings a fire in the fireplace glows cheerfully. Dennis may prepare French toast stuffed with cream cheese, crushed pineapple, and pecans and serve it with warm apricot syrup. Another morning may bring old-fashioned oatmeal-sour cream pancakes served with homemade buttermilk-butter-vanilla syrup.

What's Nearby Anacortes

Explore Anacortes on Fidalgo Island before boarding the ferries for the other islands—visit antiques shops, galleries, boutiques, vintage hardware stores, bookstores, cafes, espresso shops, and delis. Anacortes is one of the primary gateways to the San Juan Islands; the ferry terminal is busiest during peak vacation times and on weekends—have a full tank of gas, expect to wait in line, and be prepared to arrive at the ferry dock from one to two hours ahead of scheduled departure times (cash, in-state checks, and travelers checks are accepted as payment; no credit cards are accepted at the toll booths). Travelers are advised to always have prearranged accommodations for overnight stays on the islands. Those continuing on one of the international ferry runs to Vancouver Island in British Columbia, Canada, must have reservations and carry appropriate U.S. identification for going through Customs. To reserve space call Washington State Ferries, call (206) 464–6400 at least forty-eight hours in advance of desired sailing date to Canada; credit cards are accepted for these reservations. Maps and current information about all ferry schedules can be obtained from Washington State Ferries and from the Anacortes Visitors Information Center; Telephone: (360) 293–3832; Internet site: www.anacortes.org.

The Inn at Burg's Landing

8808 Villa Beach Road
Anderson Island, WA 98303
Phone: (253) 884–9185; (800) 431–5622
E-mail: innatburgslanding@mailexcite.com
Internet site:
www.angelfire.com/biz/InnatBurgsLanding

Innkeepers: Ken and Annie Burg
Rooms: 4 rooms, 2 with private bath, 2 with shared bath
Extras: Large log home on accessible island; family friendly inn
On the grounds: View of ferry landing and south Puget Sound, flower and vegetable gardens, views of Cascade Mountains
Smoking? Outdoors only
Visiting pets? No; resident German shepherd, Buddy
Credit cards: Visa, MasterCard
Rates: $–$$
How to get there: From I–5 between Olympia and Tacoma take exit 119 Dupont/Steilacoom, then follow Steilacoom Road north to Steilacoom and board the Pierce County ferry to Anderson Island; the ferry generally leaves the mainland on the hour. The inn is located just east of the ferry landing on the island—look for the pair of tall cedars that flank the driveway.

The large log inn is located on 9-mile-square Anderson Island in the southernmost section of Puget Sound, whose salty tides extend from the Strait of Juan De Fuca nearly 100 miles south as far as Olympia. Travelers reach the island on a small fifty-four-car ferry, M/V *Christine Anderson,* that in twenty minutes churns to a stop at Burg's Landing. "Pretty much the only time guests encounter cars on their walks and bike rides is when the ferry arrives," says Annie.

Guests at the inn, situated just above the sandy beach and with a view of the ferry landing, learn that the island boasts a year-round population of about 600 people. It also contains one grocery store, one restaurant, but no movie theater. At the entrance to the driveway are two 65-foot cedars, products of seeds planted in 1929 by Ken's uncle and aunt, Chester and Edna Burg. Inside the inn guests soon feel at home and are drawn to the large windows that frame views of the water, nearby Steilacoom, Fox Island, and Tacoma as well as the Cascades and Mount

Rainier to the east and south.

A tour of the inn includes the kitchen where an old wood stove dating back to the early 1900s resides. Annie offers a plate of oatmeal or chocolate chip cookies, often warm from the oven and with delicious aromas lingering. Two rooms on the ground floor have queen beds and private or shared bath. One room on the main level has a queen bed and shared bath. In the upper loft, a larger suite has a queen bed made of polished logs, a skylight, and a hydro-tub for two. The exposed logs, antique furnishings, and handmade quilts give the rooms a warm and rustic ambience.

Breakfast is served around 9:00 A.M. beginning with freshly brewed coffee, teas, hot chocolate, and assorted breakfast breads. Cream cheese–stuffed French toast or a cheese-bacon quiche may be offered. For evening dining ask about the one restaurant on the island or ferry over to Steilacoom and try the E.R. Rogers Restaurant housed in a mansion built in 1891 by an early gold prospector.

What's Nearby

On weekends the Johnson Farm Museum, maintained by the Anderson Island Historical Society is open on Otso Point Road; the farm presents island life of earlier times. Poke into the display and gift shop housed in the renovated chicken coop. Two lakes offer swimming, picnicking, fishing, kayaking, and canoeing opportunities for those who bring their own gear. Hikers can take a winding trail to the beach at Anderson Marine Park. Bicycles are perfect for the island's roads that are fairly free of traffic. Just south of the island is Olympia, the state capital. Also see What's Nearby Federal Way-Tacoma on page 227.

Other Recommended B&Bs Nearby

Mill Town Manor Bed & Breakfast offers a return to the Roaring '20s in a restored and sumptuously decorated lumber baron's estate that is now on the National Historic Register; rooms have names like Gatsby, Garbo, and Valentino; contact innkeepers Gary and Debbi Saint, 116 Oak Street, Eatonville, WA 98328; Telephone: (360) 832–6506; E-mail: milltown@ foxinternet.net. **Puget View Guesthouse,** a secluded cottage on the shore of south Puget Sound offers cozy accommodations along with a private deck, barbecue, hammock, access to the beach, and a continental-plus breakfast delivered to your door; contact innkeepers Dick & Barbara Yunker, 7924 Sixty-first Avenue NE, Olympia, WA 98516; Telephone: (360) 413–9474.

Schnauzer Crossing
Bed & Breakfast

4421 Lakeway Drive
Bellingham, WA 98226
Phone: (360) 733–0055; (800) 562–2808
E-mail: schnauzerx@aol.com
Internet site: www.schnauzercrossing.com

Innkeepers: Donna and Vermont McAllister
Rooms: 1 room, 1 suite, and 1 cottage all with private baths; 2 of these are handicap accessible
Extras: Welcome baskets in each room with fruit, homemade cookies, and snacks; rooms have private telephones; indoor aviary with canaries, finches, and doves
On the grounds: Japanese garden plantings, ponds, and garden sculpture; hot tub in secluded garden area
Smoking? Outdoors only
Visiting pets? No; 2 resident standard schnauzers, Barbel and Marilea
Credit cards: Visa, MasterCard, Discover
Rates: $$–$$$$
How to get there: From I-5 approximately 30 miles north of Mount Vernon take exit 253 and then an immediate right onto King Street; turn left onto Lakeway Drive heading east 2⅜ miles. Just beyond Euclid Street angle left on Lakeway Drive and proceed ½ mile to the inn's sign; turn left down gravel drive to second house on the left. If you miss the angle turn onto Lakeway you will be on Cable Street, and you should turn around.

When guests are welcomed and ushered into the great room, they are immediately drawn to the floor-to-ceiling cathedral windows that frame stunning views of Lake Whatcom to the north and east. "It's quite a showstopper," says Donna with a smile. "Monty and I have lived here for nearly thirty years and we never tire of the view." The inn is also located near Bellingham and Bellingham Bay, at the northernmost section of Puget Sound. Lummi Island lies to the south of the bay.

Welcome baskets in each room contain fresh fruit, homemade cookies, nuts, chocolates, and sometimes crackers and cheeses as well. Each guest room is impeccably decorated and offers a serene uncluttered nest. The smallest room features a queen bed with down comforter, floral flounce, navy bed linens and pillow covers, and handsome window treatments that allow good views of the lake. The spacious suite offers a private entrance through the tree-framed Oriental-style garden. Its wraparound windows admit sunny and intimate garden views. This elegant retreat has a king bed, wood-burning fireplace flanked by two rattan-cushioned armchairs and small table, and a solarium sitting room. The bath comes with a whirlpool tub and double-headed shower. The Cottage tucked in among 100-foot cedars is a romantic "treehouse" with its wraparound deck and views of the Lake Whatcom. Inside is a king bed dressed in shades of blue with bright red pillow accents, a gas fireplace, kitchenette, wet bar, skylight, and green-tiled bath with a whirlpool tub and a shower. The suite and cottage come with TV-VCRs and CD players; all three rooms have private telephones.

Breakfast is served in the dining area next to the great room and near Donna's open kitchen. A tall bouquet of colorful daylilies may grace the Danish-style contemporary dining table. The expanse of slanted windows let in the warm morning light. Schnauzer Crossing Blend coffee is brewing in the coffee maker and Donna serves an elegant repast of fresh hazelnut or lime scones and orange juice along with triple sec French toast, Parmesan-baked eggs, or individual quiches. For evening dining The Wild Garlic, Pacific Café, and Il Fiasco are good choices.

What's Nearby Bellingham

Near Bellingham Bay, the National Historic District of Fairhaven offers an eclectic assortment of shops, boutiques, galleries, and cafes (look for Tony's Coffee House). The Whatcom Museum of History & Art is located in one of the finest renovated structures in the entire region, the 1892 Old City Hall building. Maps and additional information can be obtained from the Bellingham/Whatcom County Visitors Bureau at 904 Potter Street; Telephone: (360) 671-3990. Twenty miles north via I-5 is U.S. and Canadian customs at Blaine, Washington; Telephone: (360) 332-8221. Travelers must carry proof of American citizenship; for traveling pets rabies vaccine documentation must be available.

Other Recommended B&Bs Nearby:

Big Trees Bed & Breakfast, Craftsman-style home near Lake Whatcom, two of the three guest rooms offer lake views; contact innkeeper Jan Simmons, 4840 Fremont Street, Bellingham, WA 98226; Telephone: (800) 647-2850.

Benson Farmstead
Bed & Breakfast

1009 Avon-Allen Road
Bow, WA 98232
Phone: (360) 757–0578
Internet site: www.bbhost.com/bensonbnb

Innkeepers: Jerry and Sharon Benson
Rooms: 4 rooms with private baths
Extras: Historic farmstead dates back to 1914; outdoor hot tub
On the grounds: English-style garden, fruit trees, berries; antique machinery garden; views of Skagit Valley tulip fields
Smoking? Outdoors only
Visiting pets? Inquire, outdoor pets only; can stay in the outbuildings; 3 outdoor cats
Credit cards: Visa, MasterCard
Rates: $–$$
How to get there: From I-5 approximately one hour north of Seattle, and about 4 miles north of Mount Vernon, take exit 232, Cook Road, and go west for 1½ miles to Avon-Allen Road. Turn left (south) here and proceed ¾ mile to the farmstead located on the left.

"**V**elkommen is the traditional Scandinavian greeting," says Sharon. She and husband Jerry welcome travelers to the North Coast area. This is a popular stop for those heading farther north to Bellingham and on to British Columbia just across border at the U.S. and Canadian customs port of Blaine. The beautifully restored 1914 farmstead and extensive grounds were once a dairy farm. The couple bought the place in the early 1980s and fully restored the two-story house with its seventeen rooms. After raising their four sons, they redecorated again and opened the farmstead to bed-and-breakfast guests in the early 1990s.

Four light and airy rooms all come with private baths. Two rooms feature old-fashioned claw-foot soaking tubs. One room has this tub set in the room along with an elegant four-poster queen bed with an Amish quilt and cozy window seats with views of the countryside. Another cheerful room offers an antique white-iron bed and a daybed with a trundle. A 1930s-style bedroom set with lace draped romantically over the queen bed decorates a third room. Overstuffed chairs, extra pillows, and period lamps offer cozy sitting places in each room. The bedside tables have floor-length coverings overlaid with lace, as well as small vases of flowers and good reading lamps. The lovely window treatments in the rooms frame pleasant views of the garden or of the Skagit Valley landscape.

Guests are invited to use the cozy parlor and common room equipped with a wood stove, TV/VCR, puzzles, and reading material. Sharon and Jerry serve their guests homemade desserts, coffee, and tea here each evening around 9:00 when couples return from dinner. "Everyone enjoys talking and chatting about their travels and sometimes about world events, even poli-

tics," says Jerry with a grin.

Breakfast is served family style around 8:30 or 9:00 A.M. and begins with fresh fruit, juice, and coffee or teas. The bountiful entree may be Swedish pancakes and sausage or crustless quiche with ham. Sharon bakes wonderful breads, coffeecakes, and muffins in her large country kitchen and these are served as well. She might be persuaded to give you a tour of the kitchen with its old-fashioned wood stove, rack of hanging copper pots over the electric stovetop, and its wide window seat with a plethora of pillows. For evening dining the best direction is toward scenic Chuckanut Drive; ask about such eateries with great views as Chuckanut Manor, Oyster Bar, and Oyster Creek Inn.

What's Nearby

See What's Nearby Mount Vernon on page 253, What's Nearby La Conner on page 245 and What's Nearby Anacortes on page 209.

Other Recommended B&Bs Nearby

Alice Bay Bed & Breakfast, one romantic suite overlooking a miniature bay on Samish Island, feather bed, hot tub, gourmet breakfasts, shorebirds and seabirds that come and go with the tide; contact the innkeeper Julie Rousseau at 982 Scott Road, Samish Island, Bow, WA 98232-0223; Telephone: (360) 766-6396. **Samish Point by the Bay,** a secluded and romantic garden estate overlooking Samish Bay, Cape Cod–style guest house for romantic getaways, stone fireplace, beach access; contact innkeepers Herb and Theresa Goldston at 447 Samish Point Road, Bow, WA 98232; Telephone: (360) 766-6610.

Inn at Barnum Point

464 South Barnum Road
Camano Island, WA 98292
Phone: (360) 387-2256; (800) 910-2256
Internet site: www.whidbey.com/inn/

Innkeeper: Carolin Barnum Dilorenzo
Rooms: 2 rooms with private baths, 1 large suite with private bath and soaking tub
Extras: Suite comes with deck, small kitchen, gas fireplace, and sleeping loft with views of the water
On the grounds: Views of Port Susan Bay looking east; access to beach for walking
Smoking? Outdoors only
Visiting pets? No; resident Akita
Credit cards: Visa, MasterCard, Discover
Rates: $$-$$$$
How to get there: Via I-5 approximately 45 miles north of Seattle take exit 212 and proceed west 5 miles on Highway 532 to Stanwood; cross to Camano Island via bridge and continue another 5 miles to chamber of commerce booth. Turn left (south) onto E. Camano Drive and follow this for 3 miles to Russell Road, just past the veterinary clinic. Turn left (east) onto Russell Road for approximately ½ mile then right onto Barnum Road for 1 mile; the inn is located at the end of the road. The drive takes about an hour from either Seattle or from Vancouver, British Columbia.

Both second-floor guest rooms in the main house offer outstanding views of Port Susan Bay looking east toward the Cascade Mountains. A high Victorian cherry-wood queen bed awaits in one room that is decorated in a nautical and seashore theme with colors of blues and white. From wide windows guests often spy blue herons walking on their spindly legs at the shoreline looking for tasty tidbits. "And sometimes in the evening," says Carolin, "the herons are seen in the apple tree just outside the windows." In the second room guests climb a small set of steps to reach their four-poster pine queen bed. This room offers both water and woods views and comes with a lodge and Northwest Native American theme. Both rooms have gas fireplaces, TV, snuggly down quilts, and private baths.

The Shorebird Room is accessed by a private stairway leading up to a deck then inside to a spacious sitting area, a small kitchen, and a loft sleeping area with great views from all sides. Guests enjoy afternoon breezes and watching seabirds and water activities either from the outside deck or from inside by the gas fireplace. During the daytime sunlight sparkles on the waters of Port Susan Bay; at night moonlight may cast long streams of light on the constantly moving waters as the tides come and go. A large soaking tub, at the ready to fill for a soothing bath, offers a view of flickering flames from the fireplace.

In this suite the kitchen is fully stocked with goodies and gourmet coffee and teas so that guests can enjoy breakfast at their leisure. For those staying in the main house, breakfast is served in the cozy dining room overlooking the bluff and the bay. Carolin serves freshly squeezed juice, a fresh fruit tray, and her homemade scones, muffins, or sweet rolls. This is followed by a hot entree such as stuffed French toast or crab-egg-spinach quiche and bacon, ham, or sausage. For evening dining ask about local restaurants such as Rene's on the island or eateries in nearby Stanwood.

What's Nearby Camano Island

There is locally produced theater and performances at Camwood Players or Lincoln Theater. Beach walks yield treasures such as driftwood, shells, and agates; find old-growth forest trails at the nearby state park. Visit artists at work in local galleries or drive past an ostrich-emu farm. Nearby Stanwood is a quaint town with many buildings dating back to the early 1900s; several Scandinavian shops reflect the ethnic background of early settlers. For maps and current information about activities and annual events throughout Island County, contact the Camano Island Visitors Information Center; Telephone: (360) 387–0434.

Ovenell's Heritage Inn Bed & Breakfast

46276 Concrete Sauk Valley Road
Concrete, WA 98237
Phone: (360) 853-8494
E-mail: breakfast@ovenells-inn.com
Internet site: www.ovenells-inn.com

Innkeepers: Norman and Eleanor Ovenell and daughters Cindy, Kris, Helen
Rooms: 4 rooms in the main house, 1 with private bath; Lookout Ridge guest house has 2 self-contained suites with common living and kitchen area
Extras: Miles of nature, riding, and bicycling trails, some along the river
On the grounds: Extensive lawn and perennial beds; gazebo, pond, and decks; views of Sauk Mountain, Sauk Valley, the North Cascade foothills, and Mount Baker; 450-acre cattle ranch and private wildlife refuge; 2-mile riverfront located 1 mile from main house; barns and corral
Smoking? Outdoors only
Visiting pets? No; 4 resident dogs (Murphy, Lexie, Yogi, Maggie), 5 cats (Coco, Bootsie, Patty, Puffy, Oreo), 4 ponies (Tawna, Lightening, Puff, Muff), 2 quarterhorses (Prize, Traveler), 180 head of cattle, numerous ducks, geese, and rabbits; inquire about space for visiting horses
Credit cards: Visa, MasterCard
Rates: $–$$$
How to get there: From I–5 about one hour north of Seattle take exit 232, Cook Road, and turn east toward Sedro-Woolley. Continue east on Highway 20 to Concrete; turn right (south) onto Concrete-Sauk Valley Road, cross the bridge, and continue left for 2 miles to the inn. The inn is located approximately 25 miles east of I–5.

Travelers who head east toward Mount Baker and the rugged North Cascades region that lies directly north of Seattle will find an extraordinary bed-and-breakfast experience at this working farm and cattle ranch, the Double O Ranch, near the community of Concrete. Nestled in a scenic valley fringed with conifers and deciduous trees, the inn is owned by the Ovenell family who share their distinct lifestyle dedicated to both environmental concerns and the conservation of fragile resources in the Sauk Valley area.

Guests can luxuriate in one of four rooms in the large main house or in one of the two suites in the separate guest house located ¼ mile from the main house, a lodging alternative for those who like to cook for themselves. The main house, built in 1915, looks out over more than a square-mile spread in Sauk Valley and is situated so that it commands prime views of the North Cascades and Mount Baker. "On a clear day the mountain looks straight at us," says Norm with a chuckle. He remembers landing his small airplane, a Cessna 120, on nearby fields back in the early 1950s when he was a young man; now in his seventies he tells guests that he prefers a four-wheel drive vehicle these days.

Your room might come with a Windsor chair, a rose-carved bureau, shadow boxes, antique fans, rose wreaths, old pictures, and reading lamps. Another has an under-the-eaves private bath. The other rooms share a bath that includes a tiled shower, pedestal sinks, luxurious towels, and robes.

Gourmet desserts and beverages are served in the evening before folks retire. Then after a good night's rest, everyone gathers in the light and airy dining room for a bountiful ranch breakfast. The table is set with fine china and antique crystal and silver. Daughters Cindy and Kris create such tasty items as soufflés and quiches, special potato dishes with cheeses, sausages and breakfast meats, and a fresh fruit platter garnished with edible flowers from the garden. On sunny and warm mornings the deck, just outside the sliding glass doors from the dining area, provides a pleasant spot to enjoy breakfast along with the great views. For evening dining consider driving 20 miles up to Marblemount for a mountainside dinner experience.

What's Nearby Concrete

The upriver area offers eagle watching, hiking, fishing, and back-country trail riding. For additional information, call information numbers at Concrete, (360) 853–7042, and at Mount Baker Ranger District, (360) 856–5700. Also see What's Nearby Mount Vernon on page 253 and What's Nearby Anacortes on page 209.

Other Recommended B&B Nearby

South Bay Bed & Breakfast, a lakeside retreat with five view rooms, private baths, gas fireplaces, sun room, wraparound porch, and private patios; contact innkeepers Dan and Sally Moore, 4905 South Bay Drive, Sedro Woolley, WA 98284; Telephone: (360) 595–2086.

Colonel Crockett Farm
Bed & Breakfast Inn

1012 South Fort Casey Road
Coupeville, WA 98239
Phone: (360) 678-3711
E-mail: crocketbnb@aol.com
Internet site:
www.members.aol.com/crocketbnb

Innkeepers: Bob and Beulah Whitlow
Rooms: 5 rooms with private baths
Extras: Romantic tables for two in dining room; redwood-paneled library with fireplace
On the grounds: Century-old trees such as holly, maple, redwood, and cedar; lilac hedges, a fish pond, wishing well, and restored barn; visiting deer, pheasants, quail, rabbits; thousands of daffodils bloom throughout the yard in the spring; views of Admiralty Inlet from second floor rooms
Smoking? Outdoors only
Visiting pets? No; 1 loveable long-haired outdoor cat, Taffy
Credit cards: Visa, MasterCard
Rates: $–$$
How to get there: From Langley and Greenbank in the southern section of Whidbey Island, proceed north on Highway 525 toward Coupeville, a distance of approximately 20 miles. At junction of Highway 20W turn left (west) toward the Keystone ferry dock; in 1⅝ miles turn right (north) onto Wanamaker Road (which promptly turns left) for 1⁷⁄₁₀ miles. Turn left onto South Fort Casey Road for ⅛ mile then left into the inn's driveway.

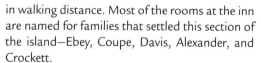

"**O**ur island is rather long and narrow, indented with one small harbor and several bays, lagoons, and coves—then small headlands and points jut out here and there along the way as well," explains Bob. "Altogether it's about 48 miles from the south end to the north end." Sandy beaches and windswept bluffs dot the island's shoreline too, with meadows and farmland stretching here and there along the center. Guests will usually not miss a visit to the restored Admiralty Head lighthouse, now an interpretive center at Fort Casey State Park, with-

in walking distance. Most of the rooms at the inn are named for families that settled this section of the island—Ebey, Coupe, Davis, Alexander, and Crockett.

Throughout five guest rooms are fine examples of antique furniture and period accessories—a canopied and draped four-poster, an

Edwardian fainting couch, a tiger-maple bed and matching dresser, an antique oak bed with a high oak headboard, an English marble-top washstand, antique brass beds, a Victorian love seat, caned chairs, and hurricane lamps.

The inn has a wonderful library, its walls and box-beam ceiling paneled in split red oak. This enticing room has a cozy fireplace and several wingback chairs, the kind that offer comfortable niches in which to curl up with a book of poetry, literature, history, or a mystery.

Five separate tables in the light-filled dining room are set with layers of linens, sometimes deep rose and pale pink. Creamy white china, stemware, antique serving pieces, silver, and bouquets of fresh flowers are attractively arranged on each couple's table. An elegant fresh fruit platter, orange juice, and hot-from-the-oven muffins like cranberry-walnut-orange accompany a hot entree such as eggs California—this comes with mild green chilies, sour cream, salsa, and slices of avocado. A Swedish sausage ring or Canadian bacon may be served as well.

What's Nearby Coupeville

In addition to Fort Casey State Park and its lighthouse interpretive center, visitors can walk, hike, and bicycle trails and paths in the Ebey's Landing National Historic Reserve. Historic Coupeville offers cafes, bistros, shops, and galleries including the Coupeville Arts Center and the Penn Cove Gallery. The Island County Historical Society Museum, adjacent to the wharf, features historical exhibits throughout the year. For maps and current information about annual events contact the Coupeville Visitors Information Center, (360) 678-5434. Also see What's Nearby Greenbank on page 243 and What's Nearby Langley on page 247.

Other Recommended B&Bs Nearby

Anchorage Inn Bed & Breakfast, a sparkling new Victorian-style inn with five rooms and private baths located near old town shops; contact innkeepers Dave and Diane Binder at 807 North Main Street, Coupeville, WA 98239; Telephone: (360) 678-5581. **The Victorian Bed & Breakfast,** 1889 Italianate-style home with family keepsakes, queen beds, private baths, and a quaint hideaway cottage; contact the innkeepers at 602 North Main Street, Coupeville, WA 98239; Telephone: (360) 678-5305.

Otters Pond Bed & Breakfast

100 Tomihi Road, Orcas Island
P.O. Box 1540
Eastsound, WA 98245
Phone: (360) 376-8844; (888) 893-9680
E-mail: otterbehere@otterspond.com
Internet site: www.otterspond.com

Innkeepers: Carl & Susan Silvernail, Andrea Wilson
Rooms: 5 rooms, 4 with private baths
Extras: Evening turndown service; gourmet breakfast fare; hot tub with shoji screen enclosure; terrycloth robes; wildflower-scented soaps, lotions, shampoo, and conditioner
On the grounds: Pond with wildlife and visiting waterfowl
Smoking? Outdoors only
Visiting pets? No; resident Pomeranians, Rusty and Bubby
Credit cards: Visa, MasterCard, Discover, Novus
Rates: $-$$$
How to get there: From Anacortes take one of the large Washington State ferries to Orcas Island, a ride of 1 hour; see specific ferry information in What's Nearby Anacortes on page 209. Exit ferry at Orcas Island taking an immediate left onto Horseshoe Highway and proceed to the community of Eastsound, a distance of 10 miles. Pass through Eastsound and bear to the right at the edge of town; proceed and pass by Crescent Bay to the STOP sign. Turn right here and proceed 2⁹⁄₁₀ miles toward Moran State Park sighting a large pond on the right; turn right past the pond on Tomihi Road, a gravel road. The inn is the second property on the right (if you reach the sign to Rosario Resort you have gone too far).

When guests arrive, they are welcomed and immediately invited to the large and inviting common room for refreshments—coffee, herb teas, or a cold beverage and a selection of cheeses, crackers, scones, or coffeecake. Rusty and Bubby, two small Pomeranians, may stop by to wag their tails and say hello; they live in the innkeepers' quarters located separately from the main house. There may be a fire in the wood stove or in the gas fireplace, the warmth erasing a late afternoon chill from the nearby waters of Puget Sound. The dark leather couch and matching chairs look inviting. Reading materials are arranged neatly on the glass coffee table, as is a welcoming bouquet of flowers.

An upholstered rocking chair sits by the wide windows. Eyes are drawn to the twenty-five-acre pond with its waterlilies and natural area located just beyond these windows and beyond the patio.

Guests learn that long-legged blue heron are regular visitors to the pond, that kingfishers dart about the waterlilies and pond grasses, and that wood ducks, mergansers, swans and other waterfowl and bird species, even hummingbirds, are seen throughout the seasons. Small deer approach at sunset and again in the early morning, following paths from within the dark forested area at the edge of the property; Douglas fir and Western red cedar are the tallest sentinels. "Almost every room in the house has a view of our wonderful lily pond and the trees," says Andrea. She, her sister Susan, and Susan's husband Carl manage the bed and breakfast with all three helping with hospitality and innkeeping duties.

Guests choose from five spacious rooms that are named for the various bird species that visit. Your room may come with a king bed covered in an elegant brocade comforter, a queen four-poster with a feather comforter, a queen brass-and-iron bed, skylights, oversized claw-foot bathtubs, and views of the lily pond and the tall conifers. Early morning here often smells like a freshly cut Christmas tree. Guests often catch a whiff of this pungent aroma in the evening, when they don swimwear and terrycloth robes and trek out to the hot tub on the wide deck.

Breakfast in the dining room on the main level is served at two seatings, 8:00 A.M. and 9:00 A.M. This gourmet affair is even more appealing because it comes with views of the lily pond and visiting wildlife. One such breakfast includes white grape-peach sorbet, brandy poached pears, bananas Foster French toast, and Orcas Island sausage. Freshly brewed coffee is always available at 7:00 A.M. The trio of innkeepers goes all out on Valentine's weekend with such fare as Cupid Crush Sorbet, strawberries Romanoff, Lover's Granola, and Count of Monte Cristo French Toast.

What's Nearby

See What's Nearby Orcas Island on page 225 and What's Nearby Anacortes on page 209.

Other Recommended B&B Nearby

Kangaroo House Bed & Breakfast, a family friendly bed and breakfast within walking distance of Eastsound, Orcas Island's largest community, offers rooms with private and shared baths in a 1907 Craftsman-style home; full breakfasts, garden hot tub; contact innkeepers Peter and Helen Allen, P.O. Box 344, Eastsound, WA 98245; Telephone: (360) 376-2175.

Turtleback Farm Inn and The Orchard House at Turtleback Farm

Route 1, Box 650
Crow Valley Road, Orcas Island
Eastsound, WA 98245
Phone: (360) 376–4914; (800) 376–4914
Internet site: www.turtlebackinn.com

Innkeepers: William and Susan Fletcher; Assistant Innkeeper: Sophie Lapas
Rooms: 11 rooms with private baths including 4 handicap-accessible rooms
Extras: Afternoon tea self-serve style, sherry, fruit, candies; fresh flowers in common rooms, dining room, and guest rooms; innkeepers offer a thorough orientation to the island and its recreational activities
On the grounds: Meadows, ponds, wildlife, and resident sheep, lambs, chickens, domestic geese, and migratory waterfowl
Smoking? Outdoors only
Visiting pets? No; spunky Jack Russell terrier, Spud, and a Briard (a French sheep dog), Shardik
Credit cards: Visa, MasterCard, Discover
Rates: $$–$$$$
How to get there: From Anacortes take the Washington State ferry to Orcas Island, the second stop on the route among the San Juan Islands; see specific ferry information in What's Nearby Anacortes on page 209. Exit ferry at Orcas Island taking an immediate left onto Horseshoe Highway; drive 2.8 miles to Deer Harbor Road, the first paved turn. Turn left here and continue .9 mile to Crow Valley Road; turn right and proceed to the inn's parking area.

There is a pair of 300-year-old maples in the meadow, six freshwater ponds, and a plethora of resident and migratory animals and waterfowl that frequent this lovely eighty-acre spot in Crow Valley on Orcas Island. "And we also often see bald and golden eagles soaring above the ponds," says Bill. The serene setting, with open fields and meadows fringed with Douglas fir, imparts an immediate sense of relaxation for vacationing urbanites. The couple completely restored and expanded the late 1800s "folk national" style farmhouse in the early 1980s; at that time the intrepid blackberry vines had taken over one section of the house.

Now however guests spend lazy afternoons on the wide sunny deck that spans the southwest side of the large farmhouse enjoying the bucolic scene. A book in hand, a cup of iced tea or steaming coffee, a lemon scone—what else could one desire?

Guest rooms are large and light. Some have French doors that open wide to outdoor decks, queen or double beds with soft down comforters and extra pillows, cozy sitting areas, claw-foot or antique tubs with showers, and pedestal sinks. One room offers a view of the two old maples in the meadow, another room overlooks the inn's flower garden, and another an ancient cork elm. The Orchard House, a cedar farmhouse set in the apple orchard and looking east to Mount Wollard, offers four spacious rooms with king beds, gas fireplaces, sitting-dining areas, full baths, and French doors that open to private decks.

Guests in the main farmhouse are served breakfast between 8:00 and 9:00 A.M. in the main level dining room or on the expansive deck. Fresh eggs from the resident chickens are used in the main entrees, and these are often served with Canadian bacon or sausage along with an assortment of teas and coffees. Susan's recipe for Baked Fruits is especially tasty—it includes apricots, peaches, dark brown sugar, candied ginger, vanilla, lemon, and other spices.

What's Nearby Orcas Island

In Eastsound, visit small shops, bookstores, Orcas Performing Arts Center, and a good assortment of cafes and restaurants such as Bilbo's, Christina's, Ship's Bay, LaFamiglia, and Compass Room at historic Rosario Resort. For additional information contact Orcas Island Chamber of Commerce & Visitors Center, P.O. Box 252, Eastsound, WA 98245 (the center is located next door to Bilbo's); Telephone: (360) 376-2273; Internet sites: www.orcasisland.org and www.sanjuanweb.com.

Other Recommended B&B Nearby

Chestnut Hill Inn Bed & Breakfast, a retreat in grand country style, offers five elegantly appointed guest rooms with four-poster canopy feather beds, gas fireplaces and private baths; contact innkeepers Marilyn and Daniel Loewke and their staff, 5157 Victorian Valley Road, Orcas Island, P.O. Box 399, Orcas, WA 98280; Telephone: (360) 376-5157; Internet site: www.chestnuthillinn.com.

Palisades Bed & Breakfast
at Dash Point

5162 SW 311th Place
Federal Way, WA 98023
Phone: (253) 838–4376; (888) 838–4376
E-mail: laporte2@ix.netcom.com
Internet site:
www.bbonline.com/wa/palisades

Innkeepers: Peggy and Dennis LaPorte
Rooms: 1 suite with private bath and 3 rooms; marble whirlpool spa and skylight
Extras: Snacks served on arrival; fresh fruit bowl, candy dish, and flowers along with hot beverage service in suite; thick terry robes and plush towels; TV/VCR with video library; office with fax and telephone; telescope for sighting watercraft, ships, and bird species; cookies/chocolates with bedtime turndown service
On the grounds: English garden terrace and gazebo; switchback trail from terrace down to sandy, waterfront beach for walking; bicycles for riding
Smoking? Outdoors only
Visiting pets? No; resident Lhasa Apso, Oreo, and outdoor Persian cat, Puff
Credit cards: Visa, MasterCard, American Express, Discover
Rates: $$$$
How to get there: From Seattle take I-5 south to Federal Way and take the 320th Street exit; turn right onto 320th and proceed to Forty-seventh Street. Turn right and proceed to Dash Point Road; turn left, then take a sharp right onto Fifty-second Street to the first house on the left. From Portland and Olympia proceed north on I-5 to Tacoma and take the City Center exit; follow Highway 509 (Marine View Drive) through to Brown's Point and on into Dash Point. Just beyond the Dash Point State Park entrance turn onto Fifty-second Street to the inn, the first house on the left.

Once upon a time this inn was a small beach bungalow with tiny windows. Perched on a cliff above south Puget Sound, it had a winding trail down to the beach covered with blackberries. That was 1972. In the late 1990s owners Peggy and Dennis have completed a total renovation of the house and offer bed-and-breakfast guests an elegant and romantic three-room dream suite on the top floor of their light-filled oasis on the cliff. A four-poster queen open-canopy feather bed with bishop-sleeve drapery faces double French doors leading to a private deck. In the sitting area the domed ceiling has recessed lighting and a hand-painted trompe d'oeil of delicate vines and ribbons. A comfortable sofa along with French Provincial desk, chairs, and coffee table are arranged near the windows and the gas fireplace. Use the telescope to spot bald eagles as they soar past on their way to the nearby Dumas Bay Bird Sanctuary. Or climb aboard the inn's bicycles and pedal over to the sanctuary and to Dash Point State Park for a closer look.

Back at the inn guests often pause in the cozy living room on the main floor to enjoy a cheerful fire in the fireplace; the handsome mantle is carved of pine. This room has a high coffered ceiling and paneling of light pine. Enjoy chilled wine in crystal wine glasses accompanied by Brie and crackers. To relax in private in your top-floor suite, walk up three marble steps and sink into the warm waters of the whirlpool tub and spa. At night a small tray of cookies and chocolates arrives with turndown service.

In the morning guests may decide to have breakfast in their suite, to come downstairs to the enormous country kitchen (it, too, has a fireplace), or be served in the formal dining room. Peggy may serve eggs Benedict and sautéed new potatoes with herbs or glazed pears in crepes with crème Anglaise and strawberry garnish, homemade low-fat granola with yogurt, blueberry scones and croissants, and gourmet coffee or espresso and teas.

What's Nearby Federal Way-Tacoma

A golfing facility is close by at Twin Lakes Golf Course. Point Defiance Park offers gardens, picnic areas, hiking trails, and large zoo. Downtown Tacoma has eclectic Antique Row, lavish Beaux Arts-style renovated Union Station, antique street lamps, the Broadway Theater District, a good selection of eateries, and nearly two dozen galleries and studios. The Tacoma-Pierce County Visitor's Center can provide local maps (800) 272-2662. Also visit Lakewold, one of the region's best historic estate gardens. Also see What's Nearby Seattle on page 261.

Other Recommended B&B Nearby

Soundview Bed & Breakfast in south Seattle offers a spacious and private king suite decorated in nautical blues and whites in a separate guest house with superb views of central Puget Sound; the guest hot tub on the deck also offers the great views; contact innkeepers Gerry and Dick Flaten at 17600 Sylvester Road S.W., Seattle, WA 98166; Telephone: (206) 244-5209.

Island Escape
Bed & Breakfast

210 Island Boulevard
Fox Island, WA 98333
Phone: (253) 549-2044
E-mail: paula@island-escape.com
Internet site: www.island-escape.com

Innkeepers/owners: Paula Pascoe and Roy Davis
Rooms: 1 suite with private entrance, private bath, gas log fireplace
Extras: On arrival sparkling apple cider and chilled goblets in ice bucket; fresh flowers; special amenities in bath such as oatmeal bar soap, herbal bath grains, herbal shampoo; whirlpool tub and recessed lighting in bath
On the grounds: Outrageous southwesterly views of south Puget Sound
Smoking? Outdoors only
Visiting pets? No; one resident tabby cat, Alice
Credit cards: Visa, MasterCard
Rates: $$
How to get there: From either Seattle or from Olympia via I–5, at Tacoma take the Bremerton exit onto Highway 16 and proceed west. After crossing the Tacoma Narrows bridge, take the Gig Harbor City Center exit and follow signs to Fox Island; cross the Fox Island bridge, drive 9/10 mile and turn right onto Cove Road. Turn right again onto Island Boulevard, drive a short distance and turn left onto Griffin Lane, a gravel road; the inn is at the end of the drive, look for the large seagull on the posts.

Looking for total privacy? You'll find it here in this large three-room suite that's the ultimate in romance. This is a place to hide and listen to the waves lapping on the shore at the base of the cliff. This is a place to snuggle together in a tropical hammock on a private patio with a superlative view of rosy sunsets on the western horizon. Visitors here do not feel pressured to do anything but relax and rejuvenate.

The mood is immediately apparent as Paula guides you through the garden arbor, across your private deck, and reaches for the door handle of your private entrance. The spacious suite is located on the ground floor of this elegant and contemporary home. The Japanese treasures displayed in the entry, including pairs of Japanese slippers and stockings, offer a subtle message that implies "this is a very special place." In the main salon Paula has created a Hawaiian paradise with treasures that she and Roy brought home from the islands after his stint in the U.S. Air Force as a protocol officer. Upholstered rattan chairs and love seat with matching bookcases and tables are grouped comfortably near the gas fireplace.

The bedroom is furnished with pieces acquired by the couple on a European tour of duty; these include a German hutch of warm wood, a matching king bed with feathery down comforter, bedside lamps, and art prints of European village scenes. The bath has a whirlpool tub, recessed lighting with dimmer, thick fluffy towels and robes, and quantities of herbal bath grains and oatmeal soaps.

In the morning breakfast magically appears on a tray outside the door about a half-hour following the appearance of a coffee and tea wake-up tray. The tempting fare might include cranberry-orange bagels; crab, ham or vegetable quiche made of farm fresh island eggs; warm mango bread with butter shells made from imported French butter; fresh seasonal fruits and chilled orange smoothies in frosty glasses; and, plenty of freshly ground and freshly brewed Kona coffee. There is no pressure to make conversation with the innkeepers. There are no other guests. This elegant oasis on Fox Island with its views over the waters of south Puget Sound is designed for one couple's enjoyment.

What's Nearby

Quaint shops, boutiques, cafes, delis, waterside taverns, and restaurants are found in Gig Harbor, a charming seaside village located just a few miles from Fox Island. For evening dining ask about the location of Italian, steak, and seafood restaurants such as Marco's, Green Turtle, Inn at Gig Harbor, Tide's Tavern, and Shoreline. The Performance Circle Theatre offers outdoor performances during summer months.

Other Recommended B&B Nearby

Beachside Bed & Breakfast, offers one suite with English country decor and beam ceilings, a wood-burning fireplace, private patio and hot tub, expanded continental breakfast, fully equipped kitchen; contact innkeepers Doreen and Dick Samuelson, 769 Kamus Drive, Fox Island, WA 98333; Telephone: (253) 549-2524. **Peacock Hill Guest House** offers views of Gig Harbor, a quiet Oriental meditation garden, Northwest Native American and Southwestern decor; spacious common area has a wood-burning fireplace, TV/VCR, CD player, and heated tile floors; gourmet breakfast; contact innkeepers Suzanne and Steve Savlov, 9520 Peacock Hill Avenue, Gig Harbor, WA 98332; Telephone: (800) 863-2318.

Duffy House
Bed & Breakfast Inn

760 Pear Point Road
Friday Harbor, WA 98250
Phone: (360) 378–5604; (800) 972–2089
E-mail: duffyhouse@rockisland.com
Internet site: www.san-juan.net/duffyhouse

Innkeepers: Arthur and Mary Miller
Rooms: 5 rooms with private baths; children over 8 are welcome
Extras: Complimentary soft drinks, fruit juices in guest refrigerator
On the grounds: English-style garden, vintage orchard, resident eagles' nest, access to private beach and water for kayaking, buoy for mooring small boats
Smoking? Outdoors only
Visiting pets? No; 1 resident outdoor cat, Mr. Duffy
Credit cards: Visa, MasterCard
Rates: $–$$
How to get there: From the Friday Harbor ferry landing proceed up Spring Street for 1 block; turn left onto First Street, which becomes Harrison Street then becomes Turn Point Road and finally turns into Pear Point Road. The inn is located 4 miles from town via this scenic route.

The main reason to take the scenic route out and around Pear Point to the inn isn't complex—it's a matter of easing oneself more thoroughly into the island's tempo. You'll get into the mindset of the local islanders who generally don't use umbrellas and are known to whine if the temperature rises much above seventy degrees. These are folks who appreciate bracing weather, brisk breezes from the water, and winter storms. Mary and Arthur, being tolerant and convivial innkeepers, won't mind if guests bring umbrellas, raingear, and galoshes. And the resident bald eagles certainly won't mind. They regard most everyone with polite though somewhat intimidating stares. "We have one eagle nest directly across the road from the inn," says Arthur. The eagle couple and a pair of eaglets are often in residence. Guests enjoy getting acquainted with the national bird, at least as much as they can from ground level looking up into the long, swaying branches of a tall Douglas fir.

One guest room offers a queen bed, white wicker accents, and a view of the eagles' nest. All the rooms are appointed with queen beds, floral chintzes, antiques, lace or ruffled curtains, and great water or garden views. One room features antique pine; its ruffled curtains frame a view of the orchard. Vintage trees include apple, pear, plum, and cherry, and fruits harvested from these are often used in tasty breakfast dishes. "I also make fruit roll-ups that guests like," says Mary.

These naturally sweet treats are set out in the afternoon in the sunken living room along with homemade oatmeal or chocolate chip cookies and freshly brewed coffee, teas, and hot chocolate. Guests often gather in this cozy area with its fireplace—a fire in its wood stove insert often crackles merrily. Navajo rugs lie on the floor. Placed about are earthen pots of native design and weavings done by Mary. A pair of deep easy chairs and a pair of sofas and reading lamps form a comfortable grouping near the fire. The front windows frame the distant mountains and the waters of Griffen Bay. Guests are invited to browse the inn's library of books and magazines including an extensive collection of material on bird watching and on whale watching. The beautifully restored mid-1920s Tudorstyle home and its friendly innkeepers exude a sense of thoughtful warmth and permission to ease into the island's quieter tempo.

You can explore the inn's English-style perennial gardens that include ivy-draped terraces and flower-bedecked rockeries. From perches on the wooden swing-style lawn chairs, peer through binoculars to spy bird species, waterfowl, even orca whales. Walks along the private beach here are a must, with driftwood, rock, and shell treasures collected along the way. The quiet waters of the bay are good for kayaking, scuba diving, and snorkeling.

By 7:00 A.M. coffee and tea are set out on the teacart in the dining room. Breakfast is served at 8:15 A.M. The long table is set with complimentary floral and solid-color linens, contrasting linen napkins, Mary's rice pattern china, and a low bowl of fresh flowers from the garden. With Arthur and Mary sharing the cooking and baking duties, the couple serves a delicious family-style meal that may consist of grapefruit halves with banana and kiwi slices, cinnamon rolls hot from the oven and hootenanny pancakes with fresh strawberries. Other mornings might bring a fresh fruit compote or melon balls with mint leaves, strawberryrhubarb coffeecake or oatmeal coffeecake with streusel topping, and cheese egg strata or berry crepe stack-up.

What's Nearby

See What's Nearby Friday Harbor and San Juan Island on page 233, What's Nearby Orcas Island on page 225, and What's Nearby Anacortes on page 209.

Hillside House
Bed & Breakfast

365 Carter Avenue
Friday Harbor, WA 98250
Phone: (360) 378-4730; (800) 232-4730
E-mail: hillside@rockisland.com
Internet site: www.hillsidehouse.com

Innkeepers: Dick and Cathy Robinson
Rooms: 5 rooms with in room private baths, 2 rooms with private baths across the hall; 4 of the rooms feature water views, 3 feature pond and waterfall views
Extras: Expansive outside decks with views of harbor and mountains
On the grounds: Small pond with rock waterfall and plantings
Smoking? Outdoors only
Visiting pets? No; 2 resident Standard poodles, Joe and Anne; 1 African grey parrot, Buddy, and 1 outside cat, Precious
Credit cards: Visa, MasterCard, American Express, Discover
Rates: $$-$$$$
How to get there: After exiting the ferry at the Friday Harbor dock, go ½ block on Front Street then left onto Spring Street and up the hill for 2 blocks; turn right onto Second Avenue—this street curves and becomes Guard Street. In ½ mile turn right onto Carter Avenue and proceed 2 blocks to the inn, located on the left.

Guests marvel at the views of distant Mount Baker in the northernmost section of the Cascades and the boats in bustling Friday Harbor located just below the inn. Although this panorama is first enjoyed from the expanse of windows in the spacious second floor common room and adjoining dining area, guests are immediately drawn to the glass doors that lead outside. The large wraparound deck that extends across the front of the inn allows an even wider view of the mountains and the waters of Puget Sound. Small tables and chairs are arranged in pleasant groupings. Guests are welcome to use the common rooms, the expansive decks, or curl up in their cozy guest rooms with a supply of coffee, herbal teas, and Dick's famous Banana-Chocolate Chip Cookies.

Inside several rooms on three levels are decorated in a sleek and sophisticated 1990s style that reminds one of the 1930s Art Deco style. The largest room commands the best view from atop the third floor and comes with king bed, sofa, large pillows, TV, wet bar, private balcony, and two-person spa tub in the bath. On the second floor one room has a comfortable 12-foot upholstered window seat that faces the harbor, a king bed, sea captain's chest, and overhead fan. Several small cozy rooms also offer oversized window seats upholstered in soft fabrics, giant pillows, along with reading lamps, and king or queen beds. Here views are to the woods in the rear and of the enclosed pond, its small waterfall, and ornamental plantings.

Coffee, juices, and granola are set out for guests between 6:30 and 7:00 A.M. Dick's gourmet buffet breakfast is served between 8:30 and 10:00 A.M. in the dining room or on blue sky sunny mornings outside on the deck with the wonderful views. One favorite menu includes Garden Quiche, lemon-walnut scones, and almond-sour cream coffee cake; another menu brings Chili Egg-Cheese Brunch with salsa and sour cream, cornmeal muffins, and strawberry pie; and another morning's fare includes a sumptuous potato casserole, Mile-High Biscuits, and Bluebarb Crunch. Most of these delectable recipes are included on the inn's Internet site.

What's Nearby Friday Harbor and San Juan Island

Friday Harbor village is full of shops, boutiques, antiques stores, an historical museum, and a good variety of eateries. Bicycle, moped, and car rentals are available for exploring roads that circle the island. The Whale Museum at First and Court streets offers splendid life-size displays of various whale species, intriguing whale sounds, and insights into the several kinds of whales that frequent Puget Sound waters in their family pods, including the dramatic black-and-white orcas. One's itinerary should include visits to Roche Harbor (the sunset flag-lowering ceremony here is especially dramatic), Lime Kiln Point, and Lime Kiln Lighthouse, as well as visits to British Camp and American Camp. These historic camps are located in two separate sections of the island and together form the San Juan Island National Historical Park—rangers and volunteers often dress in period costumes and explain events of the past including the infamous "Pig War." For maps and further information contact San Juan Island Chamber of Commerce and Visitors Information, P.O. Box 98, Friday Harbor, WA 98250; Telephone: (360) 378-5240; Internet site: www.sanjuanisland.org.

Olympic Lights
Bed & Breakfast

4531-A Cattle Point Road
Friday Harbor, WA 98250
Phone: (360) 378-3186
Internet site: www.san-juan.net/olympiclights

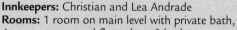

Innkeepers: Christian and Lea Andrade
Rooms: 1 room on main level with private bath, 4 rooms on second floor share 2 baths
Extras: Quantities of peace and quiet
On the grounds: Sixty acres of open meadows, wildflower meadow-garden, panoramic views of Strait of Juan De Fuca and of the Olympic Mountains
Smoking? Outdoors only
Visiting pets? No; 5 resident cats—Pia, Perry, Padra, Pepper, and Pippin
Credit cards: No; personal checks and traveler's checks accepted
Rates: $–$$
How to get there: From the Friday Harbor ferry landing drive uphill on Spring Street and turn left onto Argyle Street. In a short distance turn left onto Argyle Road, which becomes Cattle Point Road; continue to the inn's drive, approximately 5½ miles from town. If you reach American Camp you have gone too far; the inn is a large farmhouse painted yellow and cream. For specific ferry information see What's Nearby Anacortes on page 209.

Longtime innkeepers on San Juan Island Christian and Lea offer a private retreat on their sixty acres of open meadows that overlook Eagle Point and Eagle Point Cove on the southern tip of the island. This comes with superb views of the strait and of the Olympic Mountains, their craggy snowcapped peaks often poking above the clouds; on sunny blue-sky days, they provide a grand spectacle along the southern horizon. The fully renovated farmhouse dating back to 1895, sits solidly in a wide meadow near the bluff that overlooks the strait. It once housed a family of eleven children. Christian says it has withstood many winter storms.

It's a place that calls travelers to unwind, that urges them to leave city cares behind for a time. This includes a mandate from the mountains to unplug the laptop computer, turn off the modem, and leave the cell phone in the glove compartment. Guests pull on jeans, bulky sweaters, warm socks, and walking shoes to make their way past the wildflower meadow-garden, the broad meadows and fields toward the bluff or they walk down toward Cattle Point. They soak in good energy from the sun, the warm breezes, the sky, the mountains, and the salty tides. They walk on the nearby beaches. Couples may even arrange for a soothing massage in the evening.

Guests often walk over to nearby historic American Camp, part of the San Juan National Historic Park; the other site is English Camp located at the opposite end of the island near Roche Harbor. They find no crowds of tourists here at Cattle Point. Nearly everyone else is at the other end of the island. They do find a large open field and a tall flagpole with the Stars and Stripes waving in the breeze and in the spring, delicate pink wild roses blooming from thick tangles of briars that cascade over fences and hedgerows. There are beaches to explore and walk.

Back at the inn guests remove their shoes before climbing the stairs to the second floor carpeted in pale ivory. The four rooms on this floor share two full baths and come with queen beds, soft pastel colors mixed with white and ivory, touches of wicker, framed artwork by local artists. Most have views of the water, the moun-

tains, the meadow, even of the lights of Victoria B.C. at night. One room has a sitting area in soothing dusty pinks. Another on the main floor offers a private bath, king bed with a down comforter, and a large antique armoire. Also on the main floor guests are invited to use two cozy common areas and a good-sized library offers ample supplies of books and magazines as well as puzzles, board games, playing cards, and dominoes. An outdoor sitting area overlooks the strait and the mountains.

Breakfast is served at one seating at 9:00 A.M. in the kitchen and parlor; the farm table in the kitchen offers a view of the water. Great Aunt Regina's china sits at each place setting, and the silver belonged to her sister, Great Aunt Amelia. Lea's vegetarian breakfast may consist of fruit juice smoothies, locally grown fresh fruit or fresh seasonal fruit, buttermilk biscuits or apricot scones, and a tasty egg dish made from fresh eggs courtesy of the resident hens.

For evening dining arrange to pick up dinner when you leave the ferry landing and bring it out to the farm rather than driving back into town. Ask about take-out entrees from Duck Soup Inn, Springtree, Friday Harbor House, Roberto's, or a cafe called Place Next To San Juan Ferry Café.

What's Nearby

See What's Nearby Friday Harbor and San Juan Island on page 233, What's Nearby Orcas Island on page 225, and What's Nearby Anacortes on page 209.

Tower House
Bed & Breakfast

1230 Little Road
Friday Harbor, WA 98250
Phone: (360) 378-5464; (800) 858-4276
E-mail: towerhouse@san-juan-island.com
Internet site: www.san-juan-island.com

Innkeepers: Chris and Joe Luma
Rooms: 2 suites each with sitting room and private bath
Extras: Victorian ambience favors romance
On the grounds: Natural areas, meadows, ponds, woods, trails, views of distant mountains and water; visiting deer, fox, raccoon, eagles
Smoking? Outdoors only
Visiting pets? No; 1 resident cat, not allowed in guest quarters
Credit cards: Visa, MasterCard, American Express, Discover
Rates: $$–$$$
How to get there: From the Friday Harbor ferry landing drive uphill on Spring Street until the street makes a V. Turn left onto Argyle Street proceeding toward the airport then turn left onto Cattle Point Road; continue to Little Road and turn right. The inn's tower will appear as you proceed. The inn is located 3 miles from town. For specific ferry information see What's Nearby Anacortes on page 209.

The Queen Anne Victorian inn, with its handsome two-story tower and elegant stained-glass windows, would seem appropriate for an island-dwelling Rapunzel; you can just imagine the fairytale damsel waving from one of the tower windows. In one suite you step through a keyhole archway into an elegantly appointed sitting room—a tufted window seat, done in pink velvet, beckons you to recline. The antique pedestal table is dressed in white lace; a lush bouquet of flowers sits in the center and two armchairs are placed on either side. Overhead a hanging brass light glows with soft light. A dainty antique lady's desk sits near one window and next to a ficus tree. Around the edges of the largest window a checkerboard design of blue-and-white stained glass emits soft afternoon light onto the gleaming wood floor.

The queen bed is dressed in a floral comforter of mauve, pink, cream, and green;

matching pillows rest in plump array at the head, a soft ecru afghan is folded and placed at the foot. A brimmed Victorian lady's hat rests at one corner of the afghan. In the second suite another queen bed is similarly dressed in a floral comforter of soft pink, peach, and cream, its pillows done in the same print with lace edging. There's an afghan here, too, and another brimmed hat. Guests exit this boudoir through a ruffle-draped French door into their library-sitting room. This cozy space amply lit by floor-to-ceiling windows offers two walls lined with bookshelves and books. The rattan upholstered chair, antique lady's desk, area rug, handsome lamps, African style fabrics and African accent pieces evoke an *Out of Africa* ambience of mystery and romance. Both rooms have antique bureaus, reading lamps, and framed Victorian prints.

The romantic interlude continues in the morning at breakfast served in the elegant dining room. The table is set with antique linens, fine china, and silver. Matching cloth napkins are folded into artistic creations placed in the center of the china plate. The stemware may be of pale pink crystal. A floral centerpiece and array of candlesticks with tall tapers is arranged in the center of the table and placed on a graceful mirror. Tall-back chairs are tufted for comfort, and the floor-to-ceiling mahogany breakfront houses silver and china behind its tall glass doors. Chris and Joe specialize in gourmet vegetarian menus that vary each day along with the table settings and linens. On Mexican day the first course might be sweet nut tamales with strawberry-mango sauce and sopaipillas. Next comes a tortilla pudding filled with mushrooms, onions, cheese, and spices. Quinoa pilaf, made with a South American grain, accompanies this tasty dish. "We never call your mother if you don't eat everything on your plate," says Chris with a grin.

What's Nearby

See What's Nearby Friday Harbor and San Juan Island on page 233, What's Nearby Orcas Island on page 225, and What's Nearby Anacortes on page 209.

Trumpeter Inn
Bed & Breakfast

420 Trumpeter Way
Friday Harbor, WA 98250
Phone: (360) 378-3884; (800) 826-7926
E-mail: swan@rockisland.com
Internet site:
www.friday-harbor.net/trumpeter

Innkeepers: Bobbie and Don Wiesner
Rooms: 5 rooms with private baths, 2 with water and mountain views; 1 handicap-accessible room
Extras: Outdoor hot tub in gazebo with view of gardens and meadows
On the grounds: Gardens, meadows, pond; trumpeter swans visit nearby marshes during winter months; migrating birds and waterfowl visit during spring and fall
Smoking? Outdoors only
Visiting pets? No; resident 4-year-old black lab, Bud, and outdoor cat, More
Credit cards: Visa, MasterCard, American Express, Discover
Rates: $$–$$$
How to get there: From the ferry landing at Friday Harbor, proceed on Spring Street from the wharfside area for 1½ miles bearing to the right as Spring Street becomes San Juan Valley Road; continue to the inn's sign on the right, turn here and follow the lane ¼ mile to the inn. For specific ferry information see What's Nearby Anacortes on page 209.

Travelers who love wildlife, waterfowl, and trumpeter swans will appreciate the amenities offered in this country-quiet haven located a short distance from town. These who like black labs named Bud are especially welcome too, of course. The resident four-year-old canine enjoys jogging along with anyone who likes to explore the gardens, inspect the pond, and see the grand trumpeter swans with their wide wing spans flying low. "The trumpeters fly in during the winter and rest and feed in the nearby marshes," says Bobbie.

The two largest rooms come with king beds, small gas fireplaces, private decks, and south facing views toward False Bay, the Olympic Mountains, and the surrounding valley. One of these rooms on the second floor is done in pale cream accented with a striking plaid of maroon, cream, and dark green. The other, located on the first floor, is dressed elegantly in several shades of ivory. There is also a handicap-accessible room on the first floor. Additional cozy rooms with queen beds with pond and meadow views are decorated in comfortable country furnishings and in colors of pale yellow and blue or lavender, pink, and white. All rooms have good reading lamps at the bedsides, fresh flowers, down comforters, and comfortable pillows. The private baths come with hair dryers, magnifying mirrors, shampoo, and Egyptian cotton towels.

In the main floor common area are TV/VCR, a wood stove, and a supply of hot tub-towels and extra shoes to trek outdoors to the hot tub, in the garden gazebo. A hammock is also available for guests use, as is croquet. In the morning breakfast is served at individual tables set with lace cloths, fine china, and fresh flowers; guests are invited to gather in the dining room on the second floor to enjoy the bucolic views while eating and chatting. Hearty breakfasts include homemade bread and muffins or coffeecake, a fresh fruit plate and juice, and a main dish of perhaps strawberry pancake basket, apple French toast, or egg frittata.

What's Nearby

See What's Nearby Friday Harbor and San Juan Island on page 233, What's Nearby Orcas Island on page 225, and What's Nearby Anacortes on page 209.

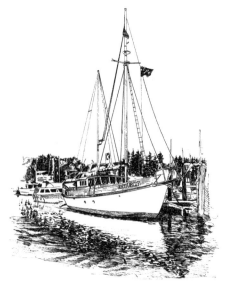

Wharfside Bed & Breakfast aboard the *Jacquelyn*

Slip K-13, Port of Friday Harbor, San Juan
Island
P.O. Box 1212
Friday Harbor, WA 98250
Phone: (360) 378–5661
Internet site:
www.san-juan-island.net/wharfside

Innkeepers: Clyde and Bette Rice
Rooms: 2 staterooms, 1 with private head and
sink, shares main shower, 1 shares main head
and shower
Extras: 60-foot, ketch-rigged sailboat moored at
Friday Harbor marina; small rowing gig and life
vests for guests use; small standing fireplace in
main salon
On the grounds: Waterside views of Port of Friday Harbor, ferry landing, north Puget Sound,
and Friday Harbor village
Smoking? Outdoors only
Visiting pets? Yes, with prior arrangement
Credit cards: Visa, MasterCard, American
Express
Rates: $$
How to get there: From Anacortes take one of
the Washington State ferries to Friday Harbor on
San Juan Island, a ride of approximately 1½
hours; see specific ferry information in What's
Nearby Anacortes on page 209. Upon exiting the
ferry at Friday Harbor turn right onto Front
Street for 3 blocks to the Port of Friday Harbor;
there is permit parking close to the main dock
(guest permit available). The *Jacquelyn* is moored
at Slip K-13, located at the far end of K Dock; visitors are advised to don deck shoes before walking down to the dock.

Captain Clyde and Betty Rice welcome guests aboard the *Jacquelyn*, their sleek 60-foot ketch-rigged sailboat. "We think we have the best seat in the house," says Betty with a welcoming smile; the couple has lived aboard for more than ten years.

One could relax in one of the deck chairs for hours, mug of coffee in hand, and take in the colorful sights, sounds, and bustling goings-on in Friday Harbor. Outdoor umbrellas and colorful windsocks wave and flap in the breezes from outside decks and village shops, restaurants, cafes, delis, and espresso shops that extend across the broad waterfront area just above the ferry landing and above the port and marina. The Washington State ferries that come and go look like wide white-and-green turtles as they lumber in and out of the landing area on their regular schedules to and from Anacortes and the other islands. Gulls sweep and dip among the small fleet of fishing boats moored at the marina. This is life on the saltwater.

Guests, or landlubbers or old salts as Clyde sometimes calls them, choose from two cozy staterooms below deck adjacent to either end of the main salon. The aft room offers a Captain Nemo elegance with a built-in velvet settee, comfy queen bed with down comforters and dual-control mattress warmers, gleaming hardwood and low-beam ceiling. The forward room has an extra-length double bed with down comforter and two seaman-sized berths that are perfect for small children. Porthole windows offer peeks at harbor activity. Grown-ups and kids are welcome to don life vests and have a go at rowing the small gig in the protected harbor area around the dock. For those who bring bicycles, the innkeepers offer deck space for secure stowage. "On a boat every inch of space is used for hanging, storing, or stowing something," says Bette with a chuckle.

Breakfast is served around 9:00 A.M. on the open aft deck weather permitting or in the main salon on the lower level. The bountiful meal starts with a fresh fruit tray, fruit soup, or perhaps poached spiced pears; raspberry cream cheese torte, apple crunch, or fresh muffins follow this. The main entree may be an egg frittata, quiche, or soufflé along with Parmesan potato crisps or latkes. Another favorite is Down Under Sausage Rolls, made with diced mushrooms, onion, and grated apple mixed with sausage that is placed inside fresh dough that's swished with an egg wash and dusted with poppy seeds before baking. "Mouthwatering," says a recent guest.

What's Nearby

See What's Nearby Friday Harbor and San Juan Island on page 233, What's Nearby Orcas Island on page 225, and What's Nearby Anacortes on page 209.

Guest House Log Cottages

24371 State Route 525
Greenbank, WA 98253
Phone: (360) 678-3115
E-mail: guesthse@whidbey.net
Internet site: www.whidbey.net/logcottages

Innkeepers: Don and Mary Jane Creger
Rooms: 5 log cottages, 1 log lodge, each with fireplaces or wood stoves
Extras: Petite kitchens in all accommodations; guest telephone in pool house
On the grounds: Wildlife pond borders log lodge; swimming pool, outdoor hot tub; Twenty-five acre forest and meadow setting
Smoking? Outdoors only
Visiting pets? No; no resident pets
Credit cards: Visa, MasterCard
Rates: $$$-$$$$
How to get there: From the Mukilteo-Clinton ferry landing at the south end of Whidbey Island, proceed north via Highway 525 for 16 miles to inn's entrance; the inn is located 1 mile south of Greenbank and 10 miles south of Coupeville.

Longtime owners and innkeepers Don and Mary Jane Creger offer romantic hideaways in five charming log cottages and in a stunning log lodge on their twenty-five acres of forest and meadow. The lodge and its wide front deck nestle at the edge of a wildlife pond, where deer are often seen; dozens of frogs chorus at evening-time, soft owl duets are often heard after dark, and cheerful birdsongs announce morning's arrival. Each cottage sits among tall Douglas fir and native rhododendron giving couples a sense of complete privacy.

The cottages come with rock fireplaces or parlor wood stoves, electric heat, small kitchens, private baths, and king or queen beds with warm quilts and comforters. Special touches may include stained-glass or criss-cross paned windows, a stained-glass arched entry door, skylights, picture windows, sleeping lofts, knotty pine walls or walls with original chinking, warm carpets, and charming print fabrics. Each cottage comes with a cozy common area arranged with a sofa, overstuffed easy chair or rocking chair, small dining table and chairs, plenty of reading lamps, attractive antiques and accessories, and TV/VCR. A library of classic and contemporary videos is available for guests to select from for the evening.

A continental breakfast is attractively arranged on a tray in your cottage suite and includes croissants or homebaked muffins, farm-fresh eggs, cheese, jam or jellies, fruit juice, and choice of hot or cold cereals with cream along with coffee, tea, and hot chocolate. Couples can also bring their own lunch and dinner supplies if they wish; there is an on-site barbecue for guests use. For dining out in the evening ask about the availability of good seafood, especially the shellfish in a classic wine, garlic, and basil broth often served at Toby's Tavern in Coupeville; Toby's Parrot Head Ale is made in the microbrewery down just the street.

What's Nearby Greenbank

Travelers can visit Whidbey Island Greenbank Farm, the 1904 home to M.W. Whidbeys loganberry liqueur; the farm features a tasting room, visitors center, and picnic grounds; Telephone: (360) 678-7700. Meerkerk Garden, a lovely eleven-acre woodland rhododendron park with paths and trails among the trees, flowering native shrubs, wildflowers, perennials, and bulbs is located about 1 mile south; Telephone: (360) 678-1912. Sassafras Herb Farm, located nearby on Day Road, offers herb gardens, herb plants, and a gift shop. Located ten minutes north of Greenbank, the Keystone ferry takes autos and travelers across Puget Sound's Admiralty Inlet to Port Townsend and the Olympic Peninsula. Also see What's Nearby Langley on page 247 and What's Nearby Coupeville on page 221.

Other Recommended B&B Nearby

Cliff House and Seacliff Cottage, one of the most romantic destinations on the island is a contemporary architectural gem whose interior rooms wrap around a glass-walled atrium filled with lush plants—you can see and hear the rain as well; sunken living room with stone fireplace, romantic sleeping loft with king feather bed allows moonlit views of Admiralty Inlet; a separate cottage comes with a petite kitchen, queen feather bed, fireplace, and cozy window seat looking out to the water; contact innkeepers Peggy Moore and Walter O'Toole, 727 Windmill Drive, Freeland, WA 98249; Telephone (360) 331-1566; Internet site: www.whidbey.com/cliffhouse.

Skagit Bay Hideaway

1740B Goldenview Avenue
P.O. Box 497
LaConner, WA 98257
Phone: (360) 466–2262; (888) 466–2262
E-mail: hideaway@skagitbay.com
Internet site: www.skagitbay.com

Innkeepers: Earlene Beckes and Kevin Haberly
Rooms: 2 large suites with private baths/decks
Extras: Each suite has a gas fireplace, private hot tub on deck, terry robes, handmilled soaps
On the grounds: Views to the west of Skagit Bay, Whidbey Island, and several smaller islands
Smoking? Outdoors only
Visiting pets? No; 2 resident felines, Misty and Stormy
Credit cards: Visa, MasterCard
Rates: $$$$
How to get there: Take I-5 about one hour north of Seattle to exit 221 and go left (west) over the freeway; take the first right toward Conway/La Conner and proceed on Fir Island Road. The road will curve right heading north and, just beyond the blinking yellow light, you will cross the Skagit River. Continue to Chilberg Road and turn left here toward La Conner. Entering La Conner take the first left onto Maple Avenue; proceed south and curve to the right crossing Swinomish Channel via the Rainbow Bridge. Take the second left onto Snee-oosh Road and proceed for about 1⁷⁄₁₀ miles. Take Sunset Drive (there is a dead-end sign and a no beach access sign) as it heads down the hill; at this point Snee-oosh Road does a sweeping turn to the right. From Sunset Drive take the second left onto Goldenview Avenue to the third house on the right. There is a parking area for the guest house adjoining the road at the top of the property.

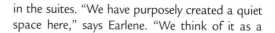

This is one of those hidden gems that provides travelers with a haven of rest and rejuvenation. Each of two suites is about 600 square feet in size and each has its own cozy living room with a gas fireplace, sofa, pillows, chairs, and reading lamps. In one of the rooms wide corner windows look south and west into the tall Douglas fir and out over Skagit Bay toward Whidbey Island. There is a selection of reading material including books on Skagit County history, a supply of games and puzzles as well as a CD/tape/radio. There's no TV in the suites. "We have purposely created a quiet space here," says Earlene. "We think of it as a place to reconnect with your partner and with your soul."

Guests walk up a flight of steps to their sleeping loft where a queen bed is dressed in a down comforter and fluffy pillows. Bedside tables hold reading lamps. From here you can step through a set of French doors out onto the upper deck where the views seem even closer. The private hot tub on this upper deck is made even more romantic with soft light coming through a double row of glass blocks set into a section of the wall next to the tub. The private baths in each suite feature large walk-in showers with double showerheads and four body sprays. It feels like bathing in a waterfall.

What else is there to do in this quiet place? Watch sunsets over Skagit Bay and stare at the ever-changing tidal waters of this north section of Puget Sound. Walk or drive to nearby Hope Island Inn for dinner; a dinner theater is also offered here. La Conner, a touristy fishing village set along picturesque Swinomish Channel, offers a number of good restaurants, cafes, delis, and espresso shops as well as gift shops and boutiques.

In the morning Earlene and Kevin bring breakfast to the suite from their quarters located below the guest house. Guests may relax in their terry robes and chat with the innkeepers as the round glass-topped table is set with colorful place mats, napkins and silver seashell napkin rings, colorful china, and stemware. The first course may be ricotta cheese hearts with raspberry sauce and fruit served on a clear glass plate that sits on the larger china plate. Fresh Dungeness crab and Havarti omelettes are often served. This comes with muffins hot from the oven, juice, and plenty of steaming hot gourmet coffee and teas. Mango tea is a special flavor always on hand.

What's Nearby La Conner

The Maple Hall Performance Center offers live theater and musical events throughout the year. The Skagit County Historical Museum on Fourth Street offers exhibits, hands-on history, and good views from its hilltop location. The La Conner Quilt Museum in the historic Gaches Mansion shows quilts from around the country and around the world. The Tillinghast Seed Company on East Morris Street offers an eclectic gift shop and a nostalgic look at days gone by in the seed and nursery business. There are establishments for renting boats, kayaks, and bicycles as well as for arranging lunch and dinner cruises and whale watching tours. The La Conner Visitor's Center can be contacted at (360) 466–4778. Also see What's Nearby Mount Vernon on page 253.

Eagles Nest Inn

4680 Saratoga Road
Langley, WA 98260
Phone: (360) 221-5331
E-mail: eaglnest@whidbey.com
Internet site: www.eaglesnestinn.com

Innkeepers: Jerry and Joanne Lechner
Rooms: 4 rooms with private baths; 1 waterfront cottage
Extras: TV/VCR in each room; ever expanding book and video library; hospitality bar and chocolate chip cookies in the inn's cookie jar; hot tub on outside deck, private hot tub at cottage
On the grounds: Adjacent to 400 acres of nature trails; views of Saratoga Passage, Camano Island, and Mount Baker
Smoking? Outdoors only
Visiting pets? No; no resident pets
Credit cards: Personal checks preferred
Rates: $$–$$$; cottage: $$$$
How to get there: Take I-5 north from Seattle for 20 miles to the Mukilteo-Clinton exit and proceed to the ferry dock. Take the 15-minute ferry ride across to Clinton on Whidbey Island and proceed north on Highway 525 to Langley Road; turn right here and continue to Cascade Avenue. Take a right on Cascade Avenue to Second Street; turn left here and proceed beyond Langley a little more than a mile to the inn (Second Street becomes Saratoga Drive). The inn is 8 miles from the ferry landing.

The contemporary octagonal-shaped inn is situated on a forested bluff so that it offers sweeping views of Saratoga Passage, Camano Island, and Mount Baker to the north. Guests enjoy walking quiet trails beneath tall Douglas fir—the fresh smell of the trees and the feel of fir needles underfoot evoke images of childhood treks through the forest. Couples can find relaxation on one of the inn's many decks, curl up with a good book, or unwind in the outdoor hot tub. Here the salty aromas and sounds of the sea and its many seabird species also permeate one's senses.

On the ground floor one airy suite is decorated in a garden motif including lacy ferns stenciled at the top of the wall. This spacious room comes with its own outside entrance, a south garden view, and a private swing just outside the door. Another room on the second level offers a large bay window with views of Saratoga Passage through tall firs, a king bed, skylight, and private bath. High atop the house and with a stunning 360-degree view from its wraparound windows and private deck, the Eagles Nest Room has a queen bed and private bath. Guests can use the upstairs lounge where a reading and video library is available and where a 10-foot bay-window seat offers restful forest views. A complimentary beverage counter and the inn's traditional cookie jar filled with scrumptious chocolate chip cookies are conveniently located here as well.

Breakfast is served in the main floor dining room or during warm summer months at tables on a lower deck that overlooks the passage. The menus, which will vary each day, consist of fresh pear pancake with caramel sauce and country sausage; alder-smoked salmon soufflé; or portobello mushroom omelet with Brie. For evening dining in the seaside village of Langley, ask about The Bistro, Café Langley, Giuseppe Italian, and Five-Ten Bar & Grill.

What's Nearby Langley

The Clyde Theatre on First Street offers year-round local stage productions and also first-run movies. In February there is an active Mystery Weekend in the area. The quaint town offers a host of galleries, artists' studios, gift shops, and charming boutiques. For maps and current information about special seasonal events in all of Island County, check the Internet site: www.whidbey.net/islandco, or contact the Langley Visitors Information Center, P.O. Box 403, Langley, WA 98260; Telephone: (360) 221–6765.

Other Recommended B&B Nearby

Country Cottage of Langley Bed & Breakfast, one of the first vintage homes in Langley to be remodeled for bed-and-breakfast travelers, original river-rock fireplace remains in common area, cozy rooms with feather beds and down comforters in old English, country style, and beach themes; two suites have fireplace, water views, and spas; charming cottage with Dutch door and window boxes; contact innkeepers Kathy and Bob Annecone, 215 Sixth Street, Langley, WA 98260; Telephone: (360) 221–8709.

Edenwild Inn

Eads Lane and Lopez Village Road
P.O. Box 271
Lopez Island, WA 98261
Phone: (360) 468-3238
E-mail: edenwildinn@msn.com
Internet site: www.edenwildinn.com

Innkeepers: Lauren and Jamie Stephens
Rooms: 8 rooms with private baths including 1 wheelchair accessible room; some rooms have fireplaces
Extras: Ferry landing, seaplane, or airport pick-up is available for guests; afternoon aperitifs available; the flat island terrain and roads are good for walking and bicycling; nearby bay is good for kayaking, tide pooling
On the grounds: Rose gardens, rose arbor walkways, formal cutting beds, herb garden, wraparound porch, views of Fisherman Bay and San Juan Channel
Smoking? Outdoors only
Visiting pets? No; no resident pets
Credit cards: Visa, MasterCard, American Express, Discover
Rates: $$–$$$
How to get there: From Anacortes take one of the Washington State ferries to Lopez Island, the first stop on the route to the other San Juan Islands; see specific ferry information in What's Nearby Anacortes on page 209. Exit ferry on Ferry Road, which becomes Fisherman Bay Road and proceed about 5 miles to Lopez Village. Turn right on Lopez Road South (if you pass the Chevron station you have missed the turn) to the inn, the first driveway on your right.

A traveler's San Juan Islands experience begins as soon as the ferry leaves Anacortes and angles across Rosario Strait toward Lopez Island. The salt air is fresh, pungent, and bracing. The cry of gulls seems close as they wheel and dip near the strait's churning tides. There may be a light breeze or a stiff breeze, there may be fog, mist, or rain, but regardless of the weather, the intrepid often congregate on the open decks and lean over the railing to snap photos of the passing scenery. Others may elect to stay inside, buy a cup of hot coffee and a pastry, sweet roll or sandwich, and watch the goings-on from wide seats and windows. Soon a few passengers go below decks to find their autos and to get ready to drive off the ferry at

Lopez Island. Most of the passengers remain aboard until reaching the larger islands—Orcas Island or San Juan Island.

The comfortable accommodations at the newly constructed Victorian-style inn include eight spacious guest rooms, one with wheelchair access. One room offers wide bay windows that allow views of the inn's colorful perennial gardens and of San Juan Channel. Another cozy room with a double bed comes with a fireplace, an antique soaking tub, and window view of wildlife. The largest room features king and queen beds, handsome artwork, and a spacious sitting area. Guests are invited to the living room for late afternoon aperitifs by the crackling fire, or they can enjoy walking the grounds to inspect the fine collection of roses, the formal cutting beds, the herb garden, and the water views. "The sunsets over San Juan Channel are especially grand," says Lauren.

Breakfast, prepared by husband and gourmet cook, Jamie, and served at 9:00 A.M., is also quite grand. Show up as late as 9:30 A.M. and still receive smiling service. Seven individual tables are set in the dining room; French doors lead out to the rose arbor and offer views of San Juan Channel and distant San Juan Island. Place mats and linen napkins in jewel tones of burgundy, deep green, and gold set off the soft grey-green walls and the creamy white place settings and silverware; the clamshell motif on the handles echo the inn's seaside location. Maple-almond granola and perhaps the positively luscious lemon-lavender scones are followed by herb rosemary-brie omelet, ricotta cheese torte with blackberry sauce, or orange oven French toast. Canadian bacon, pepper bacon, or sausage also accompanies the hot entree.

What's Nearby

The relatively flat terrain and flat roads on Lopez Island offer excellent walking and biking. Tide pools abound for exploring and the calm waters of Fisherman Bay are good for kayaking. Lopez Village offers a few eateries including a restaurant at Islander Lopez resort, Gail's (open during summer months), and nearly everyone's favorite, Bay Café.

Other Recommended B&B Nearby

The Inn at Swift's Bay has English country decor, five garden rooms, three with private baths and fireplaces along with a private beach; contact the innkeepers, Rt. 2, Box 3402, Lopez Island, WA 98261; Telephone: (360) 468-3636.

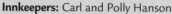

Innkeepers: Carl and Polly Hanson
Rooms: 2 rooms with water views and private baths
Extras: Access to private beach for walking; innkeeper plays the bagpipes
On the grounds: Views of Hale Passage and Strait of Georgia, north to Vancouver, B.C.
Smoking? Outdoors only
Visiting pets? No; resident chickens, rabbits, and visiting deer
Credit cards: Visa, MasterCard, American Express
Rates: $$
How to get there: Take I–5 two hours north of Seattle and Bellingham to exit 260 and go left onto Slater Road for 3⁷⁄₁₀ miles. Turn south onto Haxton Way for 6⁷⁄₁₀ miles to the Lummi Island ferry landing. The 10-minute ferry across Hale Passage aboard the *Whatcom Chief* departs hourly from 7:00 A.M. to midnight. On the island proceed to the right on North Nugent Road for 2⅘ miles; here the road turns around Point Migley and becomes West Shore Drive. Proceed ⁷⁄₁₀ mile and look for inn's sign on the left at the driveway; the mailbox is on the right. The house is octagonal in shape and faces the water.

West Shore Farm
Bed & Breakfast
2781 West Shore Drive
Lummi Island, WA 98262
Phone: (360) 758–2600

When guests enter the octagonal-shaped house and negotiate the spiral stairway to the main floor, they usually go directly to the windows and very soon ask for a geography lesson on the panoramic views. "From our windows we have a wonderful 180-degree view of the water and many of the islands," says Polly. This includes several of the smaller San Juan Islands and of Mount Constitution on Orcas Island south and west across Rosario Strait. Looking to the north guests learn the whereabouts of Matia Island, Sucia Island, Cherry Point, Point Whitehorn, Point Roberts, and Vancouver, British Columbia. "We see the lights of Vancouver at night and even lights from the Grouse Mountain Ski Area on the city's north side," explains Carl.

One settled in their rooms, couples often change into jeans and sweaters and pull on windbreakers for a trek across the road and down the stairway to the beach. The typical north coast beach yields treasures of driftwood, rocks, and shells and offers close-up views of the many seabirds that inhabit the area. Polly explains that folks can walk a mile or so along the beachfront here. You might spot seals, particularly down at Point Migley. Those who bring bicycles often enjoy biking the 7-mile loop at this northern end of the island that takes in Legoe Bay where the reef net fishermen can be seen during summer months.

The two rooms on the lower level offer king beds, cozy comforters, tables and chairs, and views of the water to the north and east. The larger room has a 1940s brown leather recliner and matching ottoman. "Folks call this vintage or antique," Polly says with a grin, "but it's really comfortable." A cupboard/closet in this room is jammed with great books and magazines and a two-drawer chest in the hallway is filled with games and puzzles. A big basket on the floor contains rolled maps of the region, many of which were taken from 450 miles in space.

Breakfast is served upstairs on the main level with the grand views. On chilly mornings and evenings, Carl builds a fire in the freestanding glass fireplace-stove. The wood crackles cheerfully and sparks swirl upward from the glass enclosure into the chimney flues—it's like having a colorful bonfire in your living room. Carl makes a great bread of several grains such as whole wheat, rye, and millet that he grinds and to which he may add cornmeal or amaranth. Guests work on their individual fruit compotes, perhaps of home-grown plums with a dollop of yogurt and raspberries or strawberries on top. Polly prepares the breakfast entree, often a tasty puff pancake baked in the oven and served in wedges with warm homemade berry sauce. Or she may do Eggs in the Garden in a large cast-iron skillet; first she takes layers of onion and tender steamed vegetables and forms them into small nests, then she breaks fresh eggs into the nests and lightly cooks the whole thing. With Carl's homemade bread fresh from the bread machine, Polly often serves organic jams and preserves, one particular favorite a ginger marmalade. The delicious breakfast is capped with steaming hot coffee, teas, or hot chocolate. For dining out in the evening ask about The Beach Store Café located on the island. You might also ask Carl to render a serenade with his bagpipes.

What's Nearby Lummi Island

The 9-mile island has 18 miles of county roads. At Legoe Bay travelers can watch local fishermen using the ancient Indian reef netting method of fishing during certain days in the summer months. Also see What's Nearby Bellingham on page 213.

The White Swan Guest House

1388 Moore Road
Mount Vernon, WA 98273
Phone: (360) 445-6805
Internet site: www.cnw.com/~wswan/

Innkeeper: Peter Goldfarb

Rooms: 3 rooms in main house share 2 baths; sunny garden cottage has a deck, kitchen, sleeping loft, and private bath; children are welcome in the cottage

Extras: Well-developed English-style perennial garden; near Skagit Valley flower fields—tulips, daffodils, and iris bloom in April

On the grounds: An acre of lawn, garden, and varieties of fruit trees

Smoking? Outdoors only

Visiting pets? No; 3 adult dogs—Shadow, a shepherd mix; black labs, Willy and Harley; orange chow puppy, Andy; none allowed in guest quarters

Credit cards: Visa, MasterCard

Rates: $-$$$

How to get there: From I-5 about one hour north of Seattle take exit 221 and follow signs to La Conner and to Fir Island Road; continue 5 miles west to blinking yellow light and bear right onto Moore Road. Proceed 1 mile to the inn's driveway located on the right.

While it doesn't feel as though you are on an island, this is small Fir Island, a peaceful farming community located just six miles from the historic fishing village of La Conner and just south of Mount Vernon. "We're close to the Skagit Valley flower fields," says Peter. "In spring much of the surrounding valley is carpeted with fields of blooming iris, tulips, and daffodils." Local growers raise these varieties for the international bulb market.

Upon arrival, Peter's bed-and-breakfast guests are immediately drawn to his large perennial garden—it blooms in lush profusion in a large area between the restored 1898 Queen Anne farmhouse and the charming Shingle-style cottage. Tall delphinium and larkspur mingle pleasantly with white and yellow daisies, pink and purple petunias, orange marigolds, peach and yellow snapdragons, and several new and old varieties of luscious roses. Many guests bring binoculars and scout about for the large birds that visit throughout the year. Perhaps the best show happens between November and March when the snow geese, white swans, and eagles visit. Visitors also bring bicycles to enjoy pedaling about the country roads; one favorite excursion is the 6-mile ride to La Conner, a touristy fishing village located along the Swinomish Channel.

Inside the large farmhouse guests find a platter of tempting chocolate chip cookies waiting on the sideboard. Three guest rooms offer king or queen beds, cozy comforters, comfortable pillows, and ample bedside reading lamps. One room features a cozy sitting nook in its adjacent turret. Peter's collection of hand-stitched needlework samplers is displayed throughout the inn amid the unpretentious country style of the common areas on the main floor. The parlor has stacks of books and piles of magazines to read; the wood stove is fired up on chilly evenings.

Mornings bring good smells of freshly brewing coffee available around 7:30 A.M. on a tray in the living room. Breakfast is served around 9:00 A.M. in the sunny yellow dining room. Homemade rhubarb sauce, applesauce, and assortment of fresh fruits may be served along with fruit juice smoothies and coffeecake or muffins filled with fresh fruit. "I'm starting my twelfth year as a bed-and-breakfast innkeeper," says Peter. "For the most part it's been fun doing this by myself. I keep hoping, but the four dogs don't lift a paw to help."

What's Nearby Mount Vernon

For current information about the annual Skagit Valley Tulip Festival that takes place during the month of April check the Internet site: www.tulipfestival.org; Telephone: (360) 428–5959. Also see What's Nearby La Conner on page 245 and What's Nearby Anacortes on page 209.

Other Recommended B&B Nearby

Storyville Bed & Breakfast, large 1904 country farmhouse, with five guest rooms and one suite, on Pleasant Ridge with views of Mount Baker and Cascades; contact innkeepers James and Francesca Embery, 1880 Chilberg Road, Mount Vernon, WA 98273; Telephone (360) 466-3207. **Valentine House Bed & Breakfast,** a newly constructed Victorian-style inn, offers three rooms with private baths, turrets, lace-covered bay windows and cozy parlor with wood-burning fireplace; outdoor weddings held on the grounds; contact innkeeper Laura Engebret-sen, 1842 Valentine Road, Mount Vernon, WA 98273; Telephone: (360) 466-3079.

Spring Bay Inn
on Orcas Island

Obstruction Pass Trailhead Road
P.O. Box 97
Olga, WA 98279
Phone: (360) 376–5531
E-mail: info@springbayinn.com;
Internet site: www.springbayinn.com

This waterfront chalet-style inn, located on Spring Bay at the far southeast corner of Orcas Island, may be the ultimate destination retreat in the islands. Innkeepers Sandy and Carl, who are retired park rangers.

If the weather cooperates, you are invited to join other guests on a guided sunset kayak cruise in the small protected bay. Warm up later in the Great Room on the main level with its large fireplace on one end, and a wood stove at the

Innkeepers: Sandy Playa and Carl Burger, retired park rangers
Rooms: 5 rooms with wood-burning fireplaces and private baths; the inn is a TV/VCR-free zone
Extras: Guided pre-brunch kayak tour (weather permitting) by innkeepers; guests can explore shoreline, wetlands, and forested trails in nearby Obstruction Pass State Park
On the grounds: Waterfront views of the bay, adjacent forests of Douglas fir and madrone
Smoking? Outdoors only
Visiting pets? No; 2 resident golden retrievers, Carson and Radcliff
Credit cards: Visa, MasterCard, Discover
Rates: $$$$
How to get there: The inn is located 20 miles from the Orcas Island ferry landing. From the ferry landing proceed on Horseshoe Highway through the community of Eastsound and continue past Rosario Resort, Moran State Park to the small community of Olga. Turn left onto Pt. Lawrence Road for ¾ mile, then turn right onto Obstruction Pass Road for ⁹⁄₁₀ mile to Obstruction Pass Park Trailhead, a dirt road. Turn here, making right fork, and proceed ¾ mile to inn's gate; from here proceed ⁹⁄₁₀ mile to the inn.

other. Getting acquainted with fellow travelers and with the innkeepers while sampling Northwest wines or herbal teas are the main agendas of this sociable gathering. Those inclined may pick up a guitar or other musical instruments and strum a tune or two. You will find no TV on the premises; this is a media-quiet zone. Couples who have signed up for one of the two hot tubs may disappear to enjoy a late evening soak outdoors with views of the water.

The five guest rooms feature high ceilings, large expanses of windows, water views, and wood-burning Rumford fireplaces. The largest suite offers great views of the bay from its twenty-eight windows as well as a queen bed and private outdoor soaking tub. All rooms come with comfortable feather beds accented with handmade quilts and all have private baths. Children are welcome at the inn but kayak tour restrictions may apply.

Mornings at the inn start at 7:30 A.M. with baskets of fresh baked pastries, fresh fruit, and coffee or tea placed outside guest room doors. At 8:30 A.M. comes a guided kayak tour with Sandy and Carl. After this invigorating adventure, a healthy gourmet brunch is then served family-style at 10:30 A.M. in the bay-front dining area. The delicious fare may include souffléd potato pancakes with smoked salmon sauce, blueberry Riesling soup, freshly squeezed orange juice, fruit smoothies, and for dessert decadent chocolate brownies. Sandy says that one can always work off the calories with a brisk late morning walk on the many trails that lace in and around the forests of Douglas fir and madrone near the inn or in adjacent Obstruction Pass State Park.

What's Nearby

See What's Nearby Orcas Island on page 225 and What's Nearby Anacortes on page 209.

Other Recommended B&Bs Nearby

Buck Bay Farm Bed & Breakfast, a traditional farmhouse near Moran State Park with views offers four rooms with private baths, one handicap-accessible room, sun room, sunny decks and porches, and hearty breakfasts; contact innkeepers Rick and Janet Bronkey, Point Lawrence Road, Star Route Box 45, Olga, WA 98279; Telephone: (360) 376-2908. **Sand Dollar Inn,** on Buck Bay with sweeping water and pastoral views features Asian antiques, comfortable rooms with private baths, and sumptuous breakfasts served in the sun room; contact innkeepers Ric and Ann Sanchez, Star Route Box 10, Olga, WA 98279; Telephone: (360) 376-5696.

La Cachette Bed & Breakfast

10312 Seabeck Highway
P.O. Box 920
Seabeck, WA 98380
Phone: (360) 613-2845; (888) 613-2845
E-mail: lacachette@moriah.com
Internet site: www.moriah.com/inns

Innkeepers: Drs. Chris and Mike Robbins
Rooms: 4 elegantly appointed rooms with fireplaces and private baths; two suites have views of Hood Canal
Extras: Formal tea served in great room at 4:00 P.M.; guests may purchase inn-prepared gourmet lunches; silver-service coffee and tea in-room each morning
On the grounds: 10 acres of forest and rolling meadows, grazing sheep, two large ponds and gazebo, many flowering ornamentals, views of Hood Canal
Smoking? Outdoors only
Visiting pets? No; no resident pets
Credit cards: Visa, MasterCard, American Express
Rates: $$$–$$$$
How to get there: From Tacoma-Gig Harbor take Highway 16 heading north toward Bremerton. At Port Orchard take Highway 3 and continue north; exit at Newberry Hill Road and proceed west for approximately 5 miles toward Hood Canal. At Seabeck Highway turn right and continue for about 3 miles; immediately after crossing Wade Road intersection in about 100 yards, turn right into the inn's driveway.

Hood Canal, the narrow body of saltwater that looks like a long finger with a crook at the end, extends southwesterly and is separated from Puget Sound by the Kitsap Peninsula. Travelers who venture along the secondary highways and byways to reach the Seabeck area will be richly rewarded by vistas largely untouched by commercial tourism. La Cachette is a French word meaning "the hideaway," and this lovely pastoral inn fits its name in every way. "We wanted to bring to our bed and breakfast a sense of the style and grace of the Ile-de-France region near Paris," explains Chris. She and her husband Mike are doctors of clinical psychology as well as a couple who have a sense of the kind of comforts that travelers appreciate.

Guests who arrive by 4:00 will be invited to formal tea in the great room to partake of luscious fruit tarts and elegant pastries served from ornate silver trays. Rooms come with a brass king bed or a luxurious canopied king bed, a gas fireplace, TV, plush robes, and an elegant private bath. One room has greenhouse windows overlooking the gardens and fountain. The grande suite on the second floor has a magnificent view of Hood Canal, rolling meadows, and ponds; the decor is deep plum and celadon. The first floor suite has the canopied king bed.

Guests are invited to explore the grounds, ponds, and forested perimeter to watch the sheep that graze on the lower lawn. The inn also prepares a gourmet picnic lunch for a romantic afternoon rendezvous by the pond, in the charming gazebo, or at nearby Scenic Beach State Park. In the morning about half an hour before breakfast, coffee and tea in silver pots are delivered to each room. Guests agree that this is a most leisurely and wonderfully civilized ritual. Breakfast is served in the formal dining room with views of Hood Canal from 8:00 to 9:00 A.M. Freshly squeezed orange juice, additional coffee and teas, morning pastries, and granola with fresh fruit comprise the first course. This is followed by home-baked breads still warm from the oven and a hot entree that highlights fare unique to the Pacific Northwest, such as alderwood-smoked salmon fillets or fresh oysters from Hood Canal waters.

What's Nearby

Antiquing in Poulsbo, fishing at Seabeck Marina, exploring the byways of this section of Hood Canal are pleasant daytime options. The Bremerton Symphony offers evening concerts throughout the year. There are numerous restaurants for evening dining in nearby Silverdale.

Other Recommended B&B Nearby

Seabreeze Cottage, a very private spot on Hood Canal for those who wish complete privacy; the tide reaches nearly to the overhanging deck; hot tub and hammock with water views, two loft bedrooms, fireplace, and well-equipped kitchen; contact owner Dennis Fulton at 16609 Olympic View Road N.W., Silverdale, WA 98383; Telephone: (360) 692-4648. **Summer Song Bed & Breakfast,** a charming Hansel-and-Gretel-style cottage complete with small living room, dining room, bedroom, bath, kitchen, fireplace, and private decks; gourmet breakfast features a wild huckleberry pastry; contact the innkeepers at 9141 Sunset Lane N.W., P.O. Box 82, Seabeck, WA 98380; Telephone: (360) 830-5089.

Willcox House

2390 Tekiu Road NW
Seabeck, WA 98380
Phone: (360) 830–4492; (800) 725–9477
E-mail: willcoxhouse@silverlink.net
Internet site: www.willcoxhouse.com

Innkeepers: Cecilia and Phillip Hughes
Rooms: 5 rooms with private baths
Extras: Gourmet meals including fixed-price dinner options
On the grounds: Outrageous views of Hood Canal to the west; boat dock; landscaped grounds, walking paths down to the dock
Smoking? Outdoors only
Visiting pets? No; no resident pets
Credit cards: Visa, MasterCard, Discover
Rates: $$-$$$$
How to get there: At Bremerton from Highway 3 go west on Kitsap Way for 1⅜ miles to Northlake Way (near the Red Apple Market) and fork left here. Proceed 1¹⁄₁₀ miles and fork left onto Seabeck Highway; go 2⁹⁄₁₀ miles and then turn left on Holly Road. Proceed 4⁶⁄₁₀ miles (past Camp Union) and turn left at stop sign onto Seabeck-Holly Road. Drive 5¼ miles to Old Holly Hill Road and fork right; go 200 yards and turn right at mailboxes on Tekiu Road. Follow narrow winding paved road downward for 1⅜ miles, bear left at the forks and drive through the gatehouse to the inn's canopied entrance.

One's reward for finding this extraordinary and historic 1930s inn is unabashed delight and wonderment. To think that a grand manor of this caliber, all 10,000 square feet of it, was constructed back in 1936 in this remote location at the edge of Hood Canal, makes one think of the likes of a Howard Hughes. "Actually our historic records show that Clark Gable once visited here," explains Cecilia. "We've named one of our guest rooms in his honor." The Willcox family had society connections far beyond the Pacific Northwest and many well-known men and women of the 1930s are reported to have visited their sumptuous manor on Hood Canal.

Guests first enjoy a tour of the main floor with its handsome great room and intimate dining room with windows facing the water. French doors open from the great room to landscaped grounds and a trail that leads down to the 300-foot private pier, floating boat dock, and beach. A fire crackles in the great room's enormous copper-faced fireplace, where a grand piano and sumptuous overstuffed sofas and chairs are grouped. The oak parquet floors are polished. It isn't difficult at all to imagine George Gershwin at the piano entertaining guests with one of his pre World War II melodies.

The couple spent fourteen months renovating, refurbishing, and redecorating the house before opening to guests in 1989. In the spacious guest rooms one may find a brass or marble fireplace, a queen or king bed with luxurious linens and comforters, and furniture and lamps of the period. One room boasts an Art Deco lighted lady's vanity in the lavish bathroom.

Breakfast is served from 8:30 A.M. in the dining room on the main floor. Elegant, tasteful, and delicious are the best words to describe Cecilia's fare—from Belgian waffles and crepes to breakfast soufflés and stuffed French toast—all served with silver, lace, glass, crystal, and fresh flowers. The couple also offers fine dining in the evening, but reservations are a must.

What's Nearby

The area abounds in Native American history, hiking, boating, and fishing and shellfishing—oysters, shrimp, crab, and clams are sought at various times of the year. Farmers' markets, floatplane tours, and golf are other activities readily available. The area is accessible to Silverdale, Bremerton, Pouslbo, Bainbridge Island, and Seattle. Also see What's Nearby Federal Way-Tacoma on page 227.

Other Recommended B&B Nearby

Lomas' Murphy House Bed & Breakfast, a few miles from Bainbridge Island via a small bridge to the Norwegian bayside village of Poulsbo; rooms come with an elegant mix of country French and Scandanavian with a touch of nautical and marine decorations; close to the harbor, marina, and parks, and village shops along Liberty Bay; contact innkeepers Bob and Barbara Lomas, 425 NE Hostmark Street, Poulsbo, WA 98370; Telephone: (360) 779-1600.

Chambered Nautilus Bed & Breakfast Inn

5005 Twenty-second Avenue NE
Seattle, WA 98105
Phone: (206) 522-2536; (800) 545-8459
E-mail: chamberednautilus@MSN.com
Internet site: www.bed-breakfast-seattle.com

Innkeepers: Joyce Schulte, Steve Poole, and Karen Carbonneau
Rooms: 6 rooms with private baths; 1- and 2-bedroom furnished suites in University Suites adjacent to the inn
Extras: Tea and homemade cookies on arrival; private phones in rooms with voice mail and dataports
On the grounds: English-style garden; native perennials
Smoking? Outdoors only
Visiting pets? No; resident teddy bears
Credit cards: Visa, MasterCard, American Express
Rates: $$-$$$
How to get there: Take I-5 northbound through Seattle to the Fiftieth Street exit; turn right on Fiftieth and follow this street to the flashing red stop light at Twentieth Avenue NE. Turn left at this light, go to Fifty-fourth Street and turn right; proceed downhill to Twenty-second Avenue and turn right. Look for the inn's sign and the large blue Georgian Colonial house; it is located a few steps upward on the hillside and faces east.

The Georgian Colonial inn, constructed in 1915 by the Gowan family, is located near the heart of the University Village Center and close to the University of Washington campus. Dr. Gowan founded the department of Oriental Studies at the university. "The area offers much to see and do," says Joyce, "including lots of green spaces, paths, and waterside trails to walk, jog, bicycle, and even rollerblade!" The 22-mile Burke-Gilman Trail around Lake Washington is nearby as are Greenlake and Ravenna parks.

In the evenings guests often congregate and enjoy the spacious common room on the main floor with its wood-burning fireplace and inviting sofa and wingback chairs; the room is amply supplied with books, newspapers, games, and a working gramophone along with a tray of hot tea and homemade cookies. French doors open to the enclosed sun porch.

Rose Chamber, one of the four spacious rooms on the second floor, features a rose-covered wallpaper from the 1930s. The polished oak antique queen bed, dresser, and armoire give the room a warm old-fashioned feel. On the top floor is a roomy hideaway with gray wood paneling, a bedside fireplace, eyebrow windows over the queen antique iron bed, and a window seat with mountain views.

Breakfast is served between 8:00 and 9:00 A.M. in either the fireplaced dining area or on the cheerful sun porch. The meal starts with fresh fruit, juice, steaming hot coffee from a local roaster, and homemade granola. This might be followed by Northwest salmon breakfast pie or marmalade-stuffed French toast with orange syrup. "Our guests leave the table more than ready for a busy day of sightseeing," says Steve with a grin. For evening dining good restaurants in the immediate area include Ciao Bella and Union Bay Café.

What's Nearby Seattle

University of Washington's Visitors Information Center, (206) 543–9198, provides helpful maps and current information on cultural and sporting events. Nearby University Village Center offers a gaggle of interesting shops, delis, cafes, galleries, bookstores, and a great weekend Farmers' Market. For information about theater and performance events at ACT, Intiman, Empty Space, Paramount, and Fifth Avenue theaters, call Seattle-King County Visitor Information at (206) 461–5840 or write to 520 Pike Street, Suite 1300, Seattle, WA 98101. Washington State online guide: www.tourism.wa.gov/012.htm; or call (800) 544–1800, ext. 012.

Other Recommended B&B Nearby

The Buchanan Inn, An Island Bed & Breakfast, in renovated 1912 Oddfellows Hall; four spacious suites with private baths, two have antique wood stoves; contact innkeepers Ron and Judy Gibbs (happy corporate drop-outs) at 8494 Oddfellows Road, Bainbridge Island, WA 98110; Telephone: (206) 780–9258. **Foxbridge Bed & Breakfast,** a new Georgian country manor-style bed-and-breakfast features gourmet breakfast fare and secluded country location; contact innkeepers Beverly and Chuck Higgins, 30680 Highway 3 NE, Poulsbo, WA 98370; Telephone: (360) 498–5599; email: foxbridge@sprintmail.com.

Roberta's Bed & Breakfast

1147 Sixteenth Avenue East
Seattle, WA 98112
Phone: (206) 329-3326
E-mail: RobertasBB@aol.com
Internet site: www.RobertasBB.com

Innkeeper: Roberta Barry
Rooms: 5 rooms with private baths; each room has a telephone/dataport/voice mail
Extras: Piano with vintage sheet music; wake-up coffee and tea on tray at room door; selection of vintage books in each room; gas fireplace in common room
On the grounds: One block from Volunteer Park, home of the Asian Art Museum and a large conservatory with an orchid collection; one block from bus line to downtown
Smoking? Outdoors only
Visiting pets? No; no resident pets
Credit cards: Visa, MasterCard
Rates: $$-$$$
How to get there: From I-5 northbound take exit 166 and proceed north and east on Olive Way, which becomes John Street; continue east to Fifteenth Avenue and turn left proceeding 8 blocks to Prospect Street. Turn right here then turn left onto Sixteenth Street to the inn.

O n one of Seattle's tree-lined residential neighborhoods, longtime innkeeper Roberta Barry welcomes travelers to her bed and breakfast in the historic Capitol Hill area. "We're just a couple of blocks from Volunteer Park, which has a fabulous view of the city," says Roberta. "It also houses the Asian Art Museum and a large glass conservatory for native and exotic flowers." There is an extensive orchid collection here as well.

The large Craftsman-style house with its wide front porch is roomy and comfortable with five spacious rooms on the second and third floors. The top-floor room offers a romantic hideaway with a window that frames a view of the Cascade Mountains to the east. An eclectic collection of books is found in each room including authors such as Agatha Christie, Iris Murdoch, and Robert B. Parker. One room on the second floor has an inviting love seat. All the rooms have been updated and refurbished within the past year with new carpets and contemporary colors. In the morning Roberta brews up a batch of coffee and provides a help-yourself tray near your guest room door.

A hearty breakfast is served at the large table in the main-floor dining room, where an antique Franklin stove in the corner seems to be overlooking the companionable event. "Sometimes we fire him up on really chilly mornings during winter months," says Roberta. Weekend guests might settle onto the sofa in front of the gas fireplace in the common room and peruse the Sunday *New York Times* before eating. Travelers often enjoy sharing adventures as they eat Roberta's freshly baked banana-nut muffins or cinnamon coffeecake along with Dutch babies, stuffed French toast, or gingerbread pancakes with lemon sauce. For dining out in the evening, ask about Café Lago (Italian fare), Coastal Kitchen (a local favorite), and Café Flora, an upscale vegetarian eatery nearby.

What's Nearby

The Capitol Hill area is great for walking with all kinds of shops, cafes, delis, and restaurants located nearby. The calm protected waters and shorelines of Lake Union offer walking and biking paths, waterside parks and nature habitats to be explored by foot, kayak, canoe, sailboat, motorboat, or seaplane. At the Center for Wooden Boats a flotilla of restored vintage rowboats and sailboats can be rented by the hour; Telephone: (206) 382-2628. The eclectic Broadway District and Fremont Neighborhood has cafes, delis, shops, and boutiques. Also see What's Nearby Seattle on page 261.

Other Recommended B&Bs Nearby

The Bacon Mansion, an Edwardian-style Tudor dating to 1909, with marble fireplaces, a grand piano, an Italian fountain, and ten stately guest rooms; contact innkeeper Daryl King, 959 Broadway East, Seattle, WA 98102; Telephone: (206) 329-1864. **Salisbury House Bed & Breakfast,** located in the Capitol Hill area offers queen beds with down comforters, some rooms have bay windows with cushioned window seats; for breakfast guests often request the favored Baked Blintzes; contact innkeepers Cathryn and Mary Wiese at 750 Sixteenth Avenue East, Seattle, WA 98112; Telephone: (206) 328-8682.

Redmond House
Bed & Breakfast

317 Glen Avenue
Snohomish, WA 98290
Phone: (360) 568-2042

Innkeepers: Ken and Mary Riley
Rooms: 2 rooms with private baths, 2 rooms with shared bath
Extras: Small ballroom with selection of big band and ballroom dance music; hot tub located in sun room; late afternoon treats and hot beverages
On the grounds: Extensive plantings of rhododendrons
Smoking? Outdoors only
Visiting pets? No; resident longhaired white cat, Lady Jane, not allowed in guest rooms
Credit cards: Visa, MasterCard
Rates: $$
How to get there: From I-5 about 30 miles north of Seattle near Everett, take the Wenatchee-Stevens Pass exit to Highway 2; cross the "trestle" and stay to the right on old Highway 2. Continue east and south and take the first exit into Snohomish; you will enter on Avenue D. Turn left (east) onto Fourth, then right onto Glen Avenue and proceed to the inn. The town is about 7 miles from I-5.

"I think our community must be antiques-hunting heaven," says Mary with a smile. "We have over 400 antique dealers here." Most of these eclectic establishments are arranged along First Avenue in the downtown area. The Snohomish River meanders just west of the avenue forming a scenic backdrop to the small community. Guests who arrive at the inn first see an array of rhododendrons planted on the grounds; when they bloom in the spring the mass of color offers a stunning frame for the 1890 Victorian. The large wraparound porch offers cozy wicker furniture and a porch swing—good places to linger with a cup of tea and a novel or the latest antiques dealers journal. Mary offers such treats in the late afternoon as her famous chocolate chip cookies and orange-cranberry bread.

Four guest rooms on the second floor offer

comfortable lodgings; two of the rooms have private baths. One of these has a king four-poster rice feather bed in handsome dark cherry. This is covered with a handmade Amish quilt done in a white-on-white with love birds stitched in each corner and in the circular center section. Lace curtains dress the windows and the carpet is a cream Berber. Two subtly striped Victorian wallpapers adorn the walls with a soft floral border dividing them at the wainscoting level. Two overstuffed chairs with reading lamps nearby complete this spacious room.

Guests are invited to relax in the downstairs parlor, in the TV sitting room, or in the 25-square-foot ballroom. A selection of big band music is available for those who want to try a lively cha-cha, a graceful waltz, a slow or fast fox trot, a jaunty swing, or a romantic rumba. Ken and Mary are avid ballroom dancers and enjoy talking "dance talk" with interested guests.

Breakfast is served at one seating beginning at 8:30 or 9:00 A.M. in the formal dining room. Mary sets the table with neutral linens and one of her six sets of china. These plates are placed on handsome silver chargers also with gold rims. Lighted candles and a bouquet of flowers add to the elegant table dressing. The meal might begin with a delicious Breakfast Parfait of oatmeal, yogurt, crushed pineapple, and slivered almonds. This is followed with a hot entree such as Dutch babies with strawberries, bananas, and kiwi with warm maple syrup or a croissant sandwich of sliced ham, scrambled egg, and Swiss cheese. For lunch or dinner options ask the innkeepers about local eateries such as Collector's Choice, Venus, Silver King Café, The Cabbage Patch, and Jordan's Café & Bakery.

What's Nearby Snohomish

In addition to hundreds of antiques dealers and dozens of antiques shops, the historic downtown area features gift shops, boutiques, cafes, delis, and parks. For additional information contact the Snohomish County Visitors' Center, P.O. Box 135, Snohmish, WA 98290; Telephone: (360) 568–2526; Internet site: www.snohomish.org.

Other Recommended B&B Nearby

Snohomish Grand Valley Inn B&B, a 1940s farmhouse where guests are treated to old-fashioned hospitality and a hearty country breakfast; children welcome; contact the innkeepers at 11910 Springhetti Road, Snohomish, WA 98290; Telephone: (360) 568–8854.

Commencement Bay
Bed & Breakfast

3312 North Union Avenue
Tacoma, WA 98407
Phone: (253) 752–8175
E-mail: greatviews@aol.com
Internet site: www.bestinns.net/usa/cb

Innkeepers: Sharon and Bill Kaufmann
Rooms: 3 rooms all with telephones, cable TV/VCR, and private baths
Extras: Dinner and massage packages available; exercise room; vintage grand piano; Game Room offers large screen TV/VCR and selection of videos; office area with modem hookup; mountain bikes
On the grounds: Views of Commencement Bay and daily boating activity, view of Brown's Point Lighthouse
Smoking? Outdoors only on back garden deck
Visiting pets? No; resident black cocker spaniel, Lady Di
Credit cards: Visa, MasterCard, American Express, Discover
Rates: $–$$$
How to get there: From Seattle/Olympia/Sea-Tac Airport take I–5 to exit 132 to Highway 16 (exit reads BREMERTON). In about 1 mile exit at Union Avenue turning right and proceeding 2 miles to North Twenty-sixth; turn left to Proctor Avenue (first traffic light) and turn right here. Go downhill to Union Avenue and turn right; the inn is the second house on the right.

The stately Colonial-style inn offers a commanding view of Commencement Bay and is located just above the scenic waterfront area that extends along Ruston Way. Guests can also see the Brown's Point Lighthouse and another lighthouse on nearby Vashon Island. Bill is active in the Coast Guard reserve and enjoys sharing information with interested guests about the navigational features in the bay and giving easy directions for exploring the myriad destinations and activities in the Tacoma area. A pin map in the Library and Game Room shows that guests from Germany, Japan, and Nigeria have joined others here from nearly every state in the U.S.

Guests often congregate in the comfortable main-floor living room with its conversational seating areas, vintage grand piano, warm area rugs, and views of the landscaped grounds and bay far below. A warm fire in the fireplace invites one to linger over a cup of coffee or tea. A soak in the hot tub on the rear deck may appeal after a day of visiting parks and gardens. You can also browse the city's Beaux Arts-style Union Station shops, Antique Row, and the Broadway Theater District. "Our fabulous galleries show everything from neon and grunge to glass and Picasso in clay," says Sharon with a friendly smile. "And we often help guests with arranging theater tickets for live theater and for musical performances."

Three guest rooms provide comfortable havens with views of either Commencement Bay or of the distant Cascade Mountains and sun rises from behind 14,000-foot Mount Rainier.

In one room done in forest green, pale rose, and burgundy, a cherry four-poster queen bed, velvet settee, and crystal chandelier enhance the luxurious ambience and the distant mountain views. In another room soft hues of peach and blue accent the rich pecan furniture, ecru bed linens, and heirloom quilt.

In the morning guests find freshly brewed coffee set out by 7:30 A.M. Breakfast is served in the formal dining room at 8:30 A.M. The chandelier is lit and soft music is heard in the background. The selection begins with seasonal fruits, juice, and fresh pastries. The main entree may be Peach Melba Dutch Babies with Red Raspberry Ecstasy from nearby Maury Island Farms or it may be poached pears with raspberry sauce or Blackberry Delight from the same farm. For lunch or evening dining ask about C.I. Shenanigans, Lobster Shop, and Old House Café.

What's Nearby

On clear days snowy Mount Rainier looms high on the eastern horizon; especially fine views are enjoyed from the scenic waterfront area along Ruston Way. Several eateries on the waterfront offer deckside eating along with the grand views. Also see What's Nearby Federal Way—Tacoma on page 227 and What's Nearby Seattle on page 261.

Other Recommended B&B Nearby

Bay Vista Bed & Breakfast, located in north Tacoma on a hillside with high sweeping views of south Puget Sound and Vashon and Maury islands; contact innkeeper Fran Borhek, 4617 Darien Drive, Tacoma, WA 98407; Telephone: (253) 759-8084.

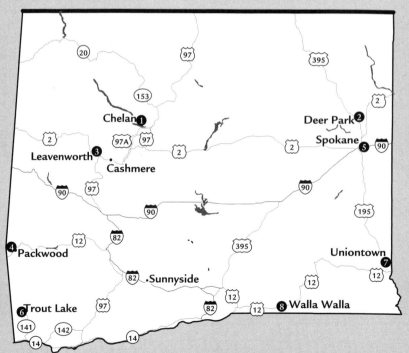

N

AK
BC
WA
OR

Chelan ❶

Deer Park ❷
Spokane ❺

Leavenworth ❸
Cashmere

Packwood ❹

Uniontown ❼

Sunnyside

Trout Lake ❻

Walla Walla ❽

Washington Cascades and Eastern Washington

Numbers on map refer to towns numbered below.

Growly Bear Bed & Breakfast

37311 SR 706
Ashford, WA 98304
Phone: (360) 569-2339; (800) 700-2339

Innkeeper: Susan Jenny Johnson
Rooms: 4 rooms, 2 with private baths, 1 is a large suite with a sitting area
Extras: Baskets of fruit, snacks in guest rooms; close to scenic drives in Mount Rainier National Park
On the grounds: Historic 1890 homestead
Smoking? Outdoors only
Visiting pets? No; no resident pets
Credit cards: Visa, MasterCard, American Express
Rates: $$
How to get there: From I-5 between Olympia and Portland take exit 68 and proceed east on Highway 12 for 32 miles to Morton. Turn north onto Highway 7 and continue 17 miles to Elbe. Turn east onto Highway 706 and proceed about 7 miles to Ashford; continue 5 miles from Ashford toward Mount Rainier National Park and just beyond mile post 12 go across Goat Creek Bridge and turn left at the inn's sign. From the Federal Way or Tacoma area, take either Highway 161 or Highway 7 south toward Elbe and follow directions above.

Travelers who venture off the beaten path into this section of the Washington Cascades are rewarded by close encounters with 14,410-foot Mount Rainier. "Lots of our guests enjoy summer and fall hiking in Mount Rainier National Park," says Susan. "Then during the winter the downhill and cross-country skiers flock to the area." Here close to the mountain at an elevation of 2,100 feet, guests can curl up in a rustic homestead house built back in 1890 when the area was first settled. They hear the whispering sounds of the wind in the firs, hemlocks, and cedars and the sounds of Goat Creek bubbling not far away beyond the garden.

Four rustic rooms offer comfortable beds and handmade quilts and two rooms come with private baths. One room has an antique iron bed and features handsplit cedar shakes and pine boards on the walls and ceiling. Another room uses wood from historic National Mill on its walls. This large room also comes with a queen sleigh bed, cozy sitting area with two sofas, a small balcony, and a private bath. Susan arranges baskets filled with fresh fruit, crackers, and candies in each guest room. A roomy guest lounge on the main floor offers sitting places, reading lamps, and a sideboard with hot and cold beverages and freshly baked cookies. Books and magazines are in ample supply here as well.

Susan serves breakfast from 7:30 to 9:30 A.M. and on chilly mornings she often cooks on her grandmother's old wood cookstove. The meal begins with the usual juices and fresh fruit plate followed by tasty egg and breakfast meat entrees. There are also fresh pastries baked by Susan such as a cream-cheese coffeecake with orange peel, a luscious strudel with apple filling, or a walnut roll with cinnamon and nutmeg. For dining out in the evening guests can walk to Alexander's, a restaurant and inn located next door.

What's Nearby Ashford

The primary destination here is Mount Rainier National Park with its numerous areas for hiking, skiing, snowmobiling, and snowshoeing. Birdwatching and photography are other active pursuits. The park celebrates its 100th anniversary in 1999; look for special events at Paradise and Sunrise, two scenic drives that lead up to panoramic locations on the mountain. Paradise is accessed from the Ashford area, Sunrise from the east side near the Chinook Pass highway. Sunrise is the more arduous drive but the rewards are many, including wonderful wildflower meadows with environmentally sensitive paths and trails among the native plantings. Additional information about Mount Rainier National Park can be obtained from park headquarters in Ashford, (360) 569-2211. For mountain pass weather reports call (206) 368-4499.

Other Recommended B&B Nearby

Jasmer's at Mount Rainier, two cozy rooms with private entrances on Big Creek; one comes with queen bed, TV/VCR, fireplace, bay window; both offer use of outdoor hot tub; in-room continental breakfast of pastries, muffins, biscotti, fruit; contact innkeepers Luke and Tanna Osterhaus, 30005 SR 706 East, P.O. Box 347, Ashford, WA 98304; Telephone: (360) 569-2682.

Love's Victorian Bed & Breakfast

North 31317 Cedar Road
Deer Park, WA 99006
Phone: (509) 276-6939
E-mail: lovesbandb@juno.com
Internet site: www.bbhost.com/lovesvictorian

Innkeepers: Bill and Leslie Love
Rooms: 3 rooms with private baths, 1 room comes with gas fireplace
Extras: Elegant Queen Anne Victorian constructed in the mid-1980s; afternoon tea served in sun room to arriving guests; picnic lunches and dinners can be arranged; parlors and common areas have fireplaces; music room with baby grand piano
On the grounds: Outdoor hot tub just outside sun room, extra towels, robes, and slippers
Smoking? Outdoors only
Visiting pets? No; resident chow, Shamoo; Doberman, Luther; Scottish fold cats, Lilly, Emma, Sweet Pea, Mittens, and Henry; Polish banty rooster and chickens
Credit cards: Visa, MasterCard
Rates: $$–$$$
How to get there: From downtown Spokane take Highway 395 heading north approximately 20 miles to Deer Park. After Dennison-Chattaroy Road take the first right and go to stop sign. Cross the railroad tracks and proceed 2⅜ miles to the inn located on the left. The inn is located about 25 minutes from Spokane.

Travelers would have difficulty missing the imposing Queen Anne Victorian-style house with its handsome cupola, miniature balcony on the second level, ample wraparound porch, and traditional gingerbread decorative trim. Although it may seem unusual to find a traditional Victorian in the wilds of eastern Washington and mountainous area north of Spokane, the Loves relate a poignant story that surrounds its construction. "Our log home burned to the ground while we were at church the day after our twenty-second wedding anniversary," says Leslie. She goes on to explain that in the ashes survived a few pages of a book of Victorian house plans, and it was this plan that Bill used to rebuild their house. He had formerly built log homes.

When guests open the picket fence gate, and walk beneath the garden archway, they seem to enter a more romantic era. Porcelain dolls sit on needlepoint pillows. French lace and dried flower arrangements are arranged over doorways and tucked into nooks and crannies. Tufted velvet chairs and elegant settees with rounded or heart-shaped backs are grouped in several parlors and in guest rooms. Windows are draped with sumptuous velvets, sheers, and handsome velveteen sconces.

In the light and airy sun room between 4:30 and 6:00 P.M., arriving guests are served tea and cookies from a corner tea table. One wall of the room is filled with vintage Gibson Girl prints and photographs. Overstuffed chairs, cozy wicker chairs with floral cushions, and small tables with old-fashioned lamps form pleasant nooks for sitting. The hot tub sits just outside the sliding glass doors and down several steps; tiny white lights hung in the trees arch over the tub to form a sparkly bower at night.

On the second floor, a guest room named for Leslie's grandmother includes her antique bed; a lace canopy is draped about the headboard and the bed comes with a feather mattress, down quilt, and crocheted coverlet. The bath offers an old-fashioned claw-foot tub. The largest room, in the turret, comes with a gas fireplace, a small balcony that overlooks the pond and small waterfall. The bed is so high that one must climb steps into this cozy nest.

Coffee is served at 8:30 A.M. just outside the guest rooms. Then around 9:30 A.M. Bill and Leslie serve a candlelit breakfast in the dining room, which has a handsome fireplace and mantle. Breakfast begins with the inn's traditional fruit compote of strawberries, blueberries, marionberries, bananas, yogurt, and brown sugar and topped with an edible blossom from the garden. French toast or waffles may be heart-shaped and served with warm maple or berry syrup. This is often followed by Bill's special egg dish. After breakfast if the weather is pleasant, you might ask Bill to take you for a spin in one of his vintage automobiles.

What's Nearby Deer Park

The area is a gateway to lakes and mountains including cross-country and downhill ski areas. The Red Shed Farm Museum has an eclectic collection of more than 500 farm tools and machinery along with a re-created 1940s bedroom. Located at 6223 Ridgeway Road, Deer Park, the museum is open by appointment; Telephone: (509) 466-2744. At nearby Gonzaga University travelers can visit a special collections room dedicated to onetime resident, singer Bing Crosby. It contains more than 150 of his treasures including an Oscar, letters, books, sheet music, and gold and platinum records; open daily; Telephone: (509) 328-4220.

Bosch Garten
Bed & Breakfast

9846 Dye Road
Leavenworth, WA 98826
Phone: (509) 548–6900; (800) 535–0069

Innkeepers: Cal and Myke Bosch
Rooms: 3 rooms with private baths; baths feature large showers, tiled floors and counter tops, large mirrors, and extra towels for hot tub use
Extras: Resident Master Gardener
On the grounds: Hot tub in enclosed Japanese teahouse with natural plantings; garden areas with roses, herbs, and alpine varieties; views of surrounding mountains
Smoking? Outdoors only
Visiting pets? No; no resident pets
Credit cards: Visa, MasterCard, Discover
Rates: $$
How to get there: From about 20 miles north of Seattle, access Leavenworth via Highway 2 and 4,061-foot Stevens Pass, or via I-90 east from Seattle to Cle Elum and north on Highway 97 over 4,102-foot Swauk Pass. Both routes are approximately 3 hours in driving time allowing more time during winter months. From Highway 2 at the east edge of Leavenworth, turn right onto East Leavenworth Road. Proceed a short distance to Mountain Home Road turning left here, then turning right onto Dye Road to the inn's parking area.

Besides the floor-to-ceiling cathedral windows in the spacious common room and the room's comfortable overstuffed sofas, wingback chairs, and ottomans, guests remark about the twenty-foot tall Norfolk pine that resides in an enormous pot next to the windows. "The pine is actually more than 25 years old," explains Myke. She is an avid master gardener and has created a number of garden areas on the grounds including ones for roses, herbs, edible flowers, and alpine varieties. She has developed an intimate Japanese planting area with hardy perennials, river rocks, and a miniature bridge where the outdoor hot tub resides.

Guest rooms on the second level adjoin a well-stocked library loft-alcove stocked with beverages and snacks. One room is furnished with bent-willow couches, a king bed, and large Southwestern paintings. Another room can be set up in either twin beds or European king bed. It features flower-stenciled furniture and walls. The third room is furnished in natural-finish pine and comes with a king bed, day bed with a trundle, and handsome cathedral ceiling. All the guest rooms feature down comforters, reading lamps, cable TV, air conditioning, cozy sitting areas, and large pillows as well as sliding glass doors to the covered upper deck with its great mountain views.

In the spacious dining area on the main floor tall sliding glass doors admit views of the nearby mountains. The large oval table and matching Danish-style curved ladderback chairs sit on warm Berber carpeting. Breakfast often begins with a fresh fruit cup of perhaps Fuji apples, D'Anjou pears, strawberries, and kiwi topped with Amaretto sauce. One favorite main entree is cottage cheese pancakes and baked Golden Delicious apple slices with sausage links. The innkeepers also like to serve Black Forest ham-and-cheese croissants with a broiled fruit stick of apples, mushrooms, and pineapple chunks. The whole tasty affair comes to a close with a dessert of luscious cinnamon rolls, chocolate mousse, German stollen bread, or banana chunks dipped in sour cream and rolled in coconut. "I think this is known as a waist-bulging breakfast," says Cal with a grin. Saturday nights at the inn are special, too: that's when the traditional decadent dessert is served in the evening.

What's Nearby Leavenworth

This four-season area in the heart of the Washington Cascades offers cross-country skiing as well as snowmobiling, ice skating, sleigh-riding, and Alaskan husky dog-team rides. Summer brings live theater offerings staged outdoors. Fall brings the harvest of hundreds of acres of fruit trees in the Wenatchee Valley. There are nearly thirty restaurants in the immediate area between Leavenworth and Cashmere including a local brewery, two local coffee roasters, and several evening coffeehouses. For maps and current information contact the Leavenworth Visitors' Information Center, P.O. Box 327, Leavenworth, WA 98826; Telephone: (509) 548–5807. Ask for directions to renowned Ohme Gardens.

Other Recommended B&Bs Nearby

Cashmere Country Inn Bed & Breakfast, a charming country house with five guest rooms and private baths, French country decor, perhaps best known for the innkeeper's gourmet breakfasts; contact innkeepers Patti and Dale Swanson, 5801 Pioneer Drive, Cashmere, WA 98815; Telephone: (509) 782–4212.

Run of the River
Bed & Breakfast

9308 East Leavenworth Road
Leavenworth, WA 98826
Phone: (509) 548-7171; (800) 288-6491
E-mail: rofther@rightathome.com
Internet site: www.runoftheriver.com

Innkeepers: Karen and Monty Turner
Rooms: 6 rooms including 1 handicap-accessible room, all with private baths; some rooms have whirlpool spa tubs; largest suite features enclosed river-rock spa
Extras: Innkeeper collects and restores vintage bicycles; rooms have views of the river and surrounding hills; binoculars for guests' use; mountain bikes for rent
On the grounds: Extensive natural perennial garden areas around the inn, Icicle River flows at the rear of the inn; outdoor hot tub on lower terrace overlooks the river
Smoking? Not allowed
Visiting pets? No; 1 friendly Airedale, Jasper
Credit cards: Visa, MasterCard, Discover
Rates: $$–$$$
How to get there: From Highway 2 at the eastern edge of Leavenworth, turn south onto East Leavenworth Road and proceed 1 mile to the inn's gravel driveway.

The words of writer John McPhee etched on an oval block of redwood tucked in one of the inn's garden areas captures the ambience that Monty and Karen have created in this enchanting log house bed and breakfast: "The Hawk Flies. The River Runs. Time Slows. Peace." "Something is always going on outdoors here," says Monty with a smile. "Kingfishers diving, eagles soaring, deer coming down to the river . . ." At an elevation of 1,230 feet on the eastern and sunnier side of the Cascades, Leavenworth brings some travelers to fish streams and rivers or to hike or mountain bike the more than 300 miles of trails in the area. Some travelers come to enjoy a host of invigorating winter activities, and many come for the gala seasonal festivals. But some come simply to rejuvenate.

When guests arrive at the inn they are welcomed into the great room with its pine logs and pine paneling. Exposed logs frame views of the Icicle River as it makes a bend at the edge of grounds. Welcome treats of homemade cookies or brownies and pecan-roasted coffee are served here. Comfortable sofas and chairs beckon. The wood stove rests on a raised tile hearth, and the wall behind it is fashioned of river rock and edged with pine. Cabin-style wood doors lead to the guest rooms.

Roomy chambers located on the main floor and on the second floor come with handsome hand-hewn log beds and handcrafted log furniture. The largest suite features two wood stoves, a loft, private deck, and a marvelous river rock-enclosed whirlpool spa. Other rooms offer private spa tubs, wood stoves, and private decks with views of the river or of the flower gardens and grounds. There are thick down comforters, piles of pillows, good reading lamps, country prints, and cozy sitting areas. The large hot tub on the lower terrace offers another relaxing place to soak and take in peaceful views of the river.

The innkeepers serve a bountiful breakfast at 8:30 A.M. in the main-floor dining area. The table is set with country-style china, pewter side dishes, and vases of fresh flowers from the perennial gardens. A yogurt and fruit plate begins the morning meal perhaps followed by cinnamon French toast along with baked egg dishes. Guests enjoy Monty's special "boat drinks," fashioned of local fruits and ciders blended in tasty combinations.

For afternoon or evening dining ask about good restaurants like Gustav's, Cougar Inn on nearby Lake Wenatchee, Alley Café, and Pewter Pot.

What's Nearby

See What's Nearby Leavenworth on page 275.

Other Recommended B&Bs Nearby

Haus Rohrbach Pension, located on a hillside with views of Leavenworth and of surrounding mountains, long-time innkeepers offer ten rooms, eight with private baths and two handicap accessible; children welcome; contact innkeepers Bob and Kathryn Harrild, 12882 Ranger Road, Leavenworth, WA 98826; Telephone: (509) 548-7024; (800) 548-4477. **Pine River Ranch Bed & Breakfast,** luxurious suites with handsome four-poster log beds, some with river-rock fireplaces and whirlpool spas; contact innkeepers Michael and Mary Ann Zenk, 19668 Highway 207, Leavenworth, WA 98826; Telephone: (509) 763-3959. **Silver Bay Inn Bed & Breakfast,** reached only by float plane or regular boat trips from Chelan; guest cabin or cozy rooms in the main house, hot tub under the stars, breakfast on deck with lake views; contact innkeepers Randall and Katherine Dinwiddie, P.O. Box 43, Stehekin, WA 98852; Telephone: (509) 682-2212. Chelan County Visitor's Information Center; Telephone: (800) 838-2324; Internet site: www.chelan.org.

Fotheringham House Bed & Breakfast

2128 West Second Avenue
Spokane, WA 99204
Phone: (509) 838–1891
E-mail: fotheringham.bnb@ior.com
Internet site: www.ior.com/fotheringham

Innkeepers: Graham and Jackie Johnson
Rooms: 4 rooms, 1 with private bath
Extras: Historic 1891 late Victorian with restored turret, tin ceilings, curved wraparound porch with elegant stained-glass window to foyer
On the grounds: Victorian garden and old rose varieties, fountain, sitting areas; oldest park in the area is directly across from the inn
Smoking? Outdoors only
Visiting pets? No; no resident pets
Credit cards: Visa, MasterCard, American Express, Discover
Rates: $$
How to get there: From I-90 eastbound take exit 280, from I-90 westbound take exit 280A. Turn north for 1½ blocks to Second Avenue turning left here; stay in the right lane and proceed for about 9 blocks to the inn located on the corner of Second Avenue and Hemlock Street and directly across from Coeur d'Alene Park.

Sometimes a house needs help. Especially an old house like the one Jackie and Graham bought in 1993 in Spokane's historic Browne's Addition. "We seem to collect things or projects that need help," says Jackie. The couple has restored Victorian furniture for more than thirty years. The 1891 late-Victorian house on the corner of Second and Hemlock waited patiently for them. Its paint was falling off, its porches were sagging, its turret was long gone, and its roof needed replacing.

Guests marvel at what this energetic couple accomplished in just two years—they even won two awards for residential historic preservation. The missing turret was researched, its design verified, and local craftsmen were employed to construct and install an authentic reproduction. It towers grandly in its original location at the front of the house, just above the wraparound porch. "The house looks and feels more architecturally complete with the turret," says Graham. Bed-and-breakfast guests agree as they stand on the sidewalk and admire the whole effect.

They amble through Jackie's old-fashioned Victorian garden as they bring their bags to the porch. Old scented roses combine nicely with clumps of lavender, ferns, hostas, columbine, phlox, delphinium, and astilbe. One would expect to see a young Doris Day on the white wicker porch swing being serenaded by a youthful Gordon Macrae—the vintage film *On Moonlight Bay* comes to mind. Near the front door soft light and pale lavender colors from the lovely curved stained-glass window follow guests into the foyer. A carved walnut headboard and marble-top dresser and commode adorn the Garden Room. The Museum Room has a canopied four-poster bed and a walnut dresser with a harp mirror. There are tin ceilings in many rooms, and hard and soft wood floors. The parlor and dining room contain restored pieces of mid-Victorian American walnut sofas, chairs, and tables.

In the evening guests are invited to Scottish tea with homemade hazelnut truffles in the parlor. Graham enjoys telling guests about his golfing experience at St. Andrews in Scotland and about the time, as a Spokane teenager, he caddied for a former resident Bing Crosby at a local golf course in the 1950s. There are now eighteen public courses in the area that golfing guests can enjoy. If possible arrange to have dinner at the Patsy Clark Mansion Restaurant near the inn. This is another outstanding example of historic preservation and offers a late Victorian ambience.

In the morning guests are thoughtfully provided coffee and tea outside their doors, then breakfast is served on the main floor in the cozy dining area. A typical menu might include berry frappe, broiled grapefruit, malted hazelnut waffles with cooked apples and hazelnut-maple syrup, and smoked chicken-and-apple sausage. Jackie and Graham also may serve baked French toast, huckleberry crepes, stradas, and omelets.

What's Nearby Spokane

The Spokane Opera House offers symphony concerts, best of Broadway shows, and the like. Manito Park Gardens feature an excellent rose garden and perennial garden, conservatory greenhouse garden, an extensive formal garden area, and an adjacent intimate Japanese garden. Nearby Finch Arboretum has large plantings of rhododendrons, native trees, and an extensive collection of lilacs. At Turnbull Wildlife Refuge located south of Cheney travelers enjoy hiking trails and the 5 ½-mile Pine Creek Auto Tour Route. Along Lake Couer d'Alene, just across the Washington-Idaho border east of Spokane, a scenic drive is especially dramatic at sunset. For maps and current information contact the Spokane Area Visitor's Bureau; Telephone: (800) 248–3230; Internet: www.spokane-areacvb.org. Also see What's Nearby Deer Park on page 273.

The Marianna Stoltz House

427 East Indiana Street
Spokane, WA 99207
Phone: (509) 483–4316; (800) 978–6587

Innkeepers: Jim and Phyllis Maguire
Rooms: 4 rooms, 2 with private baths
Extras: Tea, cider, cocoa, lemonade, iced tea, and homemade cookies provided daily; guest phone and fax machine
On the grounds: Located 5 blocks from Gonzaga University
Smoking? Outdoors only
Visiting pets? No; 2 small dogs, Brigid and Sophie, live in innkeepers' quarters and much to their dismay aren't allowed to play with guests
Credit cards: Visa, MasterCard, American Express, Discover
Rates: $–$$
How to get there: Take I-90 near downtown Spokane to exit 282 or 282A (Trent/Hamilton) and proceed north on Hamilton Street to the Fourth traffic light. Turn left onto Indiana Street and go 5 blocks to the inn, located at the corner of Indiana and Addison Streets.

Travelers who have a penchant for large early 1900s Craftsman-style houses will feel at home here. The house doesn't sit on a hill or overlook an ocean. Rather it sits squarely in a well-established residential neighborhood and in the shade of century-old trees. It has a lawn and a porch that wraps around two sides. It feels as though just around the corner should be an old-fashioned drugstore with a fountain where couples order strawberry sodas or thick vanilla milkshakes.

Guests enter the front door to receive a warm welcome from the innkeepers and move into the large common areas on the main floor. The living room, dining room, and parlor are all with leaded-glass windows, high ceilings, and fine woodwork of polished fir. Oriental rugs sit on polished hardwood floors, and there may be classical music playing softly in the background. A piano waits in the parlor. Roomy sofas and comfortable upholstered chairs are arranged in cozy groupings. Antique light fixtures and fringed lampshades mix well with the other period furnishings. Leaded-glass bookcases house books and reading material as well as chess and backgammon.

On the second floor are four tastefully decorated rooms with king, queen, or single beds and private or shared baths. Old family quilts are used on the beds and lace curtains adorn wide windows. In one suite is a soaking tub for two, with extras such as bathrobes, soaps, shampoo, lotion, blow dryers, and extra towels provided. Breakfast is served in the dining room around the antique dining table, generally from 7:30 to 9:30 A.M. Freshly ground Starbucks coffee is brewed and ready as are tea and juices. Delicate cups and saucers are Royal Doulton's Country Rose pattern. Ruby red dishes may accompany the fresh fruit platter. Entrees served on fine china sitting atop gold charger plates may consist of French toast with strawberry and mandarin orange sauce, Stoltz House Strada, or croissants with poached eggs topped with bacon and cheese sauce.

Phyllis and Jim are long-time innkeepers and they are pleased to provide their guests with information on local tours, concerts, and cultural and social events. They can also recommend good neighborhood cafes and restaurants. "We're actually close to the Spokane River that flows through the downtown area," says Phyllis. "It's fun to visit Riverfront Park, its paths and amusement areas, and see the small falls that extends across a section of the river there." The inn is located just five blocks from Gonzaga University, where the Bing Crosby collection, open to the public, is filled with musical memorabilia from the singer's life.

What's Nearby

See What's Nearby Spokane on page 279 and What's Nearby Deer Park on page 273.

Other Recommended B&B Nearby

Oslo's Bed & Breakfast, has two spacious rooms with private baths, common areas with fireplace open to large outdoor terrace, patio, garden; Norwegian theme prevails with avid gardener-innkeeper who was born and raised in Norway; delicious Scandinavian breakfast fare includes freshly baked goodies such as cinnamon coffeecake, cookies, and biscotti; especially convenient for mature guests, inn is all on one level; friendly resident pug dog, Susy; contact innkeeper Aslaug Stevenson, 1821 East Thirty-ninth Avenue, Spokane, WA 99203; Telephone: (509) 838-3175 or (888) 838-3175.

The Farm, A Bed & Breakfast

490 Sunnyside Road
Trout Lake, WA 98650
Phone: (509) 395-2488
E-mail: farmbnb@gorge.net
Internet site:
www.gorge.net/business/farmbnb

Innkeepers: Dean and Rosie Hostetter
Rooms: 2 rooms with shared bath
Extras: Trout Lake Festival of Arts held at the inn during July includes local artists and authors, wine tasting, microbrews
On the grounds: Huge vegetable garden, perennial garden, small pond, views of Mount Adams
Smoking? Outdoors only
Visiting pets? No; resident golden lab, Levi, and barn cat, Boots
Credit cards: No; personal checks accepted
Rates: $–$$
How to get there: From the Vancouver and Portland areas take I-84 on the Oregon side of the Columbia River and proceed east into the Columbia Gorge. Continue to Hood River approximately 45 miles and take exit 64. Turn left and cross the Columbia River via the Hood River bridge then turn left (west) onto Highway 14 for 2 miles. Turn north onto Highway 141 and proceed north past milepost 20 to the large sign that says Conboy Lake Wildlife Refuge. Turn here onto Warner Road and proceed about 1½ miles to the end of the road; turn left onto Sunnyside Road to the inn, the second house on the right.

This large two-story farmhouse painted soft yellow sits so close to the base of Mount Adams that guests often remark, "You can almost reach out and touch it!" The 12,000-foot mountain, one of many volcanic peaks in the Cascade Mountain range, rises above the small community of Trout Lake located several miles to the north. The snowy peak rises into view as one drives north from Hood River on the Oregon side of the Columbia River. The snowy top of 11,235-foot Mount Hood can also be seen to the south. Guests often linger on the outside deck that faces the fine view.

Guests also enjoy walking about the expansive grounds to inspect the couple's huge vegetable garden and the lovely perennial garden. The irrigation canal on the property, one of more than a dozen such canals near Trout Lake that date back to the 1890s, feeds a small pond with an old-fashioned waterwheel. The water comes from the nearby White Salmon River. Rosie and Dean offer guests the use of four mountain bikes for exploring on nearby roadways and byways.

Inside two cozy common areas beckon one to sit and chat over a cup of coffee or tea. The living room has Oriental rugs and a Victorian love seat; be sure to peek at the old barber chest that sits nearby. The sitting room comes with cushioned wicker, a Vermont Castings wood stove, TV, and a vintage pharmacy case. A Victorian mahogany table graces the dining room. On the second floor two guest rooms come with queen or double beds, antique quilts, and down comforters. In the largest room a collection of vintage American Indian baskets is displayed on a shelf that extends across one wall. Beneath this a cozy

twin bed is built partway into the wall. This room also offers a queen bed, Victorian love seat, 1920s dresser and commode, and an old oil painting of Mount Hood. Its three windows are dressed in lace. The shared bath has a large walk-in shower tiled in green and white; glass bricks form one wall of the shower area.

In the morning Rosie and Dean share cooking duties in the preparation of their hearty breakfasts. Rosie's freshly baked breads and pastries, such as orange-cranberry scones, sour cream coffeecake, or banana-pecan rolls combine nicely with Dean's wild huckleberry hotcakes, baked pears, and bacon or fresh handmade sausage from Otto's in southeast Portland (this well-known establishment is owned by their daughter and son-in-law). "Our Mount Adams area is also known for its wonderful huckleberries," says Rosie.

What's Nearby Trout Lake

The area is known for its wilderness, its hiking and backpacking trails, and its winter cross-country skiing and snowmobiling. In mid-July the lively Trout Lake Festival of the Arts is hosted here including jazz musicians, local artists and artisans, and regional authors as well as wine tasting, microbrew tasting, and good food. During summer months live theater is offered at Trout Lake Country Inn; there is also a restaurant here. The local ranger station can provide helpful information and maps for hiking, river rafting, birdwatching, wildflower meadows, huckleberry fields, and ice caves. There is a wide variety of cafes, delis, brewpubs, and coffeehouses in nearby White Salmon and in Hood River. Also see What's Nearby Hood River on page 113.

Premier Alpacas Ranch & Guest House

401 South Railroad Avenue
Uniontown, WA 99179
Phone: (509) 229-3655
E-mail: dlmiller@inlandnet.com
Internet site: www.pnaa.org/premier.html

Innkeepers: Leslee and Dale Miller
Rooms: 1 room in the main house with private bath, separate guest house with snack kitchen, sleeping loft, bunkhouse room and private bath
Extras: Indoor heated lap pool
On the grounds: Small herd of alpacas
Smoking? Outdoors only
Visiting pets? No, 2 Dalmations, Touchee and Mollie, and 1 nutmeg tabby, Meg
Credit cards: No; personal checks accepted
Rates: $-$$
How to get there: From Highway 195 at Uniontown, turn east onto Church Street and go to Railroad Avenue. Turn right (south) here and proceed to the inn, located at the end of the street. Uniontown is approximately 85 miles south of Spokane and is approximately 60 miles north of Oregon's northeastern border.

Leslee explains to guests that when she and Dale decided to leave behind the city lights of Seattle, they found a decided change of pace in the far southeastern corner of the state. "Actually Uniontown has only about 300 residents," says Leslee, "but we love our new way of life here, out of the fast lane." The couple also looked for a crop or animal to raise on their eight acres, and the small alpacas were a perfect choice for them. "The soft fleece of the alpaca was used thousands of years ago in the high Andes of South America to make clothing for members of the Inca royalty," explains Dale. We stand at the fence and look out at the small herd munching grass in the pasture. The cuddly looking alpacas, at about 36" in height, seem much less intimidating than their cousins, the tall and imperial looking llamas.

We're surrounded by the distant low hills of the Palouse country, rolling farm and ranch country often said to be the richest farmland in the U.S. This inn is a place where anyone can relax into a slower-paced lifestyle. Folks seem in less of a hurry here. The rolling hills carry the eye to the far horizon and urge one to breathe deeply. City cares drop away for awhile. In the yard a hammock swings gently beckoning one with a favorite mystery or novel. Indoors in the attached skylit sun room filled with lush green plans, the heated lap pool offers a soothing place to swim and work out the kinks. Either in the main house or in the adjacent guest house, one can enjoy hot chocolate, coffee, or tea while curled up on a sofa or chair next to a wood stove.

In addition to the cheery stove, the guest house has a spiral stairway up to the sleeping loft and also features a remodeled bunkhouse section—both offer double beds with warm quilts and comforters. A small snack kitchen comes with a toaster oven, refrigerator, and cof-feepot; hot and cold beverages also are provided. One room in the main house offers a queen bed and semi-private bath.

Leslee serves a hearty farm breakfast of such tasty items as fresh seasonal fruits or juice from the garden or orchard, pancakes, or French toast along with locally made smoked sausage, bacon, or ham. One favorite with guests is Leslee's frittata made of farm fresh eggs, spinach, potatoes, roasted red peppers, and Parmesan cheese. Freshly baked breakfast bread and perhaps lemon yogurt muffins accompany the entree along with coffee, tea, milk, and gourmet hot chocolate. For dining out in the evening ask about Eleanor's, a local saloon that offers a great selection of microbrews and is reported to serve the best hamburgers on the Palouse.

What's Nearby Uniontown

There are many antiques stores within a 20-mile radius as well as scenic byways to explore in the Palouse country. History buffs can visit a 1904 church in town, the first consecrated Catholic church in the state of Washington. The first Sunday in March brings the annual benefit Sausage Feed; since 1948 the men of the town have made sausage from a renowned secret recipe. In late February the University of Idaho, located in nearby Moscow, hosts a weeklong Jazz Festival. An old-fashioned Threshing Bee takes place in early September. Public golf links are located in nearby Lewiston and in Clarkston.

Other Recommended B&B Nearby

The Churchyard Inn, seven rooms in a 1905 Victorian with an old world setting, private baths, 1 handicap-accessible room with private bath; contact innkeepers Marvin and Linda Entel, 206 Saint Boniface Street, Uniontown, WA 99179; Telephone: (509) 229-3200.

Green Gables Inn

922 Bonsella Street
Walla Walla, WA 99362
Phone: (509) 525-5501; (888) 525-5501
E-mail: greengables@wwics.com
Internet site: www.greengablesinn.com

Innkeepers: Jim and Margaret Buchan
Rooms: 5 rooms and carriage house cottage, all with private baths; 3 baths offer old-fashioned claw-foot tubs and all come with baskets of amenities such as bath gel, glycerin and French milled soaps, and bath salts
Extras: The master suite has a fireplace, single whirlpool tub, and French doors to private deck overlooking grounds; tandem bicycles for guests use; morning coffee and biscotti served outside rooms prior to breakfast
On the grounds: Lawns and cutting flower gardens
Smoking? Outdoors only
Visiting pets? No, resident cocker spaniel, April; chocolate lab, Stan; and 2 outdoor cats Calvin (black and white) and Ray (grey and white)
Credit cards: Visa, MasterCard, American Express, Discover
Rates: $$-$$$$
How to get there: From Highway 12, accessed from the Tri-Cities area or from I-84 and Milton Freewater in eastern Oregon, take the Clinton Street exit and proceed 4 blocks to Bonsella Street. Turn right here for 1 block to the inn.

Located just a block from Whitman College and within walking distance of downtown Walla Walla, the handsome Craftsman-style house is adorned with three pointed gables. Guests negotiate its broad front steps, walk across the deep front porch, and enter a warm interior. The foyer and handsome central staircase gleams with polished wood and decorative wood trim. "The home was built in 1909 for a family who loved to entertain," explains Margaret. Every inch of its 6,000 square feet with handsome decor offers a welcoming environment to guests. The large common area, with its two fireplaces and comfortable sofas and chairs, is an inviting place to meet other travelers and to enjoy coffee, tea, cookies, and snacks. Jim, who is sports editor of the local newspaper, enjoys having guests join him here to view sporting events from around the country via the satellite TV system.

The largest room, the master suite, is decorated with mahogany furnishings. A king bed faces the wood-burning fireplace and a romantic love seat and built-in window seat offer cozy places to sit a spell. French doors open to an outside deck that overlooks the rear grounds. Another room features birds-eye maple king bed, writing desk, and armoire. A collection of Maxfield Parrish art prints graces the wall above the bed. Built in 1912, the Carriage House offers room for families with children. Its spacious bedroom comes with closet space and built-ins, a TV, king bed, and tiled bath.

In the morning freshly brewed coffee and tasty biscotti are served outside the rooms at 7:00 A.M. A full breakfast is served in the dining room on the main floor at 7:30 or 9:00 A.M. weekdays and at 9:00 A.M. on weekends. The delicious meal may consist of a green chile and cream cheese quiche served with salsa and cornbread; smoked chicken sausage with sun-dried tomatoes; or baked apples stuffed with dried fruits and topped with crème fraiche. For lunch and evening dining ask about such spots as The Homestead, The Oasis, Legends, Merchants Ltd. on Main Street, and Pastime Café an old-timer since 1927. Shady Lawn Creamery has antiques, coffee, and espresso, and Jacobi's Restaurant in one of the town's old train depots offers a nostalgic ambience for dining. In nearby Dayton the Patit Creek Restaurant is an all-time favorite for gourmet fare.

What's Nearby Walla Walla

The downtown area offers art galleries, antiques shops, theaters, and other retail shops. A number of local wineries are open to the public. The Fort Walla Walla Museum complex and the nearby Whitman Mission offer glimpses into the opening of the West to white settlers. The Frasier Farmstead Museum features a splendid old-fashioned garden. A performing arts hall and theater on the Whitman College campus offers an active schedule of events. Current information can be obtained from the Walla Walla Valley Visitors' Center, 29 East Sumach Street, P.O. Box 644, Walla Walla, WA 99362; Telephone: (509) 525-0850; Internet site: www.wallawalla.com.

Other Recommended B&B Nearby

Stone Creek Inn, four elegantly appointed Victorian rooms reflect the past in this 1883 mansion; contact innkeeper Patricia Johnson at 720 Bryant Street, Walla Walla, WA 99362; Telephone: (509) 529-8120.

III. Canada and Alaska

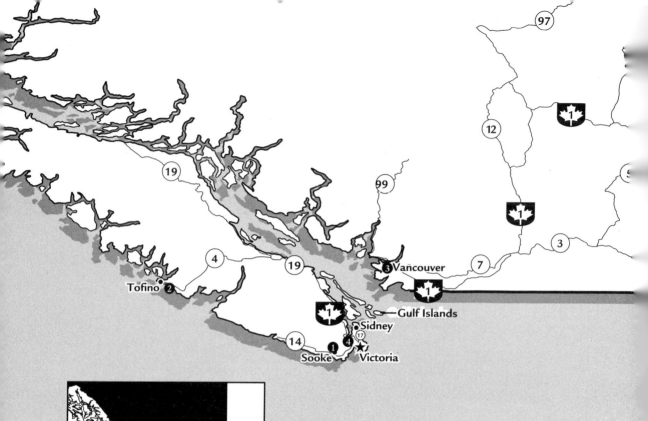

97

12

1

99

3

19

4

19

1

3 Vancouver

7

1

Tofino 2

Gulf Islands

1

Sidney

14

1 4 17

Sooke ★ Victoria

AK

BC

WA

OR

N

British Columbia, Canada
Numbers on map refer to towns numbered below.

Tramore House
Bed & Breakfast

26261-64B Avenue
Langley, B.C. V4W 3M7 Canada
Phone: (604) 857–2618; (888) 799–2618
E-mail: yodan@bc.sympatico.ca
Internet site: www.bbcanada.com/372.html

Innkeepers: Heather and Darrell Dean
Rooms: 2 rooms with shared bath
Extras: English Tudor manor in country setting
On the grounds: 6 acres including lawns, gardens, woods, and stream
Smoking? Outdoors only
Visiting pets? No; resident Doberman, Max; golden lab, Paddy; Dalmatian, Tiga; and African gray parrot, Lily, who lords it over the other three pets
Credit cards: Visa, American Express
Rates: $–$$
How to get there: From Seattle drive north on I-5 to Bellingham, take the Meridian exit onto Highway 539. Proceed north 13 miles to Lynden and continue 3 miles to the U.S./Canada border crossing at Aldergrove. Continue for 8 miles on this road, which changes to Highway 13 or 264th Street on the Canadian side; you will cross over the freeway passing Goddard's Country Market on the right and arrive at a stop sign. Proceed from here about ½ block to 64B Avenue; turn left for ⅓ mile to the inn located on the right. The inn is about 45 minutes from Vancouver, B.C.

The English-style manor is located on six acres with walking paths in the gardens, wooded areas, and about the lawns. You might enjoy a picnic lunch along the stream that borders the property. In the foyer of the house is a handsome suit of armor, its design dating back to Celtic times. In the large common area are sumptuous sofas and chairs, warm raspberry carpet, and lush window dressings with draped valences. Guests are welcome to use the extensive library as well as the TV/VCR and stereo systems. One guest room offers a double bed, the other comes with twin beds, and both rooms share a bath. A full English breakfast is served in the formal dining room on the main floor.

What's Nearby

Three winter ski areas are within easy range: Whistler, Grouse Mountain, and Mount Baker. There are twenty-one golf courses in the area as well as horseback riding, ballooning, and bike riding. Take a winery tour; visit Fort Langley, a Canadian National Historic Site; and go antiques shopping. Local eateries include The Marr House, The Bedford House, and The Lamplighter.

Other Recommended B&Bs Nearby

River Run Cottages, guests find quaint waterfront cottages with fireplaces; contact innkeepers Bill and Janice Harkley, 4551 River Road West, Ladner, B.C. V4K 1R9; Telephone: (604) 945-7778. **Tuscan Farm Gardens,** intimate retreat located in the lush Fraser River Valley; contact innkeepers Arleigh and Heather Fair, 24453 Sixtieth Avenue, Langley, B.C. V2Z 2G5; Telephone: (604) 530-1997.

Oceanwood Country Inn

630 Dinner Bay Road
Mayne Island, B.C. V0N 2J0 Canada
Phone: (250) 539-5074
E-mail: oceanwood@gulfisland.com
Internet site:
www.gulfislands.com/mayne/oceanwood

Innkeepers: Marilyn and Jonathan Chilvers
Rooms: 12 rooms all with private baths including 1 wheelchair-accessible room; several rooms come with fireplaces, decks, and soaking or hot tubs
Extras: Sauna, hot tub, bicycles and helmets, binoculars; fixed-price dinner served nightly; early morning coffee; afternoon tea and sweets served in the Garden Room; in-room continental breakfast available; the inn features specialty teas from T Botanical Teas in Vancouver, B.C.
On the grounds: Panoramic views of Navy Channel and of the southern Gulf Islands
Smoking? Outdoors only
Visiting pets? No; resident lab and cat who aren't allowed in guest quarters
Credit cards: Visa, MasterCard
Rates: $$$–$$$$
How to get there: From B.C. Ferries Terminal on Mayne Island turn right onto Dalton Drive, then turn right onto Mariner's Way, and left on Dinner Bay Road; follow this to its end to the inn, located on the left and overlooking the water. Ferries depart from Vancouver, B.C. and from Swartz Bay on Vancouver Island; Telephone: (250) 386-3431; Internet site: www.bcferries.bc.ca. The island is also accessible by floatplane from downtown Vancouver or from Victoria.

This is perhaps the ultimate in off-the-beaten-path bed-and-breakfast luxury along with views of Navy Channel and an island experience as well. Several of the southern Gulf Islands are seen from the inn including North Pender, Saltspring, Prevost, Moresby, and Portland islands. Guests can walk, jog, or bicycle about the island or elect to simply hole up at the inn and soak in the salty views from their private decks or from the hot tub. Extensive herb and vegetable gardens, greenhouse, and perennial gardens surround the inn. Those who wish can arrange for ocean kayaking with Mayne Island Kayak & Canoe Rentals; call (250) 539-2667 for information about kayaks, canoes, and instruction.

Rooms are spacious and might come with fireplaces, French doors that open to water-view balconies, vaulted ceilings, whirlpool tubs, and queen beds along with Victorian mahogany or country pine furnishings. English country chintz fabrics are used generously in window dressings and upholstery. The largest room has a soaking tub on one of its two private decks, a sunken living room with fireplace, queen bed in a raised sleeping nook, and spacious bath that opens to a small deck. Fixed-price dinners are served beginning at 6:00 P.M. and feature fresh fish, shellfish, fowl, and beef entrees. Breakfast is served from 8:30 to 9:30 A.M. at the individual tables in the fireplace dining room and solarium, and the meal comes with the splendid ocean views as well.

Other Recommended B&Bs Nearby

Eatenton House Bed & Breakfast, more ocean views from large garden sun deck, great breakfasts; contact innkeeper William Childs, 4705 Scarff Road, RR#1, Pender Island, B.C. V0N 2M1; Telephone: (250) 629-8355. **Moonshadows Guest House,** panoramic ocean views, hot tub, private baths; contact innkeepers Pat Goodwin and Dave Muir, 771 Georgeson Bay Road, S16 C16, RR#1, Galiano Island, B.C. V0N 1P0; Telephone: (250) 539-5544. **Weston Lake Inn Bed & Breakfast,** elegant country ambience, hot tub, gardens, ocean views; contact innkeepers Susan Evans and Ted Harrison, 813 Beaver Point Road, Salt Spring Island, B.C. V8K 1X9; Telephone: (250) 653-4311.

Ocean Wilderness Inn & Spa Retreat

109 West Coast Road
Sooke, B.C. V0S 1N0
Phone: (250) 646-2116; (800) 323-2116
E-mail: ocean@sookenet.com
Internet site: www.sookenet.com/ocean

Innkeeper: Marion Rolston
Rooms: 9 rooms with private baths, sitting areas, and private entrances; some feature soaking tubs for two, private balconies, patios, and skylights
Extras: Morning silver service with coffee and flowers outside doors; spa services include mud facials, herbal wraps, seaweed wraps, ocean nutrient treatments, and special massages; guests can learn and practice tai chi, yoga, meditation
On the grounds: Five acres of old-growth rain forest; seals and whales in waters of Strait of Juan De Fuca, bald eagles and seabirds; private beach, hiking trails
Smoking? Outdoors only
Visiting pets? No, 2 outside cats, Dino (black and white) and Pandora (white)
Credit cards: Visa, MasterCard, American Express
Rates: $$-$$$$
How to get there: Located 30 miles west of Victoria follow Highway 1 to Colwood/Sooke exit and proceed on Highway 14 to the village of Sooke. Proceed beyond the only traffic light and continue for 9 miles; the highway becomes West Coast Road. Note: street numbers stop at 10,000 and restart at 100 just before reaching the inn.

It may seem like the end of the world to travelers who reach this log country retreat in the far southwest corner of Vancouver Island, and in many ways it is—you notice the old-growth rain forest and see where the forest meets the sea. "This place would soothe anyone's tired soul," said one journalist. Guests come for wilderness hiking, beach walking, whale and bird watching. They can also indulge in mud facials, ocean nutrient treatments, herbal wraps, seaweed wraps, and learn tai chi, yoga, meditation, and massage. Guests can also arrange for private time in the outdoor hot tub situated in a romantic Japanese gazebo beneath the trees.

Guest rooms and suites on either the top floor or on the main floor feature a variety of ocean, mountain, and forest views. Queen beds come with soft comforters and lavish fabric canopies and floor-length corner drapings. Soft floral carpets warm the polished wood floors. Deep upholstered chairs and couches offer comfortable sitting areas in each room; antique floor lamps and table lamps offer ample reading light. One could retreat here for many days and not be inclined to depart or rush about. Mornings bring coffee or tea at your door, then breakfast either in your suite or with other guests in the log dining room. Entrees may include French toast with blueberries, scrambled eggs, apple sauce with orange sauce along with homemade biscuits, muffins, cinnamon swirls, and homemade granola and jams.

What's Nearby

There are hiking trails and picnic areas in East Sooke Park. Nearby eateries include Sooke Harbour House, The Good Life Book Store & Restaurant, the dining room at Point-No-Point, and The Country Cupboard. Driving north to Tofino brings travelers closest to the ocean and its elements.

Other Recommended B&Bs Nearby

Sooke Harbour House, twenty-eight sumptuous guest rooms, many with four-poster queen beds, romantic sitting areas, private indoor or outdoor hot tubs, and great views of the Olympic Mountains, Strait of Juan De Fuca; herb and perennial gardens, award-winning restaurant; room amenities include decanters of port, cookies, fruit, robes, morning newspapers, and large continental breakfasts; contact innkeepers Sinclair and Frederique Philip, 1528 Whiffen Spit Road, Sooke, B.C. V05 1N0; Telephone: (250) 642-3421. **The Tides Inn Bed & Breakfast,** waterfront rooms some with seaside decks, fireplaces, whirlpool tubs; hot tub, private baths, full breakfast; contact innkeepers Valerie and James Sloman, 160 Arnet Road, Box 325, Tofino, B.C. V0R 2ZO; Telephone: (250) 725-3765. **Wilp Gybuu** (Wolf House), contemporary home overlooking Duffin Passage and Clayoquot Sound, spacious rooms decorated with Native American art by artist innkeeper; queen beds, warm comforters, fireplaces, private baths; full breakfast, resident cat; contact innkeepers Wendy and Ralph Burgess, 311 Leighton Way, Box 396, Tofino, B.C. V0R 2Z0; Telephone: (250) 725-2330;

Johnson Heritage House Bed & Breakfast

2278 West Thirty-fourth Avenue
Vancouver, B.C. V6M 1G6 Canada
Phone: (604) 266–4175
E-mail: fun@johnsons-inn-vancouver.com
Internet site:
www.johnsons-inn-vancouver.com

Innkeepers: Sandy and Ron Johnson
Rooms: 3 rooms with private baths
Extras: Antiques and restored collectibles such as carousel animals, vintage coffee grinders, and an old-fashioned gasoline pump displayed in common areas and guest rooms
On the grounds: Perennials and rhododendrons; located in Kerrisdale district with tree-lined avenues, quiet neighborhoods, near University of British Columbia (UBC)
Smoking? Outdoors only
Visiting pets? No; no resident pets
Credit cards: No; personal checks accepted
Rates: $–$$
How to get there: Proceeding toward Vancouver from the U.S./Canadian border at Blaine via Highway 99, this becomes Oak Street. Turn left onto Thirty-third Avenue and continue 1½ miles passing traffic lights at Granville and Arbutus streets. At Vine Street turn left, then turn left again onto Thirty-fourth Avenue to the inn.

Those who love colorful stories about house renovation will love this 1926 Craftsman-style house and its energetic owners. This kind of renovation has numerous chapters and scenes that detail minor and major disasters. Waterfalls appeared from the ceiling, three sides of the house had never been equipped with drain tiles, they had to remove the entire roof structure just prior to a ten-day rainstorm. This in addition to removing a raccoon family who lived in the attic, shoveling out debris from the eccentric and reclusive former owner who reportedly wore elbow-length white gloves. "It only took us seven years to clean up, shore up, re-roof, and completely redo this place from top to bottom," says Sandy. She and Dean did most of the work themselves.

The results are just short of spectacular. The kitchen cabinets are made of solid cherry and the floor of quartzite quarry rock from Denmark. Large carved stone figures from Indonesia grace the garden areas where lush hostas and perennials thrive and where more than seventy-five rhododendrons bloom during late April and May. An Indonesian iron four-poster king bed graces one of the guest rooms. Another room has a romantic four-poster white-iron queen bed draped in creamy ruffles. The fir floor is adorned with Persian area rugs and collectibles displayed include carousel animals, horned-gramophones, and a vintage gasoline pump. Another room features views of Grouse Mountain. One bath is done in a whimsical barbershop theme. A larger bath goes with a mermaid theme with stunning leaded-glass windows, cushioned wicker, green plants, and sinks and soaking tub placed on a raised tile dais.

Breakfast is served in the dining room decorated with a carousel horse, a 6-foot cast-iron coffee grinder, an 1896 music box, and tropical plants. The hearty meal is served at the large oak table with a view of the vegetable and rhododendron garden through cottage windows.

What's Nearby

Fabulous gardens to visit include Van Dusen Gardens, Queen Elizabeth Park and Gardens including Bloedel Conservatory of tropical plantings, Nitobe Japanese Garden at UBC, and several other notable gardens at UBC including the Native Garden, Physick Garden, and the unforgettable Asian Garden. Stroll by the grand restored Edwardian mansions in the nearby Shaughnessy district. Sprinklers Restaurant at Van Dusen Gardens offers lunch, afternoon tea, and dinner; Telephone: (604) 261–0011.

Other Recommended B&B Nearby

Lighthouse Retreat Bed & Breakfast, romantic suites and perennial gardens, located near the ocean and Tsawwassen ferries; contact innkeepers Hanna and Ron Pankow, 4875 Water Lane, West Vancouver, B.C. V7W 1K4; Telephone: (604) 926–5959.

"O Canada" House
Bed & Breakfast

1114 Barclay Street
Vancouver, B.C. V6E 1H1 Canada
Phone: (604) 688-0555
Internet site:
www.vancouver.bc.com/OCanadaHouse/

Innkeeper: Jim Britten
Rooms: 6 rooms with private baths; biscotti, mints, fresh flowers, teddy bears in rooms; robes and hair dryers in baths
Extras: Sherry served in front parlor in the early evening; on-site parking and luggage storage provided; close to downtown shops, restaurants, and theater and entertainment; concierge service for guests during their stay
On the grounds: Garden with fountain and benches; quiet downtown neighborhood
Smoking? Outdoors only
Visiting pets? No; no resident pets
Credit cards: Visa, MasterCard
Rates: $$–$$$
How to get there: Take Highway 99 to downtown Vancouver crossing the Granville Island bridge and onto Granville Street. Turn left at Smithe Street, then turn left at Thurlow Street; from here turn right onto Barclay Street to the inn.

The inn features a spacious main floor that contains a large entry with an open staircase, handsome painted woodwork, two elegantly appointed guest parlors with fireplaces, and a large dining room with an adjoining pantry. This serves as a guest kitchen and is stocked with complimentary snacks, tea, coffee, and juices. The guest rooms are spacious and include sitting areas and private baths. Decorated in eclectic furnishings from the 1930s to late Victorian, the rooms feature tasteful window dressings, luxurious comforters with elegant duvets on queen or king beds, comfortable overstuffed chairs, TV/VCRs, small refrigerators, and telephones. The largest penthouse suite, nearly 800 square feet, comes with two queen beds and a spacious sitting area. Handsome antique lighting fixtures and lamps grace the rooms and the common areas.

The gourmet breakfast, accompanied with lace and silver and fine china, may include homemade apple-cinnamon muffins, salmon crepes, grilled dill potatoes, and a handsomely presented plate of freshly cut fruit garnished with strawberries, orange wedges, and herbs. Orange juice and Colombian coffee round out the delicious meal.

What's Nearby

Ford Theater, Vancouver Playhouse, Queen Elizabeth Theatre, Stanley Park, and Gastown. Visit the Dr. Sun Yat-Sen Garden, a Ming dynasty-style Chinese picture garden, a miniature delight. Sunset strolls on the promenade walkway around False Creek are especially grand with sailboats bobbing and flags waving in the evening breezes. Plan shopping forays to the South Granville neighborhood and to nearby Granville Island. Find brewpubs in Yaletown and Gastown. In North Vancouver explore the 395-acre Capilano River Regional Park, the Capilano Pacific Trail, and the Capilano Suspension Bridge that spans a narrow section of the river.

Other Recommended B&Bs Nearby

Alta Vista Chalet Bed & Breakfast, a charming alpine chalet that overlooks Lake Alta, close to Whistler Village and winter ski areas, children are welcome; contact innkeepers Tim and Yvonne Manville, 3229 Archibald Way, Whistler, B.C. V0N 1B3; Telephone: (604) 932–4900. **Thistledown House,** a restored heritage inn with antiques and art, private baths and fireplaces, afternoon tea and gourmet breakfasts; European hospitality and German-speaking hosts; contact innkeepers Ruth Crameri and Rex Davidson, 3910 Capilano Road, North Vancouver, B.C. V7R 4J2; Telephone (604) 986–7173.

Penny Farthing Inn Bed & Breakfast

2855 West Sixth Avenue
Vancouver, B.C. V6K 1Y2 Canada
Phone: (604) 739-9002
E-mail: farthing@uniserve.com
Internet: www.pennyfarthinginn.com

Innkeepers: Lyn Hainstock
Rooms: 4 rooms with private baths
On the grounds: Garden plantings, perennials, large porch with wicker
Smoking? Outdoors only
Visiting pets? No; three resident felines, Hendrix (named after Jimi), Frisky (he sometimes plays the piano), and Melody (usually hiding behind the clock on the mantle); none is allowed in the guest rooms
Credit cards: No; personal checks accepted
Rates: $-$$$
How to get there: Via Highway 99 heading into Vancouver, at West Twelfth Avenue turn left and proceed to MacDonald Street. Turn right (north) here to Sixth Avenue, the flashing pedestrian controlled crossing, and continue to the inn, a bright blue heritage house located on the right.

Located near English Bay in the Kitsilano area of Vancouver, the large 1912 Craftsman-style house is furnished with antiques brought from England by Lyn. Polished wood floors, a floral area rug, and walls that echo the soft peach tones in the rug offer a welcoming framework for the common area on the main floor.

Arranged in a grouping around the gas fireplace, are an antique armoire, glass-topped coffee table, deep-seated sofa, and comfortable easy chairs. The 1886 Heintzman piano nearby may be waiting for Frisky the cat who has been known to play a tune. Guests find ample reading material throughout the house including novels, mysteries, and colorful coffee-table books on a variety of subjects such as gardening, travel, interior decorating, and antiques. "We have a paperback collection for guests, too," says Lyn.

The room at the top of the house has

sloped ceilings with a built-in skylight, warm carpeting, a brass queen bed, pine chests, and a sitting room with a sofa bed, TV/VCR, stereo with CD player, tea and coffee makings, and telephone. This room also offers mountain and water views. On the second floor another room features polished wood floors, a pine four-poster queen bed, and a cozy sitting area with a gas fireplace and a pair of hunter green wing-back chairs. Matching windows are dressed in floral curtains with sheers and between them a French door opens to the balcony. One room offers a small porch with cushioned rattan furniture and overlooks the front perennial garden. Lyn's bountiful breakfast features freshly baked breads, croissants, muffins, or scones served with jams and jellies along with fresh fruit and a warm entree such as blueberry yogurt waffles, an apple-brie fritatta with cranberry salsa, strawberry crepes, or shells filled with mushrooms in a velouté sauce. During warm weather breakfast may be served outdoors on the brick patio in the English country garden.

What's Nearby

Vancouver City Museum-Planetarium-Maritime Museum complex is located nearby. Other destinations to check out include the Canadian Craft Museum, the Motorcycle Museum, and Burnaby Heritage Village. Nearby restaurants include Tapastree on Robson Street, Bridges on Granville Island, and Ecco el Panni on Broadway.

Other Recommended B&Bs Nearby

Cedar Cottage Bed & Breakfast, travelers find a private guest cottage and suite in a tranquil English garden setting; contact innkeepers Barrie and Ann Wall, 910 Third Street, West Vancouver, B.C. V7T 2J3; Telephone: (604) 926-0950. **Heritage Harbour B&B,** luxurious waterfront accommodations in quiet park setting, old world ambience, fireplaces, large baths, guest lounge with water and city views, close to beach and Granville Island; contact innkeeper Debra Horner, 1838 Ogden Avenue, Vancouver, B.C. V6J 1A1; Telephone: (604) 736-0809.

The Beaconsfield Inn

998 Humboldt Street
Victoria, B.C. V8V 2Z8 Canada
Phone: (250) 384-4044
E-mail: beaconsfield@islandnet.com
Internet site:
www.islandnet.com/beaconsfield/

Innkeepers: Con and Judi Sollid
Rooms: 9 rooms with private baths; several rooms feature wood-burning or gas fireplaces, private patios, and whirlpool soaking tubs for two
Extras: Restored Edwardian mansion; champagne, chocolates on arrival; afternoon tea and evening sherry; nighttime tea makings and biscotti in library; sun room conservatory overlooks front garden
On the grounds: English-style garden plantings
Smoking? Outdoors only
Visiting pets? No; no resident pets
Credit cards: Visa, MasterCard
Rates: $$$–$$$$
How to get there: From the Inner Harbor area near the waterfront and the Parliament Buildings, proceed north on Government Street to Humboldt Street; turn right 4 blocks to the inn.

Those seeking a romantic downtown hideaway will find one here in one of Victoria's elegant mansions close to the Inner Harbor and downtown area. The inn was built in 1905 as a wedding gift for the owner's only daughter and it is now fully restored and handsomely decorated as a small urban inn. The inn's name comes from a luxurious London hotel frequented by King Edward VII prior to World War I. Today guests find sumptuous rooms that may feature original stained-glass windows, wood-burning or gas fireplaces, Ralph Lauren stripes and florals, French doors leading to private patios, period armoires, partial or half-canopied queen beds, antique writing desks, and cushioned window seats. One room is done in colors of teal and apricot with a fox hunt theme while another offers a medley of blue velvet and blue cotton chintz. Several rooms have whirlpool tubs for two.

Breakfast is served in the dining room and

in the sun room conservatory overlooking the English-style perennial garden. Morning offerings may include lemon yogurt bread, mushroom frittata, rosemary-roasted potatoes, or sweetheart oat and corn waffles with winter compote and crème fraîche. For lunch or evening dining ask about restaurants such as Il Terrazo, Camille's, Serendipity, and Herald St. Café.

What's Nearby

Victoria retains its British traditions with wonderful gardens, high tea, and great shopping and dining. Walk the Inner Harbor causeway to see moored sailboats and yachts, stroll through Old Town, Market Square, or Chinatown. The handsome Parliament Buildings and the Royal BC Museum are adjacent to the harbor. Browse galleries, museums, and specialty shops. Exemplary gardens include the romantic Italian Garden and intimate Japanese Garden at nearby Hatley Castle and the renowned Butchart Gardens.

Other Recommended B&Bs Nearby

Arundel Manor Bed & Breakfast, a romantic waterfront inn circa 1912, elegant and comfortable decor, king and queen beds; contact innkeeper June Earl, 980 Arundel Drive, Victoria, B.C. V9A 2C3; Telephone: (250) 385-5442. **Carberry Gardens Bed & Breakfast,** restored 1907 gentry home features stained-glass windows, fireplaces, and three spacious rooms with private baths; friendly pup, Max; hearty breakfast; contact innkeepers Julie and Lionel Usher, 1008 Carberry Gardens, Victoria, B.C. V8S 3R7; Telephone: (250) 595-8906. **Scholefield House,** 1892 Victorian with three rooms and decorated with antiques, quilts, linen, and lace; private baths; sherry, coffee, tea, and cookies in the library; five-course champagne breakfast in fireplaced parlor; herb and rose gardens; contact innkeeper Tana Dineen, 731 Vancouver Street, Victoria, B.C. V8V 3V4; Telephone: (250) 385-2025; Internet site: www.scholefieldhouse.com.

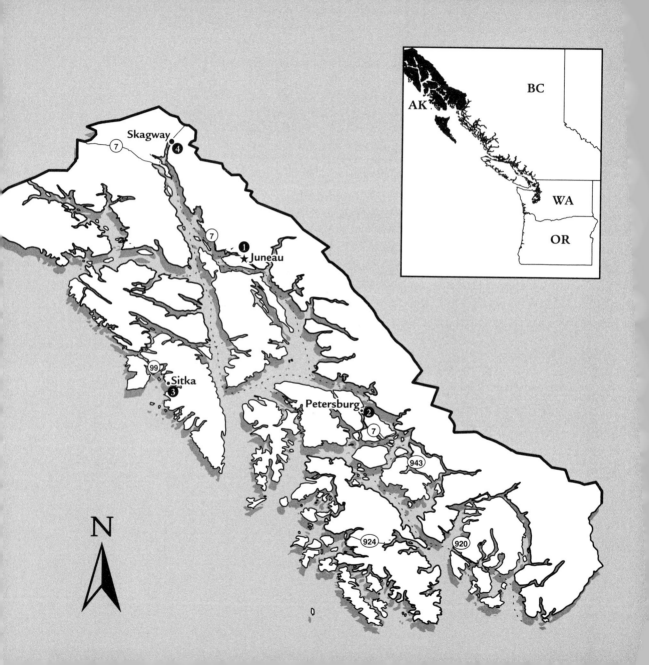

Southeast Alaska: A Sampling

Numbers on map refer to towns numbered below.

Alaska Wolf House

1900 Wickersham Drive
P.O. Box 21321
Juneau, AK 99802
Phone: (907) 586-2422; (888) 586-9053
E-mail: akwlfhs@ptialaska.net
Internet site: www.wetpage.com/akwlfhse/

Innkeepers: Philip and Clovis Dennis
Rooms: 6 rooms, 4 with private baths and 2 with shared bath
Extras: Maritime/wildlife eco-tours available aboard the couple's classic wooden yacht, M.V. *Peregrine*
On the grounds: Views of Gastineau Channel; glacier hiking-jogging-bike trail located nearby
Smoking? Outdoors only
Visiting pets? No; no resident pets
Credit cards: Visa, MasterCard
Rates: $$–$$$
How to get there: The inn is located 12 miles from the Alaska Ferry Terminal and 6 miles from the Juneau Airport. Proceed south toward town on Egan Drive; watch for Channel Marina on the right. After the marina turn left onto Old Glacier Highway for 1 mile. Turn left onto Wickersham Drive and bear left as the street climbs the foot of Mount Juneau; the house is the fifth one on the right. Enter from the lower level and stairway.

"We like to describe our bed and breakfast as Alaska friendly with a touch of class," says Clovis. Indeed the 4,000-square-foot western red cedar log home overlooking Gastineau Channel and the mountains of Douglas Island offers a haven in which to rest and rejuvenate. The cedar walls, woodwork, and ceilings have an inviting outdoorsy smell, like living inside a Christmas tree. The Juneau area also offers a good location from which to explore southeastern Alaska. "From glaciers to grizzly bears," says Philip with a grin. "But folks need to be forewarned—we're Juneau Alaskan American chauvinists and complete nature lovers!" It isn't difficult to see why with the wildness of the sea, the craggy mountains, and the cool blue glaciers. One could even imagine pulling up stakes and heading north for a spell.

Guests find six rooms, all with splendid views and various Northwest themes. One room named for Jack London features a quilted queen bed and pictures, books, and memorabilia honoring this author who wrote about the wilds of Alaska and about wolves. The spacious honeymoon suite comes with fireplace, skylights, and comfortable furnishings. Another room offers a private bath with a spa that looks out to pristine views. A smaller room has quilted twin beds and a delightful Russian theme that honors Clovis's heritage. Each room has good reading lamps, a selection of books and reading material, and Alaskan art and treasured memorabilia.

Both Clovis and Philip love to cook and mornings in the glass sun room are lively and filled with good conversation and high humor over their bountiful breakfasts. The view of the water and thick forests of spruce and hemlock is splendid regardless of the season, whether the layers of green during summer or the quiet and serene snowfalls and frosty mornings of winter. Baked apples, a spinach-cheese quiche, ham, and bran muffins warm from the oven are favorites, served with local jams and topped with steaming coffee served in the inn's wolf mugs. "Guests often become friends," says the couple. "It doesn't get much better than that."

What's Nearby

Using Juneau as a base, travelers can access by air or by marine highway such destinations as Glacier Bay, Gustavus, Skagway, Tracy Arm, Taku River, and Admiralty Island. In town check on plays and performances at Perseverance Theatre and annual events such as the Folk Festival, Jazz Festival, and Friday night concerts in the park.

Blueberry Lodge
Bed & Breakfast

9436 North Douglas Highway
Juneau, AK 99801
Phone: (907) 463–5886
E-mail: jayjudy@alaska.net
Internet site: www.alaska.net/~jayjudy

Innkeepers: Jay and Judy Urquhart
Rooms: 5 rooms all with shared baths; children are welcome
Extras: Hot tub on outside deck with views; arrangements can be made ahead for dinner at the inn; guest laundry available
On the grounds: Views of Gastineau Channel, Thomas Glacier, and the Mendenhall Wetlands State Game Refuge including freshwater streams and tidelands; resident eagle family's nest; trails to rain forests and alpine meadows located nearby
Smoking? Outdoors only
Visiting pets? No; 2 resident dogs
Credit cards: Visa, MasterCard, American Express, Discover
Rates: $$
How to get there: Take Egan Drive into Juneau and at first traffic light cross the Juneau-Douglas Bridge; turn right onto North Douglas Highway and proceed 6 miles to the inn located on the beach side of the road.

The 4,000-square-foot log home built by Jay is situated on an acre of woods and from its nearly 1,500 square feet of decks, guests gaze out to the inland ocean waterway, Gastineau Channel, and to spruce and hemlock forests beyond. The lower deck overlooks the water as well as the Thomas Glacier, a small hanging glacier, and the changing tidelands of the Mendenhall Wetlands State Game Refuge. This is a gathering place for great blue heron, Canada geese, and some 100 species of other visiting waterfowl. "We also have a family of eagles close by," says Judy. She adjusts the spotting scope near the living room windows. "See, the eagles' aerie is in that hemlock tree, about 200 feet away from the window." The eagle parents fly in with fish for their eaglets;

Judy says that usually a pair is born each year.

The enormous lodge-style common room has a lofty ceiling three stories tall but is warm and cozy with a large fireplace, two deep-seated paisley sofas, oversized pillows, and cushioned bent-willow and alder chairs and matching loveseat. A spinet piano and a game table and chairs sit nearby. A cozy library common area is also available for guests to use. Five comfortable guest rooms sport names of Alaskan wild berries; two lower-level rooms each contain two double beds and one has a queen bed. These three rooms share a full bath and a half bath. On the second level two rooms come with double and queen beds and share a full bath.

Breakfast is served in the dining room-kitchen area, a large room that overlooks all the views. Early rising guests often ease onto stools at the 7-foot island and sip welcome cups of coffee while Jay and Judy prepare the ample country breakfast. Tasty entrees might include sourdough Belgian waffles with homemade rhubarb sauce, homemade blueberry sausage, or blueberry pancakes with both maple syrup and homemade spruce-tip syrup. One of the most requested recipes is for the couple's delicious gingerbread pancakes served with lemon curd.

What's Nearby

The inn is located close to the Eaglecrest Ski Area on Mount Juneau, with two chairlifts and one surface lift serving some thirty alpine trails and more than 10 miles of cross-country ski trails. The base lodge includes lockers, restrooms, and food service. Located nearby is a renowned shore scuba diving area; Channel Dive Center offers complete dive packages including dry suit certification. October to April are suggested as the best months to dive in this area. Good areas for mountain biking, fishing, and kayaking.

Crondahls' Bed & Breakfast

626 Fifth Street
Juneau, AK 99801
Phone: (907) 586-1464
E-mail: jcrondah@ptialaska.net
Internet site: www.ptialaska.net/~jcrondah

Innkeepers: Judy and Jay Crondahl
Rooms: 2 rooms with shared bath; children are welcome
Extras: Complimentary aerobic workout, 49 steps lead up to the inn from streets below
On the grounds: Outstanding views of the city, the ocean waterway, and surrounding forested mountains
Smoking? Outdoors only
Visiting pets? No; black lab, Schwartz, and 2 cats, Scooter and Whiskers, willingly accept guests' attention and affection
Credit cards: No; personal checks accepted
Rates: $-$$
How to get there: From Juneau airport or ferry terminal take shuttle or cab to town. From Fifth and East Streets the inn is located 49 steps uphill; from Fifth and Kennedy Streets the inn is located 46 steps downhill. On-street parking is extremely limited.

The walk—either up 49 steps or down 46 steps—is definitely worth it for those who are in good shape physically. "Bring your sturdy walking shoes," advises Jay with a smile. The multi-level house is located in the historic Starr Hill neighborhood and adjacent to Chickenyard Park. "You don't need a car," says Judy. "Everything is within walking distance!" Upstairs or downstairs, of course, but you get rather used to it after awhile. Most of Juneau's houses, shops, restaurants, and other commercial buildings seem hung from the surrounding hillsides. Everything is arranged in a comfortable jumble on a narrow strip of land and hills around Gastineau Channel with views of Mount Bradley, Mount Ben Stewart, and Mount Juneau.

Guests including families with children have free range of the outdoor decks and the living room, dining room, and kitchen areas. The comfortable house is filled with art, books, magazines, and games. The whimsical prints of renowned Alaskan artist Rie Munoz are displayed in several areas of the house. One of the guest rooms comes with a double bed and spectacular view of the city and the ocean waterway. A second room offers double and twin beds. Guests and hosts share the single bath which includes laundry facilities. Children are especially welcome and enjoy playing at Chickenyard Park located just next door.

Morning often starts with a cheerful wake-up call from Judy, tooted on her euphonium, a mellow sounding brass horn. The lively family-style breakfast served in the dining room on blue and white country china may include sourdough pancakes made from a vintage starter obtained by the Crondahls in the 1970s. Other days might bring Jay or Judy's homemade bread and one of Judy's breakfast dishes such as quiche, egg burritos, egg and cheese ramekins, or chile egg puff. Also served are fresh fruit, juices, and freshly ground organic coffee from Kalani Organica. "One of the reasons we enjoy having a small bed and breakfast," says Judy, "is that we are able to spend some time with our guests if they wish." The Chrondals' Internet site offers helpful links to Juneau doings.

What's Nearby

Juneau-based organizations offer numerous musical events throughout the year—Juneau Symphony, Juneau Lyric Opera, Jazz and Classics Festival, Douglas Little Theater, Juneau Chorale, the high school drama department, and the Juneau Volunteer Marching Band. Check the Juneau Internet site: www.juneau.com, for helpful information and links.

Mount Juneau Inn
Bed & Breakfast

1801 Old Glacier Highway
Juneau, AK 99801
Phone: (907) 463-5855
E-mail: mtjunoin@ptialaska.net
Internet site: www.mtjuneauinn.com

Innkeepers: Karen and Phil Green
Rooms: 7 rooms and 1 cottage with kitchen; 2 rooms with private baths, others share a bath
Extras: In-room phones, evening refreshments, guest kitchen, laundry and freezer facilities, barbecue deck overlooking the waterway, bicycles for guests use; separate cottage
On the grounds: Gardens, wetlands, and native carved totem poles; nestled at foot of Mount Juneau overlooking Gastineau Channel.
Smoking? Outdoors only
Visiting pets? No; resident McKenzie River husky, Leo, and 2 cats, Gizmo and Gremlin
Credit cards: Visa, MasterCard, Discover
Rates: $-$$
How to get there: From the ferry terminal or the airport head south toward downtown Juneau. Proceed past the intersection of Egan Drive and Channel/Glacier Highway. Turn left at the next Glacier Highway sign, then right ¼ mile to the inn.

A handsome native carved totem pole stands sentry duty in the yard facing the channel waters; colors of red, blue, and cream decorate its carved images. It's a harbinger of things to come as all of the guest rooms are named for important animals in the native Tlingit culture such as raven, orca, and eagle. Photographs of Alaskan outdoor scenes and native art that captures the particular animal in its natural environment adorn each room. One room comes with a queen bed with an old-fashioned Dresden plate design quilt, antique pine armoire, and private bath. Other rooms have queen or twin beds, antique dressers, pine armoires, writing tables, and an ample supply of reading lamps. Five of the rooms have panoramic views of the grounds, water, and surrounding mountains. The cottage showcases the scenery of the Juneau area and it comes with a fully equipped kitchen as well as cozy sitting areas and private bath.

From the inn guests can walk 1½ miles to the historic downtown area and explore its shops, galleries, and eateries. Or borrow one of the inn's bicycles and pedal the area's roads and trails. Leo the 130-pound Mackenzie River husky loves to be photographed and may accompany guests about the grounds if they wish. "These huskies were the original freight-carrying dogs of the North," explains Phil. "He's our 'anything for a quick biscuit' guy!" The innkeepers share a great recipe for Leo's Tastee Dog Biscuits to interested guests who have dogs of their own.

Breakfast at the inn is a family affair; with guests seated around the large dining table to enjoy homemade granola and fresh fruit salad along with sourdough or banana oat pancakes, ham and egg scramble, spinach delight casserole, cheese strata, eggs Benedict, or oven pancake with glazed apples. Karen's wild berry jams and fireweed honey are often on the table along with Phil's homemade sausage. Fresh ground coffee and herbal teas are served as well.

What's Nearby:

Whale-watching, flight-seeing over the glaciers and glacier hiking, fishing, and gold panning at historic Gold Creek Basin.

Other Recommended B&B Nearby

Meadow's Glacier Bay Guest House, located 50 miles from Juneau is reached by air taxi or by ferry during summer months, guests find a stunning contemporary home graced with tasteful Alaskan art and Danish-style furnishings; views from guest rooms of surrounding meadows, Salmon River, and the rugged coastline; room rates include full breakfast, free airport and ferry pickup, and use of the inn's bicycles, fishing poles, and kites; transportation to Glacier Bay National Park can also be arranged; friendly border collie in residence; contact innkeepers Chris Smith and Meadow Brook, P.O. Box 93, Gustavus, AK 99826; Telephone: (907) 697–2348; Fax: (907) 697–2454.

Pearson's Pond Luxury Inn & Garden Spa

4541 Sawa Circle
Juneau, AK 99801
Phone: (907) 789-3772
E-mail: pearsons.pond@juneau.com
Internet site:
www.juneau.com/pearsons.pond

Innkeepers: Diane and Steve Pearson
Rooms: 3 rooms with private baths, decks, and pond or garden views
Extras: Fruit and bread basket on arrival, fresh flowers in summer, relaxing music; each room comes with a stocked kitchenette; afternoon tea or wine with cheese and snacks or marshmallows for roasting
On the grounds: Two outdoor hot tubs under the northern lights and midnight sun; extensive garden plantings, decks, private spaces for walking and sitting
Smoking? Outdoors only; there is a smoking bench adjacent to the property
Visiting pets? Permitted October through April if kenneled; no resident pets
Credit cards: Visa, MasterCard, American Express, Diners Club
Rates: $$-$$$$
How to get there: The inn is near Mendenhall Glacier; from the ferry terminal turn right out of the parking area and onto Veterans Memorial Highway. Turn left onto Mendenhall Loop Road, away from the water, and continue for about 1½ miles; just after the campground turnoff, turn right onto River Road toward trail. At Kelly turn right (north), and at Sawa turn west.

It may seem a bit unusual to have an enormous glacier in your backyard, but the Mendenhall Glacier forms an impressive icy blue river of ice several hundred feet to the rear of the inn and is visible through the branches of old-growth trees that border the property. "Actually the glacier created our pond when it retreated about 200 years ago," explains Diane. She is a master gardener and has coordinated all of the extraordinary landscaping around the two-story cedar home. Hanging baskets of greenery and perennials along with large pots of ferns and flowers sit in groupings on the outside decks. Tall spruce trees enclose shady glens and the sun filters paths and walkways. Two outdoor hot tubs are placed in separate bowers to ensure privacy for guests.

Garden views are available from all three spacious guest rooms and a sense of privacy permeates the inn, rooms, and grounds. Guests remove their shoes inside the house and are provided soft terrycloth slippers to pad about in. Rooms come with their own entries and decks as well as queen beds with warm quilts and comforters, small kitchenettes, fireplaces, and cozy sitting areas. One room features a view of the pond. Rowboats are available for paddling about the lilies, and kayaks are available for an excursion to a nearby deserted island for a picnic. You can use the inn's portable exerciser or join Diane for a morning walk or hike.

Guests may do breakfast in their own room from fresh fruit and items in the fully stocked refrigerator or they can go upstairs to the large common area between 9:00 and 10:00 A.M. for an expanded continental breakfast with fellow travelers. Diane serves a nice variety of morning foods including yogurt, cereal, juices, fresh fruit, and gourmet coffees and tea along with fresh breads, rolls, and scones with fresh jams. Bagels with cream cheese, egg dishes, and smoked salmon may accompany the buffet. During warm weather guests take their plates out to the deck to spot birds and wildlife.

What's Nearby

Take a tram to see the Mendenhall Glacier up close or arrange a helicopter sight-seeing flight over this and other nearby glaciers and scenic areas such as Tracy Arm. Activities such as bird watching, bear watching, and whale watching abound as well as mountain biking, horseback riding, and hiking. For evening dining restaurants in the Juneau area include Fiddlehead, Chan's Thai Kitchen, Summit, Armadillo, Hanger, and Red Dog Saloon.

Other Recommended B&B Nearby

The Historic Skagway Inn is in the Klondike Gold Rush National Historic Park within walking distance of Skagway shops, eateries, hiking trails, and historic sites such as the Trail of 1898 Museum and the famous Red Onion Saloon; 32-mile Chilkoot Trail and trailhead located 9 miles from the inn; courtesy van service from the ferry, airport, or train; contact innkeepers Don and Sioux Plummer, Seventh & Broadway, P.O. Box 500, Skagway, AK 99840; Telephone: (907) 983-2289.

Water's Edge
Bed & Breakfast

705 Sandy Beach Road
P.O. Box 1201
Petersburg, AK 99833
Phone: (907) 772-3736; (800) 868-4373
E-mail: bbsea@alaska.net
Internet site: www.alaska.net/~bbsea

Innkeepers: Kathy and Barry Bracken
Rooms: 2 rooms with private baths; TV/VCR and video library; kitchenette and shared common area
Extras: Well-stocked library of natural history, Alaskana, and novels; bicycles and canoe for guests use; hosts are teacher and biologist/naturalist—guests can arrange for whale-watching and fishing tours with Captain Barry aboard his boat M.V. *Island Dream*
On the grounds: Waterfront views of Petersburg and the mountains, beach for walking and wildlife watching
Smoking? Outdoors only
Visiting pets? No; no resident pets
Credit cards: No; personal checks accepted
Rates: $$
How to get there: Located on an island between Ketchikan and Juneau, Petersburg is reached by twice-daily jet air service and by the ferry system, Alaska Marine Highway. From city center head north on Nordic Drive for about 1 mile; the road then curves right at Hungry Point and becomes Sandy Beach Road. Continue ¾ mile to light brown two-story house on the beach side. The inn is approximately 1½ miles from downtown Petersburg. The innkeepers will also provide courtesy transport for guests.

With unobstructed views of Frederick Sound, the forested hills and mountains, icebergs, and wildlife, this inn is where guests are greeted with, "Velkommen to the heart of southeast Alaska's Inside Passage area!" Karen and Barry share that the town was settled in the 1890s by Norwegian fishermen and their families. "Petersburg proudly shares its Scandinavian roots with travelers," says Karen. Fishing boats, sailboats, luxury yachts, and research vessels call at the town's three harbors. "It's a lively and fun place to explore," says Barry.

There are two nicely appointed rooms on the first floor. One features a king bed and futon and commands an outrageous view of Frederick Sound from its five windows. The second room offers a queen bed, large adjacent private bath, and overlooks the creek that runs through the property. Folks awaken to the sound of gentle waves lapping at the beach and to the bubbling creek; a brisk morning walk may be in order regardless of the weather. "There is something in a shoreline bathed in mist that quiets my soul—and something in eagles, whales, and herons that sets it free," said a recent guest.

Kathy and Barry serve a deluxe continental breakfast from 6:30 to 9:30 A.M. that includes freshly ground and brewed gourmet coffee, teas, cocoa, and juices along with homemade breakfast breads, muffins, bagels, cream cheese, jams, fresh fruit, cereals, and yogurt—all served along with the best view in town.

What's Nearby

The largest concentration of humpback whales in Alaska, tidewater glaciers, and world-class sport fishing. Tongass National Forest, the world's largest temperate rain forest, offers byways and hiking trails to explore. Visit the marina to see Petersburg's commercial fishing fleet, one of the most productive in the state. Petersburg's Internet site: www.petersburg.org/visitors/welcome, offers information, photos of the area, and links. One of the best and most scenic ways to access the area is to fly to Ketchikan, then ferry north to take in Petersburg, Sitka, Juneau, all the way north to Skagway, then return to Juneau and fly south from there.

Alaska Ocean View Bed & Breakfast

1101 Edgecumbe Drive
Sitka, AK 99835
Phone: (907) 747–8310; (800) 800–6870
enter PIN number 520 at the tone
E-mail: aovbb@hotmail.com
Internet site: www.wetpage.com/oceanview

Innkeeper: Carole and Bill Denkinger
Rooms: 3 rooms with private baths; phones in each room with separate numbers
Extras: All rooms feature TV/VCR and CD entertainment centers; umbrellas and raingear for guests use
On the grounds: Panoramic views of Sitka Sound and Fuji-like Mount Edgecumbe; wide decks with patio chairs; hot tub on covered patio surrounded by ferns, lush perennial plantings, and rock gardens
Smoking? Outdoors only
Visiting pets? Restrictions, inquire; resident husky mix, Gizmo, greets visitors from her outdoor kennel
Credit cards: Visa, MasterCard, American Express, and personal checks
Rates: $–$$$
How to get there: Sitka is reached by air or ferry via the Inside Passage from Ketchikan. From the ferry terminal a shuttle bus to town costs $3.00; a taxi to the inn costs approximately $15. Arrangements can be made to have a rental car waiting for you.

The multi-level, Alaska all-cedar home with wide decks and three-story open staircase is located in a quiet neighborhood just 1 block from the beach near the Tongass National Forest. The main floor parlor, dining room, and breakfast nook offer comfortable sitting places and great views of Sitka Sound. The parlor features a vaulted ceiling of tongue-and-groove red cedar. Soft music plays in the background and cappuccino, coffee, teas, and snacks are available afternoons and throughout the evening. Light plays on the ever-changing ocean and creates a romantic feeling at day's end. "Our sunsets are glorious," says Carole with a smile.

Three rooms named Dogwood, Rose, and Fireweed, native Alaskan flowers, are outfitted with every possible comfort. One features a super king bed, fantastic ocean and mountain views, and a Japanese-style whirlpool tub in its private bath. A second room comes with a brass king bed or twins. The spacious third room on the garden level with easy access to the outdoor hot tub, has two brass beds, queen and double, and a private patio. All rooms come with TV/VCR and CD entertainment centers, small refrigerators, and comfortable sitting areas, extra pillows, and good reading lamps.

You'll awaken to the aromas of freshly baking cinnamon rolls or muffins, brewing gourmet coffee, and the great views of the water and mountains surrounding Sitka. Breakfast might feature crepes with strawberries and whipped cream, smoked sockeye salmon, five-grain hot cereal with apple chunks, sliced nectarines with blueberries and yogurt, and Carole's fabulous cinnamon rolls without raisins. The whole sumptuous affair comes to life beneath the soft light of the dining room's Australian crystal chandelier.

Ask Carole about the Tlingit Indian Storyteller and dinner, a good option for learning about the area's roots. Other restaurants nearby include Marina, which offers free shuttle service from the inn and specializes in fresh Alaska seafood, pastas, and prime rib; Channel Club located about 5 miles out Halibut Point Road offers good steak dinners.

What's Nearby

Snowmobiling on Harbor Mountain, snowboarding on Mount Verstovia and Harbor Mountain. Visit the Sheldon Jackson Museum, Russian Bishop's House and Russian Cathedral, National Historical Park-Totem Park, and arrange for wildlife and whale-watching cruises in Sitka Sound. The Alaska Raptor Rehabilitation Center is located near the museum and bike path that meanders throughout the town. Sitka is a small town with just one traffic light and is great for walking and browsing.

Indexes

B&Bs Far from City Lights

B&Bs Near Vineyards, Wineries, and Tasting Rooms

B&Bs Welcoming Families

B&Bs with Lake or River Views

B&Bs with Mountain Views and All-Season Recreation/Sports Areas

B&Bs with Ocean Views and/or Beach Access

B&Bs with Separate Cottages/Carriage Houses

City B&Bs

Romantic B&Bs

About the Author

After nearly twenty years of traveling into the nooks and crannies of the Pacific Northwest, Myrna Oakley remains an unabashed devotee of its scenic and historic treasures. From the lush Willamette Valley to the high Cascade Mountains and the high desert regions, from the scenic and accessible coastal areas to the far-flung islands of Washington, British Columbia, and Southeast Alaska she delights in finding special bed-and-breakfast inns and their welcoming innkeepers. After all these years she still loves the goosedown comforters, cozy conversations by the fire, cream in her coffee, and muffins without raisins that she finds at the inns. A native Oregonian, she lives in the Portland area. In addition to her writing projects she teaches at local colleges and universities about the business of freelance and travel writing. She also dreams about writing a mystery novel for young adults and plans to sneak away one of these days to one of the islands with her voluminous files and laptop computer.